Creating an Internationally Competitive Economy

Creating an Internationally Competitive Economy

Edited by

Harry Bloch
Professor of Economics
Curtin University of Technology
Perth
Australia

and

Peter Kenyon
Professor and Director
Institute for Research into International Competitiveness
Curtin University of Technology
Perth
Australia

Editorial matter, selection and Chapters 1 and 2 © Harry Bloch
and Peter Kenyon 2001
Chapter 4 © Peter Dawkins and Peter Kenyon 2001
Chapter 6 © Harry Bloch 2001
Chapters 3, 5, 7–14 © Palgrave Publishers Ltd 2001

First published 2001 by
PALGRAVE
Houndmills, Basingstoke, Hampshire RG21 6XS and
175 Fifth Avenue, New York, N. Y. 10010
Companies and representatives throughout the world

PALGRAVE is the new global academic imprint of
St. Martin's Press LLC Scholarly and Reference Division and
Palgrave Publishers Ltd (formerly Macmillan Press Ltd).

ISBN 0–333–77277–6

This book is printed on paper suitable for recycling and
made from fully managed and sustained forest sources.

A catalogue record for this book is available
from the British Library.

Library of Congress Cataloging-in-Publication Data
Creating an internationally competitive economy / edited by
Harry Bloch and Peter Kenyon.
    p. cm.
    Includes bibliographical references and index.
    ISBN 0–333–77277–6
    1. International economic relations. 2 Competition, International.
3. Foreign trade and employment. 4. Developing countries—
—Foreign economic relations. I. Bloch, Harry, 1946– II. Kenyon, Peter.
    HF1352 .C74 2000
    337—dc21
                                                    00–052421

MR 10   9   8   7   6   5   4   3   2   1
     10 09 08 07 06 05 04 03 02 01

Printed and bound in Great Britain by
Antony Rowe Ltd, Chippenham, Wiltshire

Contents

v

N A

Acknowledgements

In putting together the conference 'Creating an Internationally Competitive Economy' and this volume which resulted from it, a lot of people contributed along the way. We wish to take this opportunity to acknowledge their contributions and to thank them for their work.

First, we would like to thank the authors for responding to our call for papers and for presenting their ideas to the conference. The conference was uncommonly stimulating, not only in the formal sessions, but also in the many discussions and conversations that took place in and around Fremantle in August 1998 and subsequently. The authors also responded quickly to the opportunity to turn their conference papers into contributions for this book, adding considerable value to those initial papers. The published versions represent, we believe, valuable statements about the multiple facets of international competitiveness.

Part of the reason for this value-adding came from the formal comments of the discussants to each of the papers at the conference. We would like to take this opportunity to thank deeply each of the discussants for their most valuable and thoughtful contributions. The discussants were Helen Cabulu, Geoff Crockett, Sandra Hopkins, Ian Kerr, Gary Madden, Michael Olive, Thorsten Stromback, Michael Thorpe and Dave Western all of Curtin University of Technology, Phil Lewis and Gavin Wood, both of Murdoch University, and Jakob Madsen and Yanrui Wu of the University of Western Australia.

Also adding value to the discussions were the comments of many of the other participants who attended the conference. We acknowledge their excellent contributions, too. The discussions of papers were lively and highly informative.

The administration of a conference and the putting together of a volume of papers for publication involves a large amount of administrative skills. The administrative team at Curtin's Institute for Research into International Competitiveness (IRIC) of Val Smith, Madeleine Linton and Sue Lomax contributed significantly in ensuring a happy and productive conference for all, and a professionally produced set of papers for publication. As always, their skills were invaluable, as was their good humour and cheerfulness in dealing with tight deadlines and last-minute glitches.

Activities such as those represented by the conference and this volume require financial support to make them happen. In this case, Curtin

University of Technology through the Executive Dean of its Business School and the University of Melbourne through its Vice-Chancellor collaborated to find the necessary funds to finance this scholarly endeavour at a time when Australian universities face extreme pressure on their financial resources. We are most grateful for this demonstration of confidence in our work.

Perth, Australia   HARRY BLOCH
                                                                                     PETER KENYON

As this volume was going to press, we sadly learned of the death of James Gapinski on Sunday, 19 November 2000, in Tallahassee, Florida. Jim was a prolific and enthusiastic scholar. His research interests were in macro-economics, cultural economics and public policy, with a career-long interest in economic growth. He loved jazz, and Monday nights in August at the Hyde Park in Perth will be the sadder for his passing. Jim was a happy and humourous man with a wide circle of friends from Tallahassee to Perth. He will be missed greatly. We dedicate this volume to his memory.

Notes on the Contributors

V.N. Balasubramanyam is Professor of Development Economics, Lancaster University, England.

Harry Bloch is Professor of Economics, Curtin University of Technology, Perth, Australia.

Peter Dawkins is Professor and Director, Melbourne Institute of Applied Economic and Social Research, University of Melbourne, Australia.

Donald Feaver is Senior Lecturer, School of Applied Economics, Victoria University of Technology, Australia.

James Gapinski was, until his untimely death in late 2000, Professor of Economics, Florida State University, USA.

David Greenaway is Professor and Pro Vice-Chancellor, University of Nottingham, England.

Tim Hazledine is Professor of Economics, University of Auckland, New Zealand.

Peter Kenyon is Professor and Director, Institute for Research into International Competitiveness, Curtin University of Technology, Perth, Australia.

Donald Lamberton is a Visiting Fellow, Research School of Social Science, Australian National University, Australia.

Jeffrey Petchey is a Postdoctoral Research Fellow, Curtin University of Technology, Perth, Australia.

David Prentice is Lecturer in Economics, La Trobe University, Australia.

Mark Rogers is a Fellow, Harris Manchester College, Oxford University.

Mohammed Salisu is Lecturer in Economics, Lancaster University, England.

David Sapsford is Professor of Economics, Lancaster University, England.

Perry Shapiro is Professor of Economics, University of California at Santa Barbara, USA.

Peter Summers is a Senior Research Fellow, Melbourne Institute of Applied Economic and Social Research, University of Melbourne, Australia.

Richard Upward is a Research Fellow, Leverhulme Trust Programme, University of Nottingham, England.

Kenneth Wilson is Professor of Economics, School of Applied Economics, Victoria University, Australia.

Peter Wright is Lecturer in Economics, University of Nottingham, England.

Part I
Preliminaries

1 BR Title's

Introduction

Harry Bloch and Peter Kenyon N | A

Countries differ enormously in the material standards of living of their citizens, and the search for the causes of these differences has been a driving force in the development of modern economics. At least since Adam Smith's 1776 classic, *An Inquiry into the Nature and Causes of the Wealth of Nations*, this search has largely focused on the interplay between government policies and the workings of the market mechanism. In Smith's own analysis and in recent literature comparing the economic performance of nations there is a heavy emphasis on the role of international trade. The present volume contains a series of papers that can be viewed as further contributions to the long-running quest for understanding how the economic success of nations is linked through government policy and the market mechanism to international trade.

Our approach to the topic recognizes that the growth of international trade and investment has proceeded to a point where the causes and consequences of international competitiveness extend deep into the core of all modern economies. Rather than separate the analysis of international trade and investment from that of national economic performance, the contributions in this volume provide an integrated analysis to identify how market institutions and government policies impact on economic success through international trade. Hopefully, this will contribute to the design of institutional and policy reforms for achieving a higher level of national economic performance. Hence, our choice of title is *Creating an Internationally Competitive Economy*.

We choose to illustrate the extent to which domestic market institutions and policies have become tied to the global economy by emphasizing the role of institutions and policies that are often considered from a purely domestic viewpoint. Demonstrating the clear implications of these institutions and policies for competitiveness in a global economy is a common thread linking many of the papers. After some preliminaries concerning the meaning and measurement of international competitiveness, we consider particular aspects of domestic labour markets and product markets, emphasizing import competition in product markets and structural adjustment in labour markets. We then examine government policies on communication, fiscal harmonization and 'dumping' of imports. The final part of the volume is devoted to international comparisons of economic performance, with particular attention to the impact of microeconomic reform, exports, foreign direct investment and the diffusion of technology.

Part 1: preliminaries

Following the introductory remarks in this chapter, there are two contributions that attempt to clarify the concept of international competitiveness. Achieving clarity is no easy task, given the confusion and controversy that has accompanied the expansion of interest in the subject over recent years. Different views often reflect different definitions and measures, compounding any conflict arising from divergent assessments of causal relationships.

Our own contribution as editors, 'The Meaning and Measurement of International Competitiveness', emphasizes different conceptual approaches that each derive from the economic analysis of the determinants of international trade. By focusing on approaches that have a common analytical core, it is possible to demonstrate how different assumptions lead to different conclusions concerning the sources of international competitiveness. In the process, we are able to demonstrate how the causes and consequences of competition between countries differ from those relating to the generally more familiar competition between firms.

One important way in which competition between countries differs from that between firms is that the trade between a country and the rest of the world tends to be balanced, particularly over the longer term. In addition, each country taken as a whole tends to benefit through its bilateral trade with other countries. In this sense, countries do not compete when trading. This undermines the natural inclination to use the size of a country's net exports as a measure of success, by analogy to the use of profit as a measure of success for a firm. Our discussion of the meaning and measurement of international competitiveness recognizes a role for exchange rates, costs of production and product prices in influencing a country's position as a net exporter or net importer in the short term. However, our main focus is on the longer term in which competitiveness is usually reflected in both higher exports and higher imports, suggesting an analogy with a firm's size rather than its profit.

The key issue in our discussion of competitiveness over the longer term becomes determining which products a country exports and which products it imports. Early approaches to the analysis of the determinants of international trade focus primarily on conditions affecting the supply of products to international trade, culminating in the Heckscher–Ohlin theorem that identifies a country's factor endowment as the critical determinant of its pattern of exports and imports. More recent approaches recognize a key role for product demand conditions, leading to the identification of market structure, product innovation and non-price competition as factors affecting a country's trading pattern.

Our conceptual discussion suggests a large number of potential measures of competitiveness. In practice, the number of measures has been even higher. First, there are generally no exact measures corresponding to any of the concepts, leading to use of a number of imperfect proxies in each case. Second, there are measures of competitiveness that derive from approaches to understanding competitiveness that lie outside of our restricted scope of economic analysis.

James Gapinski tackles the large array of measures of competitiveness in Chapter 3, 'Developing ICOM: An Index of International Competitiveness'. He notes that a standard response to the multitude of individual measures is their combination into an index. There is then a tendency to prefer indexes with a greater number of component measures on grounds that they are more inclusive. However, Gapinski argues in favour of simplification. He describes the development of ICOM, the Index of International Competitiveness, which is envisioned from the outset to involve a small number of component series. First, the general components of the competitiveness index are discussed, with particular reference to the index published by the World Economic Forum (WEF). Gapinski notes that the WEF index is based on hundreds of individual data series, and then demonstrates that for a group of 13 Asia-Pacific countries a small index containing only ten series can perform well, providing virtually identical rankings to those of the WEF.

Gapinski proposes ICOM as an index based on alternative series to those included in his simplified index of WEF series. The advantage is that data for the alternative series are more readily available, including data on forecast values. He uses the ICOM to rank the 13 nations for three historical years 1975, 1985 and 1995, and for two 'out' years 1998 and 1999. Among the results on international competitiveness are a strong showing by Singapore and grim forecasts for Korea, Thailand and Indonesia.

Part II: market institutions in a global economy

One of the more important themes to have emerged in recent economic policy discussions concerns the effect of the increased exposure of economies to international trade and factor flows on labour markets and labour market outcomes. With globalization has come concern that not everyone is benefiting from the increasing international integration of markets for goods and services, factors and technology. Has international competition helped or harmed workers? What effect has the enormous increase in world trade had on wages and jobs? Has globalization contributed to the widening wage dispersion in many countries? Has globalization affected employment opportunities for some groups of workers? What should be the institutional and policy response? These are the questions addressed in Chapter 4, 'The Labour Market and International Competitiveness', by Peter Dawkins and Peter Kenyon.

Over the last two decades in many countries the wage distribution has widened and this appears to be based on skill differentials between workers. In many countries also, unemployment has risen and, again, the increase in unemployment has impacted more than proportionately on unskilled workers. Standard trade theory, operating through the Stolper–Samuelson theorem, attributes these effects to the adverse consequences of globalization. However, Dawkins and Kenyon conclude that the evidence points to relatively small effects of trade on less skilled workers' wages and employment in the industrialized countries. Thus, it appears that increasing globalization and international competitiveness (in the sense of more participants in world markets) cannot explain more than a small amount of the increased income inequality between skilled and less-skilled labour in those countries.

An alternative explanation for recent labour market developments is that technological progress, which is biased against unskilled workers, has increased over the last several decades. Here, Dawkins and Kenyon find that there is more compelling evidence for the proposition that technical change is capable of explaining the widening wage distribution based on skill differentials. However, most of the empirical studies of the effects of technological change on wages and employment do not link technological change with trade. Where studies do mix trade explanations with biased technological change, the evidence is mixed – both trade and technological change have affected the wage structure, but technical change may have contributed more to the change.

Dawkins and Kenyon conclude their chapter with some policy ideas relating to the interface of wages, taxes, social security, education and training in responding to recent labour market developments, and whether these changes are due to trade or technology effects. These policy ideas attempt to circumvent any 'diabolical trade-off' between increasing income inequality and persistent unemployment. Dawkins and Kenyon argue that a systematic approach to labour market programmes, reform of the tax and welfare systems to reduce effective marginal tax rates and a continual upgrading of the education and training system are the medium- to long-term ingredients in this strategy.

Chapter 5, 'Sectoral Mobility in UK and US Labour Markets', by David Geenaway, Richard Upward and Peter Wright provides an empirical examination of the degree of mobility of labour among sectors in major industrialized economies. Gains from international trade occur when the domestic economy adjusts to world prices by shifting production towards areas of comparative advantage. In an otherwise fully-employed economy, this requires reducing production in areas without comparative advantage. Hence, in an era of trade liberalization and shifting comparative advantage, the mobility of productive resources becomes a key ingredient to creating an internationally competitive economy. Labour mobility is particularly important, because inadequate mobility of labour may result in employment mismatches, and unemployment that encourages political resistance to free trade.

Greenaway, *et al.* show that the UK and the USA both experienced restructuring processes during the 1970s and 1980s, with a net flow of labour from extractive industries and manufacturing to service sectors, particularly business services, banking and finance. They seek to gain insight into the adjustment process leading to these net flows by examining the gross flows of individuals changing jobs across sectors. Comparing the USA and the UK, they find that gross flows are pro-cyclical in both countries, with individuals more likely to switch jobs in all sectors in boom periods. An important difference noted between countries is that gross flows in the USA are higher than for the UK in all periods and all sectors, so labour mobility is clearly at a higher level in the USA.

Particularly important to the issue of creating an internationally competitive economy are the characteristics of individuals who are most mobile. Here a complex pattern emerges with differences between the USA and the UK as well as between expanding and declining sectors of the economy. Greenaway, *et al.* are able to expand the set of transition possibilities for the UK data to include movements into and out of the labour force and into and out of unemployment. Here, they find housing tenure plays a particularly strong role, with occupiers of private rental accommodation much more likely to move out of the declining sectors than owner-occupiers or individuals in public rental accommodation. They close by suggesting that much more research is needed to clarify the contributing factors to a flexible workforce.

Chapter 6, 'Market Power and Foreign Trade: Implications for Competition Policy', by Harry Bloch, provides a review of the link between foreign trade and the intensity of competition in domestic and foreign product markets. The basic issue addressed is whether increasing openness to trade provides an effective constraint on the abuse of market power. If so, the traditional objective for competition policy, namely the regulation of the abuse of market power, can be increasingly left to the market as trade barriers are reduced. Thus, globalization has the potential to fundamentally change the content of appropriate competition policy by altering the conditions of competition in product markets.

Bloch notes that foreign trade increases the number of firms supplying any market beyond the group of domestic producers and also means that firms who export generally have a group of offshore producers as competitors. This suggests a substantial increase in the structural competitiveness of markets at home and abroad, particularly if one focuses on the number of potential competitors rather than the market shares of actual competitors in each market. However, a survey of models of market behaviour with foreign competition suggests that the impact of additional potential competitors on the abuse of market power is dependent on the degree of substitutability between domestic and foreign products, as well as on the interaction between foreign and domestic firms. No general prediction emerges as to the likely impact on the abuse of market power that can be expected from opening markets to foreign trade. Thus, in spite of a clear increase in structural competitiveness when markets are opened to foreign trade, there is no guarantee that the abuse of market power is substantially reduced.

Bloch then turns to a survey of empirical evidence relating to markets with foreign competition. First, he notes that studies of the linkage in prices across countries, suggested by purchasing power parity and the law of one price, provide evidence of substantial segmentation of national markets in spite of the movements towards trade liberalization over recent decades. This weakens the case for expecting foreign competition to restrain the abuse of domestic market power. Further, studies of competition in markets with foreign competitors provide evidence of implicit collusion between foreign and domestic producers, with foreign producers setting prices above their own marginal costs in export markets. This also weakens the case for foreign competition acting as a restraint on the abuse of domestic market power. Finally, studies of the pricing behaviour of domestic producers fail to provide much evidence of a restraining influence from pricing of competing foreign products. The only notable exception occurs in the case of Canada, where proximity to the relatively competitive USA market seems to exert a considerable restraining influence on domestic pricing in industries without tariff or natural barriers to trade.

David Prentice provides a case study of domestic producer behaviour when faced with import competition in Chapter 7, 'Investment, Imports and Productivity Growth in the US Cement Industry'. The cement industry in the USA provides an excellent subject for a case study of the impact of import competition. Over the period studied there is a substantial rise in the import penetration from negligible to a 20 per cent share of sales, which Prentice attributes to increased openness to imports following declines in water shipping costs. Further, as Prentice explains, there are really two industries: there are cement plants located in proximity to water shipping, the coastal industry, and there are plants located away from water shipping, the inland plants. Given the high costs of land transport for cement, only the coastal plants face any effective competition from imports. Thus, there is a natural control group, the inland plants, to compare with the group affected by increasing imports, the coastal plants.

Prentice identifies investment as the key ingredient to productivity growth and competitiveness in the Portland cement industry. Savings in factor inputs and, hence, costs in the industry have been associated with the introduction of new plant and equipment, rather than the application of new techniques to established productive capacity. For this reason, firms in the industry would be expected to use investment and disinvestment as their primary competitive strategy. Prentice examines the investment behaviour of USA Portland cement producers over the period from 1970 through 1990. Perhaps surprisingly, he finds little evidence of strategic behaviour by the producers. Instead, investment and exit decisions appear to be driven by long-run demand and plant cost considerations. This suggests that exposure to import competition has not been necessary to pressure domestic producers towards competitive behaviour, as this seems to be their natural behaviour, in spite of the highly concentrated structure of the domestic industry.

Part III: government policy issues

The design of domestic government policies for achieving national economic success in a global economy is the direct concern of the contributions in the third part of this volume. The particular policies examined concern communications, the international harmonization of tax and spending policies and the application of anti-dumping policies. Each of these areas of economic policy has become increasingly important to national economic performance in the global economy. However, our purpose is more to illustrate the breadth of government policies that have impact on international competitiveness than to provide a comprehensive treatment of all such policies (a task well beyond the scope of any single volume). In particular, we illustrate the variety of approaches that are relevant to addressing policy design in a global economy, including a conceptual approach to communications policy in Chapter 8, a theoretical approach to fiscal policy harmonization in Chapter 9 and an empirical approach to anti-dumping policy in Chapter 10.

In Chapter 8, 'Trade and Communication', Don Lamberton discusses the policies of national governments and international organizations towards communication in light of increasing international integration. He notes the impact of new communication and information-processing technology on the enormous expansion of communication and information flow both within and across countries, which presents both opportunities and threats for the improvement of national economic performance.

Lamberton challenges us to see the very broad nature of the communication and information revolution, along with implications for the way we think about international competitiveness. Against the potential for encouraging convergence towards a high living standard through the common access to technology, Lamberton warns of the threat of enhancing inequality through differential information handling capability. He notes that indivisibility is a basic characteristic of information, so the 'information-intensive economy looks set to be a fertile field for large organizations'. Networks provide a potential means to overcoming the advantages of large size, but this will depend on the ability of firms to build alliances. Here, dominant firms and countries may play a blocking, rather than enabling, role. He also argues that the use of information requires investment in more than computers, particularly in telecommunications infrastructure and education (including language training), areas in which rich countries can enhance their existing advantages.

Along with the challenges to our understanding of the nature of competition with expanding information and communication, Lamberton suggests a number of challenges for public policy at both the national and international level. The challenge to national governments in the provision of communication infrastructure and education follows directly from the changing nature of competition noted above. A further challenge is posed by the regulation of the networks and alliances arising from information and infrastructure sharing, such as encountered in the national and international regulation of telecommunication alliances. At a more basic level, there are issues of intellectual property rights and the implications of ownership of information for the ability of non-dominant players to compete in the global economy.

In Chapter 9, 'Economic Integration and Regional Policy Cooperation', by Jeffrey Petchey and Perry Shapiro, the emphasis is on intergovernmental cooperation rather than competition. In particular, Petchey and Shapiro explore the implications of the increasing integration of economic markets for the need to achieve greater integration in economic policy. The particular context they examine is where integration has moved beyond trade in products to encompass the movement of factors of production.

Petchey and Shapiro demonstrate that the welfare of sovereign states in an integrated regional factor market, such as the one emerging in Europe, is affected by the policy choices of all member states. This is due to the interdependence induced by mobility of capital and labour. If nation-states choose tax and spending policies competitively, the spatial allocation of mobile factors is inefficient. Instead, cooperation between states is shown to be efficiency enhancing, with tax and spending policies chosen to maximize joint or regional interests.

Two general difficulties are encountered when governments implement policies to achieve public objectives. First, governments generally lack adequate information to maximize the impact of their policies. This is a particularly serious difficulty when the policy aims to correct the effects of a 'market failure', as in this case market prices do not provide accurate indicators of social costs or benefits. Second, private interests generally conflict with the public purpose of the policy, creating a potential for the 'capture' of public policy in the pursuit of private gain. This potential is particularly ripe when the private interests are the source of information required to implement public policy.

A vivid example of the difficulties encountered in the implementation of public policy towards achieving international competitiveness is provided by Chapter 10, 'Inside Australia's Contingent Protection Black Box', by Donald Feaver and Kenneth Wilson. Anti-dumping determinations and the imposition of countervailing duties have become an integral part of the regulation of unfair trading practices under GATT and WTO regimes. Feaver and Wilson examine the implementation of the anti-dumping and countervailing duty (AD/CVD) process in Australia, with particular emphasis on the role played by the lack of complete information and the conflict between private interests and the objectives of public policy. Feaver and Wilson focus on *material injury determination* as the most technically complicated and least transparent step in the AD/CVD decision-making process. It is also the stage where, if the law is misinterpreted or improperly administered, bias can be surreptitiously injected into the AD/CVD decision-making process under circumstances that are difficult to detect and, therefore, difficult to legally challenge as unfair. Under the GATT Anti-Dumping and Subsidies Codes, the material injury determination is the central regulatory mechanism of the AD/CVD process and contains the requirement that only dumped or subsidized goods that *cause or threaten material injury* will be subject to anti-dumping or countervailing action. Before AD/CVD duties can be granted, a causal link between dumping and material injury must be established.

Feaver and Wilson note that it is unclear what method, if any, the Australian regulator, the Antidumping Authority, uses to establish whether a causal link exists between dumped imports and industry injury. They then go inside the black box of Australian contingent protection to examine the causation analysis in order to obtain an understanding of the process by which the ADA makes causation findings. Several empirical models are developed to test a range of hypotheses concerning the causation decision process. The results support the belief that the ADA uses a method for determining causation that is highly vulnerable to error and, more importantly, open to manipulation and bias. Thus, both incomplete information and the conflict between private and public interests are seen to play important roles in frustrating the implementation of public policy towards the regulation of unfair trading practices.

Part IV: international comparisons of economic performance

Growth in per capita income provides the most compelling testimony to international competitiveness. Not only do the forces associated with income growth, such as technical progress, improvements in input quality and enhanced market efficiency, contribute to competitiveness on world markets, but income growth is the best available proximate indicator of a country's success in the competitive struggle. The contributions in the final part of this volume each focus on a particular factor identified in the literature as explaining cross-country differences in income growth. They examine, in turn, export orientation, diffusion of technology, foreign direct investment and microeconomic reform.

Chapter 11, 'Export-led Growth in Asia: Long-run Relationships and Structural Change', by Peter Summers, examines the relationship between output growth and several factors including export growth for Japan, Korea, Malaysia, Taiwan and the USA over the period from the late 1960s through the mid-1990s. He estimates cointegrating relationships for the selected variables and finds clear evidence of structural breaks in the estimated relationship for each country.

The structural breaks that Summers finds occurred for the USA and Japan in the early 1980s, and for the other countries a few years later, around the time of the Plaza Accord. Each of the breaks is associated with a sharp reduction in the estimated elasticity of output with respect to exports. This suggests that the case for export-led growth has diminished, so the countries hardest hit by the Asian economic crisis will find it difficult to export their way out of recession. A clear message for creating an internationally competitive economy is that what works at one point in time for one country may not work for other countries at other times.

In Chapter 12, 'The International Diffusion of Technology: Technological Catch-up and Economic Growth', Mark Rogers explores the role of technology in explaining differences across countries in the rate of growth of per capita income. In particular, Rogers examines whether countries with lower levels of per capita income are able to grow faster by closing the gap in technology between themselves and richer countries. The key to such catch-up as identified by Rogers is the capacity of a country to absorb the more advanced technology.

Absorptive capacity is an abstract concept, so Rogers proceeds to nominate a number of potential proxy measures of this capacity. Five measures are specified: study abroad measures, telecommunications measures, publications measures, patent measures and international trade measures. A total of twenty measures are used alternatively as an additional regressor in equations explaining differences in per capita income growth rates across 61 countries. The regression results show that income growth is positively and significantly related to several measures whether they are entered separately or interactively with the technology gap. These key proxy measures are: the number of students studying abroad in either social sciences or engineering, the number of telex subscribers, the number of patent applications relative to GDP and exports of equipment relative to GDP.

A particular vehicle for international technology transfer that has been widely discussed in the literature is foreign direct investment (FDI). This is the context for the approach of Chapter 13, 'Foreign Direct Investment and Economic Growth in LDCs', by Balasubramanyam, Salisu and

Sapsford. In particular, they follow up their earlier work on the role of FDI in the economic growth of less-developed countries by examining the conditions under which FDI contributes positively to economic growth. Their approach, as with the Rogers study, is to estimate cross-country regressions explaining growth in per capita income, but here the focus is on the extra contribution of FDI.

Among the results to emerge from the Balasubramanyam *et al.* study is that the contribution of FDI to economic growth is positive and statistically significant only in countries that can be considered to be following export-promoting policies (hence establishing a clear link to the Summers study). Further, there is clear evidence of a positive interaction between foreign direct investment and a proxy measure of human capital, suggesting, as in the Rogers study, that technology transfer is enhanced by the absorptive capacity of the domestic economy.

In Chapter 14, 'Transaction Efficiency in New Zealand and Australia, 1961–96', Tim Hazledine examines whether microeconomic reform contributes to income growth. These reforms are generally too discontinuous and too idiosyncratic to be captured by a variable in regression equations, so Hazledine adopts a different methodology than those used in the other contributions to Part IV. His approach is to compare the experiences of two countries, New Zealand and Australia, where one country, New Zealand, has experienced a much more substantial range of reforms than have occurred over the study period in the other country, Australia.

Hazledine notes that growth in GDP and productivity in Australia exceeds that in New Zealand over the post-reform part of the study period, even though performance of the two countries was very similar prior to the beginning of the New Zealand reforms. He then proceeds to identify why microeconomic reform might worsen a country's growth and productivity performance, at least in the short run. Here he finds evidence that microeconomic reform has been associated with substantially increased transaction costs in New Zealand, where these costs are measured by the proportion of the workforce engaged in transaction-type activities. A greater proportion of the labour force engaged in such activities can enhance allocative efficiency in the economy, but it also reduces the workforce remaining to engage in transformation activities that directly lead to measured output.

A clear implication flowing from the three chapters containing studies of per capita income growth, Chapters 11–13, is the existence of synergies among policies designed to enhance international competitiveness and, thereby, achieve superior performance in per capita income growth.

Export orientation, domestic absorptive capacity (enhanced through education and other forms of human capital) and foreign direct investment (as a vehicle for technology transfer) interact to promote competitiveness and growth.

Unfortunately, no such clear story emerges from the chapters that examine aspects of the role of market liberalization. In the concluding chapter, Hazledine identifies a negative influence of moves towards commercialization in New Zealand (through increased divergence of labour from transformation activities to transaction activities). Further, in Part II dealing with market institutions, the role of trade competition in encouraging domestic competitiveness and of domestic labour market mobility in enhancing the ability of the economy to adjust to trade shocks are both left subject to substantial doubt. Finally, in Part III dealing with government policies, the studies analysing the design and implementation of communication, tax and trade policies designed to enhance competitiveness can be seen as raising more issues than they answer. There is still much to learn in the process of *Creating an Internationally Competitive Economy*. We hope that this volume at least contributes to answering the questions: What does 'international competitiveness' mean? What can countries do to achieve international competitiveness?

2
The Meaning and Measurement of International Competitiveness

*Harry Bloch and Peter Kenyon**

F11

Introduction

Discussions of economic policy and performance focus increasingly on the concept of international competitiveness. The enormous growth in world trade over recent decades means that the forces influencing trade between countries have substantial impact on the well-being of all citizens of modern economies. International competitiveness has become the catchphrase used to describe the ability to achieve desired outcomes in this era of globalization. However, with this popularity has come a fair degree of confusion. So much so that one of the world's leading economists in international economics has concluded that the term when applied to cross-country comparisons '. . . is a largely meaningless concept' (Krugman, 1996, p. 17). Part of this confusion is the implied hypothesis that in order to achieve increased living standards, countries must be able to successfully participate in this growth in international trade and that somehow this is a competitive struggle among countries, with winners and losers, both internationally and domestically.[1]

Fagerberg (1988, p. 355) defines international competitiveness broadly as 'the ability of a country to realise central economic policy goals, especially growth in income and employment, without running into balance-of-payments difficulties'. Our approach is to provide a focus to the discussion of international competitiveness by relating its meaning and measurement to the economic analysis of the forces that determine

* We are grateful to our discussant, Jakob Madsen, and other participants at the Creating an Internationally Competitive Economy conference for helpful comments and suggestions. Not all of the suggestions have been followed and complete responsibility for any errors or oversights remains with the authors.

international trading patterns. Analysis of the forces that determine international trade can be traced back at least as far as to the founder of modern economics, Adam Smith. In *The Wealth of Nations*, Smith ([1776] 1937) identifies differences in the productivity of labour across countries as providing the impetus for trade. He then demonstrates that all countries stand to gain from trade based on differences in productivity.

Differences in productivity across countries play a key role in modern discussions of international competitiveness and in the measurement of competitive advantage. However, the range of factors considered in assessing international competitiveness now extends beyond labour productivity. Our aim in this paper is to utilize economic analysis to identify a range of factors that might affect patterns of international trade and the distribution of gains from this trade. We then consider how to quantify the influence of these factors to obtain measures of international competitiveness.[2]

Traditional approaches to the analysis of international trade by economists are reviewed in the next section. We start with Smith's analysis of absolute advantage, before considering David Ricardo's analysis of comparative advantage and the neoclassical analysis of trade with general equilibrium. Each of these analyses examines the determinants of balanced trade, where the value of exports equals the value of imports. We close that section with the analysis of situations where trade is unbalanced, due to either offsetting private capital flows or government intervention in foreign exchange markets.

Recent developments in the economic analysis of international trade have focused on the role of imperfect competition. With imperfect competition, a country can improve its well-being through strategic intervention in product markets. This has led to the development of a literature concerned with the design of strategic trade policy, and in the following section we consider the implications of strategic trade theory for the meaning and measurement of international competitiveness.

Associated with the development of strategic trade theory has been the notion that competition between countries is analogous to competition between companies.[3] This view strengthened during the period in which there was apparent success for intervention by governments of some newly-industrializing Asian countries in stimulating export-oriented growth. Paul Krugman (1996) has mounted a scathing attack on this approach, which he terms pop internationalism. The pros and cons of pop internationalism and their implications for the meaning and measurement of international competitiveness are discussed, before we close this chapter with a few observations on the state of play for international competitiveness.

Traditional approaches

In this section we review approaches to the analysis of international competitiveness that have been at the core of international economics over the two centuries from the publication of Adam Smith's *Wealth of Nations*. We start with Smith's own theory of absolute advantage, before moving to Ricardo's theory of comparative advantage and its modern extension to focus on the role of factor endowments in determining comparative advantage in general equilibrium. The section concludes with a discussion of the relation between international competitiveness and balance of payments disequilibrium. A primary focus in this review is to identify the type of measure of international competitiveness relevant to each approach.

Absolute advantage

Adam Smith ([1776] 1937) demonstrates that nations can each gain from engaging in international trade. In Smith's analysis, each country has an absolute advantage in at least one product, in the sense of achieving higher labour productivity in that product than its trading partners do. The pattern of trade in Smith's analysis is determined by absolute advantage. Countries export products in which they have an absolute advantage and they import products in which they have an absolute disadvantage. Each country gains from trade in the sense that they can achieve a higher level of consumption of all products by concentrating their available labour force in the production of outputs with relatively high productivity. Thus, the measure of international competitiveness for each product as suggested by Smith's analysis is the productivity of labour achieved in a country relative to its trading partners.

Measure 1 – absolute labour productivity
A country is internationally competitive in those products for which its output per unit of labour effort exceeds that in its trading partners.

Application of the measure of absolute advantage is limited because Smith's analysis is carried out in terms of individual homogenous products and a single factor of production with exogenously determined productivity. Measures such as tonnes of wheat per worker can be compared across countries only where the product is of the same quality. Secondly, labour productivity can be altered through capital accumulation and thus can be changed by a country, so labour productivity alone cannot be a final explanation of international competitiveness. In general, comparison across products is not possible, as there is no suitable standard for this purpose in the analysis of absolute advantage.[4]

Comparative advantage

David Ricardo ([1821] 1973) extends Smith's argument concerning the gains from trade, demonstrating that gains can be achieved from international trade regardless of the absolute level of labour productivity as long as relative labour productivity differs across products between the trading partners. The pattern of trade in Ricardo's analysis is determined by comparative advantage. Countries export products in which they have high (exogenously determined) labour productivity relative to trading partners, and import products with low productivity relative to trading partners. Obtaining those products in which a country has low relative productivity through international trade allows the country to shift labour to products where it has relatively high productivity. The net effect is to expand the overall level of consumption possible in the country.

Measure 2 – comparative labour productivity
A country is internationally competitive in those products for which its output per unit of labour effort exceeds that in its trading partners by the greatest amount. The country lacks international competitiveness in those products for which its output per unit of labour input is lowest relative to that of its trading partners.

Application of the measure of comparative advantage is limited for the same reason as with the measure of absolute advantage, namely the difference in relative values of products across countries. The essential notion of both absolute and comparative advantage is that countries differ in the relative productivity of labour across industries. This implies the existence of differences in the relative values of products across countries, making comparisons of aggregates across products invalid. Furthermore, the use of comparisons of aggregates is contrary to the spirit of the analysis, as each country must have an absolute or comparative advantage in at least some range of products for there to be gains from trade. In the analyses of both absolute and comparative advantage, international competitiveness is a characteristic of some, rather than all, sectors of a country's economy.

General equilibrium with international trade

Both Smith and Ricardo base their analyses of the gains from trade on the labour theory of value, in which the amount of labour required to produce an output is a valid indicator of its relative worth. Modern economic analysis abandons the labour theory in favour of value determination through simultaneous equilibrium of all product and input markets. This approach to value determination alters the interpretation of productivity measures of competitiveness, as productivity becomes endogenously determined in the general equilibrium of prices and trade flows between countries.

An important implication of the general equilibrium analysis of international trade is that the pattern of trade depends on the relative scarcity of inputs to production. In particular, the Hecksher–Ohlin theorem tells us that countries will export products that heavily use inputs with which they are relatively well-endowed compared with their trading partners, and will import products that heavily use inputs that are relatively scarce.

Measure 3 – relative factor endowment
A country is internationally competitive in those products that most heavily utilize the factors of production with which the country is most abundantly endowed relative to other countries. The country lacks international competitiveness in those products that heavily utilize factors of production that are scarce relative to their availability in other countries.

The most obvious illustration of the impact of factor endowments on international trade involves differences in natural resource endowments. It is easy to understand that Australia, with a relatively abundant supply of arable land, is internationally competitive in the production of land-intensive agricultural products, such as wheat and wool. Likewise, Saudi Arabia is internationally competitive in the production of crude petroleum and Canada is internationally competitive in the production of softwood timber.

It should be noted that competitiveness according to general equilibrium trade theory is about relative factor endowments and not the amount of trade *per se*. This theory says nothing about the merits of the size of the traded goods sector. Therefore simple measures of international competitiveness that extol the virtues of a large traded goods sector, or a high exports to GDP ratio have no theoretical basis in terms of the Heckscher–Ohlin theory. Further, the theory explicitly denies that any single sector, say manufacturing, is more important as an exportable sector than any other, such as agriculture or services. Of course, changing overall patterns of world demand and supply might make the maintenance of competitiveness in a particular sector more difficult as the terms of trade faced by a country change over time, despite initial relative factor abundance.

The role of labour and capital in determining international competitiveness is more complicated because a country's endowment of each is at least partially endogenous. Firstly, both labour and capital can move across national boundaries. They can be expected to move from where they are relatively abundant to where they are relatively scarce, especially when scarcity (abundance) is reflected in high (low) prices.

Secondly, the quantity of labour and capital available in a country changes through processes of population growth and capital accumulation, respectively. These changes may only partially reflect price or scarcity and the impact on aggregate quantities of labour and capital may be slow. However, there is much greater opportunity for changing the composition of the labour force in terms of skills or occupations and changing the composition of capital in terms of its physical form and distribution between industries. Indeed, the modification of capital and labour endowments through government intervention is suggested as a possible strategy for enhancing competitiveness in modern trade theory as discussed below. Also, government intervention to influence labour and capital endowments plays a central role in new growth theory. If a country embarks on such government intervention, it will be affecting its industrial structure and the capacity of particular industries to compete internationally.

Unbalanced trade

The analysis reviewed above is based on the assumption that the trade between countries is balanced, so that the value of each country's exports is equal to the value of its imports. Also, there is no allowance for movement of factors of production between countries, so there are no capital flows. Hence, the analysis assumes the existence of external balance. Much recent discussion of measures of international competitiveness focuses on the use of measures that can indicate a lack of external balance. In particular, Boltho (1996, p. 2) suggests that a country is internationally competitive if it can achieve internal balance, in terms of a desired combination of domestic inflation and unemployment, without encountering an undesired deficit in its balance of payments or instability in its exchange rate.

Under a fixed exchange regime, the balance of payments provides a measure of external balance. In the absence of offsetting capital flows, a balance of payments deficit requires a country to intervene in foreign exchange markets to buy up domestic currency. The country's ability to intervene is limited by the size of its foreign exchange reserves. Hence, recourse to domestic austerity or currency devaluation could be expected in the face of sustained balance of payments deficits. In this sense, a balance of payments deficit indicates a lack of international competitiveness.

Measure 4 – balance of payments
A country that maintains a fixed foreign exchange rate lacks international competitiveness if it runs a sustained balance of payments deficit. The country is internationally competitive if it has external balance or a balance of payments surplus.

Under a floating exchange rate regime, balance of payment deficits or surpluses have no special significance. They are simply offsets to government operations in foreign exchange markets, undertaken for purposes that are unrelated to maintaining external balance. The most commonly used measure of international competitiveness for countries that maintain floating exchange rates is the real exchange rate.

Measure 5 – real foreign exchange rate
For a country that maintains a floating foreign exchange rate, international competitiveness is inversely related to the country's real exchange rate.

The real exchange rate between the currencies of two countries is the exchange rate deflated by a measure of the relative price or cost levels in the countries. The use of the real exchange rate as a measure of international competitiveness is justified by appeal to the purchasing power parity theory of exchange rates. In equilibrium with costless trade and perfect information, the exchange rate adjusted price of any homogenous traded product is equalized across countries according to the 'law of one price'. If all products are traded, the exchange rate between any two currencies is then inversely proportional to the ratio of domestic price indexes (assuming that the indexes are calculated using the same weights on each price). Of course, not all goods are traded and so domestic price indices are weighted averages of the prices of traded and non-traded goods, and the proportions of traded to non-traded goods change over time. Also, prices of exports and imports may not move together as we discuss below.

Evidence from empirical studies tends to weigh heavily against the law of one price (see, for example, Ceglowski, 1994; and the survey by

Goldstein and Kahn, 1985). Yet, it is widely observed that countries with a relatively high rate of inflation do tend to experience depreciation of their currencies. The implication is that purchasing power parity provides at best only a crude explanation of foreign exchange rates. Thus, interpretation of changes in the real exchange rate as implying weakness or strength in a country's overall trading position is fraught with danger.[5]

The balance of payments and the real exchange rate each measure international competitiveness in a way that relates to a country's aggregate trading position. These measures are thereby distinguished from Measures 1–3 above. In deriving the earlier measures, it is assumed that there is external balance in terms of balanced trade and no capital flows. External imbalance can coexist with gains from trade of the type associated with the sector-specific measures of competitive advantage.

Along with the aggregate measure of competitiveness, given by the real exchange rate, there is a potentially diverse set of price comparisons for individual products. Comparison at the level of the individual product is made by calculating the ratio of the product prices in each country expressed in a common currency. These prices are identical when the law of one price holds, but otherwise reflect aspects of external imbalance, as revealed in real exchange rates, as well as aspects of comparative advantage.

Measure 6 – relative product price adjusted for exchange rate
A country is internationally competitive in those products with prices lower than for identical products from foreign countries. It lacks international competitiveness in products with prices higher than for identical products from foreign countries.

Comparative advantage can be reflected in relative product price through the impact of factor endowments on input prices and production costs. If trade were costless and without restriction, relative prices for inputs would be equalized across countries according to the Stolper–Samuelson theorem. This would lead towards equalization of relative production costs in all countries, so relative prices would be equalized under conditions of perfectly competitive equilibrium. However, with transaction costs and impediments to trade, neither relative input prices nor relative product prices can be expected to equalize across countries. In this case, comparative advantage is associated with a low domestic product price, which tends to reduce the exchange-rate adjusted price for the domestic product relative to identical foreign products.

Modern trade theory

There has been immense growth in trade in differentiated and sophisticated products. These products do not fit comfortably within the traditional models of international trade, based as it is on the assumption of perfect competition among producers of homogenous goods. Recent developments in the theory of international trade deal with the changing structure of trade by stressing the roles of imperfect competition, increasing returns and product variety (see for example Krugman, 1990, and Grossman and Helpman, 1991). Imperfect competition introduces an extra element of endogeneity into the determination of competitiveness. Firms set product prices taking account of the price and quality of competing products as well as production costs and market demand. Thus, a worsened competitive position, say due to an improvement in the quality of a competing foreign product, may be at least partially offset by a decrease in the firm's profit margin and price. In this sense, high profit margins may be taken to reflect a strong competitive position and low profit margins a weak competitive position.

Measure 7 – relative profit margin (product level)
A country is internationally competitive in those products with profit margins higher than for competing products from foreign countries. It lacks international competitiveness in products with profits lower than for competing products from foreign countries.

Relative profit margin, Measure 7, is most useful as a measure of international competitiveness when used in conjunction with the corresponding relative price, Measure 6. A product that earns a high profit margin in comparison with competing foreign products and is sold at a relatively low price is clearly internationally competitive. In this case, the competitive price is achieved without resort to cutting profit margins, leaving the firm in a strong position to enhance product variety and quality as well as to deter competitive entry through an aggressive investment strategy.[6]

Product variety and quality are important determinants of a firm's competitive position in the new theory of international trade. In the simplest model of product variety, the quantity sold by a producer is proportional to the number of varieties it offers in the market. Both the number of product varieties and the quality of products on offer are endogenous. Thus, a measure of product variety and quality could be used

as a measure of international competitiveness in a manner similar to the
relative profit margin measure. However, there are no reasonable indexes
of product variety and quality generally available to be used for this
purpose.

In the place of direct measures of product variety and quality it is
common to use proxy measures that are associated with the production of
variety and quality. The most common of these is a measure of
technological activity, usually the level of R&D expenditures or the
number of scientists and engineers employed.

Measure 8 – relative R&D intensity (product level)
A country is internationally competitive in those products with higher
R&D activity, measured by expenditures or personnel, than for
competing products from foreign countries. It lacks international
competitiveness in products with lower R&D activity than for
competing products from foreign countries.

Although appealing, this measure of international competitiveness is
problematic. To the extent that R&D is driven by the profit motive, it may
well depend on factor endowments and thus be left to market forces to
determine its quantum and direction. Indeed, if R&D activity were simply
a private good and government policy intervened in a way which
conflicted with market forces by relocating R&D in areas lacking
comparative advantage, there would be a waste of resources and the
world R&D effort would diverge from the optimal level. Grossman and
Helpman (1991, p. 341) go so far as to say that in such a circumstance
'every country finds itself sharing in the loss'.

In addition, it is argued that the benefits of R&D can be readily imported
through being embodied in imported technology from countries with a
comparative advantage in the actual production of R&D. According to
this view, it is a waste of a country's resources to engage in R&D activity in
industries in which it lacks comparative advantage. The particular country
can more cheaply obtain the benefits of R&D from others through
importing the latest technology that embodies the world's best R&D.

Nevertheless, the production of R&D has a public good aspect to it.
First, it is not obvious that increasing the R&D effort in one country will
reduce it in another. Secondly, much of the 'development' part of R&D
depends on the 'research' part – innovation and diffusion are hard to
distinguish in practice (Bell and Pavitt, 1995). Technical change begets
technical change. Finally, R&D abilities often have to be created and
fostered in a way that will not be undertaken optimally through market

forces, but require public policy intervention for all the usual reasons: non-rivalry in consumption, non-excludability from much research output, and information asymmetries about the risks involved.

The level of R&D spending that a country undertakes (and, associated with it, the amount of spending that it devotes to human capital formation) is seen by some researchers to be important in another way as a measure of its international competitiveness. Recent developments in the theory of economic growth suggest that devoting resources to human capital development and to the process of technological advance enables countries to guide their rate of economic growth and thus choose to grow faster if they wish to do so.[7]

Instead of technical progress being exogenous, as in the original Solow–Swan neoclassical growth model, technical change and so growth are seen as being endogenous. R&D and human capital enhancement have spillover effects, which affect productivity across many sectors. A country's pattern of development and trade is, therefore, determined in the long run, in part, by the resources that it devotes to technological change and research and development, broadly defined. This raises the possibility of a country fashioning its comparative and competitive advantage as a policy option.

Measure 9 – relative R&D activity (national level)
A country is internationally competitive when it devotes relatively more resources measured by expenditures or personnel to R&D activity compared with other countries. It lacks international competitiveness compared with foreign countries to the extent that its R&D effort falls behind other countries.

Consideration of the role of public policy and public goods in relation to R&D expenditure raises two other related areas where government activity can increase the productivity of the private sector through judicious use of public expenditure and taxation policy. These are government investment in physical infrastructure and human capital enhancement. It is well-known that governments can target both physical and human capital, which enhances the infrastructure for areas of actual or emerging comparative advantage, thereby reaping Marshallian industry externalities. There is an emerging empirical literature that supports at least a role for public infrastructure spending in enhancing private sector productivity.[8]

In addition, where there are (internal) economies of scale there is scope for strategic trade policy, so that a country may capture a whole market ahead of other potential entrants. Similar arguments can be made for investment expenditure in R&D. The theoretical case for such expenditures is watertight.[9] It is in this area of 'strategic trade policy' that the concept of international competitiveness as a race with winners and losers comes closest to formal international trade theory.

The so-called 'new trade theory' (it is now approaching its twentieth birthday!) provides some justification for the view that governments can and should intervene in specific sectors or in particular ways to increase economic welfare and that such an increase may be at the expense of other countries' welfare. This directly challenges the benign idea from conventional trade theory (a world of constant returns and perfect competition) that, by and large, all trade is welfare-enhancing and that *laissez-faire* is the best trade and industry policy.

Measure 10 – relative strategic industry policy expenditure
A country will be internationally competitive in those products that it supports more strongly than its trading partners through strategic industry policy expenditure, including expenditure on industry-specific physical and human capital enhancing infrastructure, export subsidies, R&D expenditure and the like. A country that does not pursue strategic industry policy will lose international competitiveness.

This is perhaps the most controversial measure discussed here. Even one of the inventors of the case for strategic trade policy has questioned the need for policy intervention, coming down on the side of free trade as the best policy (Krugman, 1987). The dangers associated with providing private interests with an excuse for public expenditure in their favour is viewed as too fraught with potential for harm.

A basic critique is that resources that are targeted to specific uses in order to reduce marginal costs in one sector must be drawn from other sectors, thereby increasing marginal costs in those sectors. One sector's subsidy is another sector's cost. Of course, as a result the affected sectors will find it more difficult to be competitive in *their* markets. Secondly, if one country can engage in strategic industry and trade policy, other countries can, too. The resulting trade policy war may, under fairly reasonable assumptions, be welfare-reducing for both countries, trapping them in a vicious Prisoner's Dilemma. Thirdly, there is the problem of foresight. Often, 'winners' from strategic industry policy are only able to be seen from the perspective of hindsight. For example, targeting R&D or the strategic targeting of infrastructure is a very risky proposition. The problem is even more difficult in a world of imperfect competition (as is nearly always the case where strategic policy may be advantageous). It is very difficult to know *a priori* that a particular sector, particularly one that is developing new technology or a new product, is likely to turn out successful. It is not just the threat from other countries that may prevent success. There are a whole raft of issues that must be addressed depending on the nature of the specific industry policy. For example, if export subsidies are to be implemented to assist a 'strategic sector', the sector will be motivated to direct more product to export markets, most likely to the detriment of the welfare of domestic consumers. Or, if R&D is subsidized so as to capture economy-wide spillover effects, how is the value of the externality ascertained? By their nature, externalities are difficult to value. Hence, comparing the costs and benefits of the subsidy against the external benefits is problematic. Also, what is to prevent new knowledge spilling over to other countries? This may lead to free-riding elsewhere in the world, with the ultimate effect of increasing other countries' overall competitiveness at the subsidizing country's expense.

Finally, there is the problem of rent-seeking. Opening up the possibility of subsidies or special treatment from government, no matter how well-justified in theory, will immediately give rise to an industry of lobbyists who will expend resources up to the point where the marginal subsidy or benefit equals the marginal cost of lobbying. It is not at all certain that even if there are rents to be had through strategic trade policy, they will not be dissipated by the political economy of rent-seeking.

Pop internationalism

The term pop internationalism has been used by Paul Krugman (1996) to characterize the view that the gains from trade between countries are achieved in a manner analogous to the gains achieved by companies through competition with their rivals. In particular, competition between countries in this view is taken to involve winners and losers. Krugman is severely critical of pop internationalism, noting that the fundamental insight from the traditional economic analysis of international trade is that all countries gain from trade. Less obvious, but nonetheless just as important, is the further insight from standard trade theory that technological advances in one country also increase living standards in other countries with whom the innovating country trades.

We are broadly sympathetic with Krugman's critique. Our review of traditional approaches to the analysis of trade emphasizes comparative advantage as the basis of gains from trade. We associate comparative advantage with differences between countries in relative measures of productivity, factor endowments, pricing, profitability and technological activity. In our analysis, each country is more competitive, or at least expected to become more competitive, in some range of products.[10] Thus, our analysis does not support the notion that some countries gain from trade while others lose.

A major qualification to our support for the Krugman critique relates to the distributional impact of international trade. Firstly, the gains from trade need not be, and generally are not, evenly distributed across countries. Maizels (1992) argues forcefully that developing countries have been disadvantaged in international trade because the prices of the primary commodities they export are subject to short-run instability and a long-run downward trend relative to the prices of manufactured goods.[11] He attributes these adverse outcomes at least in part to protectionist policies in the developed countries. Bloch and Sapsford (1997) attribute the downward trend in primary commodity prices relative to the prices of manufactured goods to a combination of technological change and the market power held by manufacturers and the unionized labour they employ. In any event, the decline in purchasing power with the adverse movement of the terms of trade for primary product exporters works against any gains they would otherwise obtain from trade.

Another distributional issue arising from trade is the adverse impact of trade on the income of some factors of production. The Stolper–Samuelson theorem holds that free trade will lead to a decline in the real income of a country's relatively scarce factors of production when there is competitive equilibrium. This provides a solid analytical basis for groups within most countries that feel threatened by trade, particularly if they are a relatively scarce group within the country (such as low-skilled workers in the rich industrialized countries).

In spite of our reservations, we share Krugman's concern that the main potential source of benefit is often overlooked in debates about the competitive position of countries. In particular, just as in a closed economy, the fundamental source of improved economic well being in open economies is growth in productivity, particularly labour productivity. We come to the same conclusion as Porter, that in the context of improving international competitiveness 'the only meaningful concept of competitiveness at the national level is national productivity' (Porter, 1990, p. 6). Thus, it is appropriate to use relative labour productivity for the country as a whole as a summary measure of a country's performance relative to other countries, recognizing that trade and international competitiveness may only represent some of the channels through which labour productivity contributes to this overall performance.

Measure 11 – relative labour productivity (national level)
A country achieves international competitiveness and a high level of economic performance relative to other countries when its labour productivity is high relative to these countries.

Several observations can be made about the usefulness of relative labour productivity as a measure of economic relative economic performance over the long run. First, there is considerable empirical evidence for the proposition that the key to raising per capita income over a long period is productivity growth and especially labour productivity growth (see, for example, Baumol, Blackman and Wolff, 1989; and Haque, 1995).

Secondly, aggregate labour productivity as a measure of economic efficiency ignores the contribution of other factors, especially capital, and so ignores the fact that countries using, say, more capital-intensive techniques will have higher measured labour productivity without necessarily being more efficient in the use of *all* inputs. However, it is the case that, empirically, labour and capital tend to be complementary in production and are less substitutable than the simple textbook story suggests. Also, changes in factor prices tend to lead firms to cut costs by seeking techniques that are absolutely superior rather than comparing the cost of different factor combinations (that is, firms try to 'shrink' unit isoquants inward towards the origin, rather than shift between points on a given isoquant). Therefore, at least over the long term, a ranking of countries in terms of labour productivity is likely to reflect a ranking of superior techniques, and thus overall productive efficiency in the use of all factors, rather than just differences in factor intensities.[12]

In any case, even if low labour productivity countries can successfully compete with high labour productivity countries, they can only do so by paying lower real wages. If such a country wishes to increase wages and living standards, it can only do so by increasing labour productivity and this is likely to be by adopting techniques more like those utilized in high labour productivity countries. Thus, the rate of growth of labour productivity can be taken as an indicator of the adoption of more efficient techniques.

A necessary caveat is that all of this is long-term. For example, in the short term, changes in employment, unemployment and the labour force participation rate will affect the nexus between per capita income and labour productivity. Similarly, changes in the terms of trade will also affect per capita incomes independently of labour productivity. However, over the long term, *trends* in these factors are likely to be small or non-existent.

Concluding comments

In this chapter we have set forth and commented on the meaning of 11 measures of international competitiveness. We have explored these measures from the perspective of the analysis of the forces that determine the pattern of international trade. The traditional approach of the economic analysis of international trade suggests that international competitiveness is very much a micro concept. Trade is based on comparative advantage, which means that individual products or industries are internationally competitive in the sense of having low cost and price relative to the same product or industry in trading partners. Countries are not internationally competitive in the aggregate, as it is impossible to have a comparative advantage in all products and industries.

Pop internationalism treats international competitiveness as a macro concept. Some countries are internationally competitive, while others are not. The former countries grow and prosper, while the latter fail to keep up or enter into decline. Government intervention plays a key role in determining to which group a country belongs.

A common element in the micro and macro approaches to international competitiveness is the idea that competitiveness is associated with productivity growth. An increase in productivity reduces cost at either the micro or the macro level, allowing for a reduction in price relative to trading partners. This then permits an expansion of sales, output and employment. General equilibrium analysis implies that the macro level reduction in relative price can only be transitory. To restore general equilibrium, the reduction in cost requires an offsetting appreciation of the foreign exchange rate or increases in input prices. However, the general equilibrium adjustments to a reduction in cost for a particular product or industry are spread over the whole economy and do not alter the qualitative predictions based on a partial equilibrium analysis. Thus, the improvement in the competitive position of a product or industry can be permanent.

The transitory nature of improvements in international competitiveness at the macro level does not imply that the benefits of these improvements are ephemeral and unimportant. Appreciation of a country's foreign exchange rate or increases in prices of domestic factors of production are associated with a rise in the standard of living in general equilibrium. Further, endogenous growth theory identifies conditions under which gains in production can be reinvested to provide for a continual rising standard of living.

Modern trade theory specifies conditions under which governments can intervene to enhance domestic economic welfare through strategic tax and subsidy policies. Endogenous growth theory also supports interventionist policies, especially in the areas of technological development and human capital formation, again under specified conditions. The identification of economic circumstances that match the conditions specified in theory is fraught with danger, due to both inadequate knowledge of the processes of economic development and the temptation to use public interest arguments as a justification for the pursuit of private interests.

Where does this leave the concept 'international competitiveness' as an operational concept in both theoretical and policy analysis? Clearly, the concept is multidimensional and situation-specific. A single measure can not capture all the relevant aspects for any product, industry or aggregate economy. Also, the most appropriate set of measures will differ across, products, industries and aggregate economies depending on market institutions. It is hoped that this chapter has set the scene for addressing these issues.

The contributions in the remainder of this volume tackle the complexity of the concept of international competitiveness from a number of different angles. First, James Gapinski implements an averaging procedure that provides an index based on several different measures of competitiveness, taking full cognizance of limited accuracy of any such index. Next, the contributions in Part II more closely examine market institutions to determine the precise mechanisms that affect international competitiveness under a specific set of institutions. This is followed in Part III by contributions that apply economic analysis to examining the impact of particular government policies within a specified market and institutional context. Finally, the contributions in Part IV use methods of data analysis to identify factors that are associated with differences in economic performance.

Notes

1   The title of Lester Thurow's book *Head to Head: The Coming Economic Battle among Japan, Europe and America* (1992) gives the flavour of this view. Krugman (1996, n. 1) lists a further ten influential books that by and large have the same thesis – that international economic relations are a competitive struggle with winners and losers.

2   Our objective is to identify 'indicators' of international competitiveness as contrasted with the 'targets' identified in Fagerberg's definition or with the 'instruments' of government policies that encourage competitiveness. Of course, the separation among targets, instruments and indicators is often tenuous at best, so some of our measures, which are meant to be indicators of

competitiveness, may very well be used by other commentators as either targets or instruments.

3 This metaphor is a favourite amongst politicians. For example, Krugman (1996, p. 4) reports President Clinton's view that each nation is 'like a big corporation competing in the global market place'.

4 The difference in absolute advantage across countries means that each country has its own relative value of products in terms of either labour content or price. It is not possible to aggregate outputs in one country using its own relative values and then compare consistently with an aggregate of the same products in another country that has been formed using the other country's relative values. The practical counterpart of this conceptual difficulty occurs with comparisons of national incomes based on purchasing power parity exchange rates.

5 A counter example is illustrative. Suppose a country, say Australia, experiences an improvement in its terms of trade because there is an increase in the price of its exports, for example wheat and rice, due to foreign shocks, such as a drought abroad. Before any adjustment in the value of Australian currency, this would imply an appreciation of Australia's real exchange rate. The interpretation of this change in the real exchange rate according to our Measure 5 is that Australia has lost international competitiveness, even though her external balance position has strengthened. Also, a depreciating real exchange rate may lessen the ability of a country to enjoy imported goods and services and thus may result in a lowering of living standards, and so although international competitiveness may have increased according to Measure 5, this is hardly a desirable outcome.

6 Relative unit cost and relative unit labour cost are commonly used measures in discussions of international competitiveness. We do not include these in our set of measures as they are covered implicitly by the combination of our measures of relative price and relative profit margin. Low relative cost implies either low relative price or high relative profit margin.

7 There is now an enormous literature addressing endogenous growth theory. Key pioneering articles are Lucas (1988) and Romer (1986). A comprehensive recent treatment is given in Aghion and Howitt (1998). For an empirical application to explaining differences in growth performance across countries see the contribution by Mark Rogers in this volume.

8 A large literature has been generated by Aschauer (1989), which basically answers a qualified 'Yes' to the question posed by him in the title to his initiatory article.

9 Among the pioneers are Krugman (many key articles are gathered in Krugman, 1990) and Brander and Spencer (see, Brander and Spencer, 1983 and 1985, for example). Having said this, it must be stressed that the theoretical cases are often very model-specific, and sometimes do not generalize beyond the assumptions of the particular models (see Eaton and Grossman, 1986, for example).

10 A country that is expected to become competitive over some range of products may run a balance of trade deficit offset by a private capital inflow.

11 A similar adverse impact is felt by developed countries, such as Australia and New Zealand, whose exports are dominated by primary commodities.

12 Salter observed as early as 1966 that, 'technical advances which lead to absolute savings in labour unaccompanied by absolute saving in capital (both

measured per unit of output) are exceptional, and the more usual case is that of advances which involve some absolute saving of both factors' (Salter, 1966, p. 33). Haque (1995) discusses more recent empirical evidence of the correlation between high labour productivity and high capital productivity across a range of countries.

References

Aghion, P. and Howitt, P. (1998) *Endogenous Growth Theory*, Cambridge, Mass.: MIT Press.

Aschauer, D.A. (1989), 'Is Public Expenditure Productive?' *Journal of Monetary Economics*, vol. 23, pp. 177–200.

Baumol, W.J., Blackman, S.A. and Wolff, E.N. (1989) *Productivity and American Leadership: The Long View*, Cambridge, Mass.: MIT Press.

Bell, M. and Pavitt, K. (1995) 'The Development of Technological Capabilities', in I. Haque (ed.), *Trade, Technology and International Competitiveness*, Washington, D.C.: The Economic Development Institute, World Bank.

Bloch, H. and Sapsford, D. (1997) 'Some Estimates of Prebisch and Singer Effects on the Terms of Trade between Primary Producers and Manufacturers', *World Development*, vol. 25, pp. 1873–84.

Boltho, A. (1996) 'The Assessment: International Competitiveness', *Oxford Review of Economic Policy*, vol. 12, pp. 1–16.

Brander, J.A. and Spencer, B.J. (1983) 'International R&D Rivalry and Industrial Strategy', *Review of Economic Studies*, vol. 50, pp. 707–22.

— and — (1985) 'Export Subsidies and International Market Share', *Journal of International Economics*, vol. 18, pp. 83–100.

Ceglowski, J. (1994) 'The Law of One Price Revisited: New Evidence on the Behaviour of International Prices' *Economic Inquiry*, vol. 32, pp. 407–18.

Eaton, J. and Grossman, G.M. (1986) 'Optimal Trade and Industrial Policy under Oligopoly', *Quarterly Journal of Economics*, vol. 101, pp. 383–406.

Fagerberg, J. (1988) 'International Competitiveness', *Economic Journal*, vol. 98, pp. 355–374.

Goldstein, M. and Kahn, M.S. (1985) 'Income and Price Effects in Foreign Trade', in R.W. Jones and P.B. Kenen (eds), *Handbook of International Economics*, Amsterdam: North Holland.

Grossman, G.M. and Helpman, E. (1991) *Innovation and Growth in the Global Economy*, Cambridge, Mass.: MIT Press.

Haque, I. ul (1995) 'Technology and Competitiveness', in I. ul Haque (ed.), *Trade, Technology and International Competitiveness*, Washington, D.C.: The Economic Development Institute, World Bank.

Krugman, P. (1987) 'Is Free Trade Passé?', *Journal of Economic Perspectives*, vol. 1, pp. 131–46.

— (1990) *Rethinking International Trade*, Cambridge, Mass.: MIT Press.

— (1996) *Pop Internationalism*, Cambridge, Mass.: MIT Press.

Lucas, R.E. (1988) 'On the Mechanics of Economic Development,' *Journal of Monetary Economics*, vol. 22, pp. 3–42.

Maizels, A. (1992) *Commodities in Crisis*, Oxford: Clarendon Press.

Porter, M. (1990) *The Competitive Advantage of Nations*, London: Macmillan.

Ricardo, D. ([1821] 1973) *The Principles of Political Economy and Taxation*, London: J.M. Dent & Sons.

Romer, P. (1986) 'Increasing Returns and Long-run Growth', *Journal of Political Economy*, vol. 94, pp. 1002–37.

Salter, W.E.G. (1966) *Productivity and Technical Change*, Cambridge, UK: Cambridge University Press.

Smith, A. ([1776] 1937) *The Wealth of Nations*, New York: Modern Library.

3
Developing ICOM: An Index of International Competitiveness[†]

James H. Gapinski[*]

'Well, well', said he presently with an exclamation of satisfaction, 'things are turning a little in our direction at last. Why, Watson, I do honestly believe that we are going to pull it off, after all.'

Sherlock Holmes in *The Adventure of the Bruce–Partington Plans*

Introduction

At one level, international competitiveness is a vague concept that means different things to different people. At another level, however, it is a fairly precise concept that has intuitive appeal. Surely, anyone acquainted with the principles of economics has a feel for the notion of competitiveness,

[†] James Gapinski died on 19 November 2000, in Tallahassee, Florida. Vale Jim!

[*] I sincerely thank Peter Kenyon and Harry Bloch at Curtin University of Technology, first for the chance to develop ICOM and second for the chance to develop it in Perth, one of my favourite places. It should be noted, however, that the ICOM endeavour was truly a team effort. Noelle Doss provided valuable input on the construction of the index, and her energy together with her knowledge of databanks kept the work moving on a tight schedule. She, perhaps more than anyone else, can appreciate the pertinence of the Holmes quotation at the start of this piece. Helen Cabalu and Michael Dockery volunteered instructive thoughts as well. David Western, a mate of long-standing, ran important parallel work and adroitly presented the results at the ICOM session of the Conference. There, Sandra Hopkins served as discussant and in that capacity offered thorough and insightful comments. Madeleine Linton disassembled numerous computers to configure one to fit the purpose at hand, and Marek Zawada modified the software to make it operate. Sue Lomax and Val Smith amiably handled the word processing at Curtin. At Florida State University, Karen Wells processed words in her characteristically diligent manner, and Peter Krafft drew figures in his characteristically masterful fashion. The ICOM project spanned the globe, and thanks naturally assume global proportions. Blame, though, rests entirely with me.

and it may not take much to extend that notion into the international context. In that global setting countries may be viewed as having different degrees of international competitiveness: some may enjoy high levels of success while others may post dismal records. Pursued a bit further, logic suggests that nations might be ranked by their competitiveness, and this chapter develops a simplified index that establishes such a ranking. Concentrating on the Asia Pacific region, the index begins with a definition of international competitiveness. It then specifies series to make the definition quantifiable, and gathers data on those series and combines the numbers under various weight structures. Formally called the Index of *I*nternational *COM*petitiveness, it is known as ICOM for short.

The next section offers a definition of concept and addresses the question of index size and performance. Building on a performance test, we then recast ICOM with series drawn from standard sources and determine country rankings for the mid-decade years 1975, 1985 and 1995 and for the 'out' years 1998 and 1999. We then move to an enhanced ICOM and repeat the exercise, finally concluding with thoughts on alternative orientations for ICOM and on prospects for future work.

Definition, size and performance

International competitiveness can be defined in numerous ways as the contributions by Hopkins and Cabalu (1993, pp. 10–12, 27) and Manzur (1996, p. 1) illustrate. Such definitions have merit because they bring precision to the concept. For present purposes, international competitiveness is defined as *the ability to provide internationally a quality product promptly at a reasonable price*. According to this proposition, the concept has five dimensions: the ability to provide, international scope, quality product, promptness and reasonable price. ICOM specifies series to capture each of those dimensions. It should be observed, however, that from the very beginning ICOM was envisioned to be managed by a small staff in recognition of the resource constraints that customarily bind academic outfits, and consequently involves a small number of series. By contrast, the World Economic Forum (WEF) publishes an international competitiveness index that includes hundreds of series. Cited in popular publications such as the *Wall Street Journal* (King, 1998), the WEF index represents a commendably ambitious undertaking as even a casual reading of *The World Competitiveness Report 1995* (World Economic Forum, 1995) makes evident.

Against the huge number of series behind the WEF index, ICOM musters ten. Hence, the question that immediately arises concerns performance. Can a small index generate reliable results? Can a small index generate roughly the same pattern of competitiveness rankings produced by a large measure such as the WEF index? To answer that question, ICOM is first constructed using ten series from the 1995 *Report*. Comprising the ten are five sets of two series chosen to capture each of the five components of the competitiveness definition. That is, two series reflect the ability-to-provide aspect, two represent the international slant, and so on down the line. The results of this test for 1995 are presented in Table 3.1.

As regards format, Table 3.1 spans 13 countries in the Asia Pacific region. These are the four East Asian tigers of Hong Kong, (South) Korea, Singapore and Taiwan; the three Southeast Asian lions of Indonesia, Malaysia and Thailand; the Philippine gaur; the China panda; and the four elephants of Australia, Japan, New Zealand and the United States.[1]

In covering the 13 nations, Table 3.1 looks at four weight structures for ICOM. First, it considers equal weights for the ten series followed by double, triple and quadruple weights for the two trade variables, the greater emphasis on the external components being motivated by the deliberate international orientation of the index. Once assigned, the weights combine with the component series to determine ICOM by the expression:

$$\text{ICOM}_j^z = \sum_{i=1}^{10} \alpha_i z_{ij} \tag{1}$$

where, for some time t like year 1995, z_{ij} denotes the normalized value of series i for country j and where α_i designates the corresponding weight.[2] Superscript z in ICOM_j^z identifies the measure as being represented in basic or unadjusted form. Under equal weights, $\alpha_i = 0.10$ for all series. For double trade weights, $\alpha_3 = \alpha_4 = \frac{2}{12}$, the international elements being taken as series 3 and 4. Each remaining weight for the double-trade-weight scenario amounts to $\frac{1}{12}$. Similarly, for triple trade weights, $\alpha_3 = \alpha_4 = \frac{3}{14}$ with the balance of weights being $\frac{1}{14}$ each. Quadruple weights split into $\frac{4}{16}$ versus $\frac{1}{16}$. It may be observed that under all four regimes, ICOM_j^z is a convex combination of its z factors. Hence, for any country ICOM_j^z must lie between the highest and lowest z values for that country. Likewise it may be observed that after calculation by equation (1), ICOM_j^z is then scaled for purposes of presentation to give the top-ranked country a score of 100 and the bottom-placed nation a score of zero.[3] Whereas ICOM_j^z can be negative for some countries, ICOM – the scaled ICOM_j^z – never can be negative.

Table 3.1 International competitiveness rankings and scores by the WEF index and by ICOM for 1995

		ICOM			
Rank	WEF index	Equal weights	Double trade weights	Triple trade weights	Quadruple trade weights
1	USA	Sing (100.0)	Sing (100.0)	Sing (100.0)	Sing (100.0)
2	Singapore	Jpn (93.2)	Jpn (83.1)	Jpn (77.7)	HK (75.2)
3	Hong Kong	USA (88.6)	HK (75.4)	HK (75.3)	Jpn (74.3)
4	Japan	HK (75.7)	USA (72.2)	USA (63.4)	USA (57.8)
5	New Zealand	Tai (69.1)	Tai (61.7)	Tai (57.8)	Tai (55.3)
6	Taiwan	Aus (67.4)	Aus (57.9)	NZ (54.0)	Mal (53.5)
7	Australia	NZ (61.2)	NZ (56.5)	Aus (52.8)	NZ (52.5)
8	Malaysia	Kor (53.3)	Mal (49.5)	Mal (51.9)	Aus (49.7)
9	Korea	Mal (45.3)	Kor (46.1)	Kor (42.3)	Thai* (42.5)
10	Thailand	Thai (38.4)	Thai (40.5)	Thai (41.7)	Kor* (40.0)
11	Indonesia	Indo (12.3)	Indo (16.0)	Indo (18.1)	Phil (20.1)
12	China	Chi (0.4)	Phil (10.5)	Phil (16.4)	Indo (19.5)
13	Philippines	Phil (0.0)	Chi (0.0)	Chi (0.0)	Chi (0.0)

Notes: Parentheses indicate competitiveness scores. Asterisks indicate block differences in rankings between the WEF index and ICOM.

Table 3.1 contains much information, but the main conclusion is that ICOM tracks the much larger WEF index rather well. For example, the ICOM scenario having equal weights matches the WEF country blocks exactly. Block 1 for ICOM contains Singapore, Japan, the United States and Hong Kong, just as the WEF block 1 does. Similar equivalence holds for blocks 2 and 3. Moreover, identical matches between ICOM and WEF continue through double and triple trade weights. Quadruple weights show a minor block reversal for Korea and Thailand, suggesting that quadruple weights give a bit too much emphasis to trade factors.

The results are encouraging inasmuch as they answer the performance question in the affirmative: a simplified index *can* generate roughly the same pattern of rankings produced by a large index.

Recasting ICOM

The good news from the performance test invites further work on ICOM, an obvious need being reformulation of the component series into another set of ten elements whose data can be readily obtained from standard sources. The proviso of ready availability is dictated by the commitment to keep ICOM manageable by a small staff.

In the new collection of series, *ability to provide* is represented by (1) the rate of growth of real GDP expressed as a per cent. Plainly, a greater rate of production implies a greater ability to supply goods and services internationally. Also included is (2) the unemployment rate in per cent to reflect slackness in the labour market. A higher unemployment rate means that more output can be forthcoming without fueling unit cost and price. The *international* property is captured by (3) openness, calculated as exports and imports taken in combination as a per cent of GDP. Greater openness signifies greater involvement in foreign trade. The other international series is (4) exchange rate volatility, defined as the ratio of the current exchange rate relative to the exchange rate in the base year 1989. Exchange rate volatility is bad for trade because of the uncertainty and turmoil that it causes.[4]

Quality of product is gauged by three series. One is (5) gross fixed capital formation as a per cent of GDP, the thought being that smart (new) capital creates smart (quality) products. Next comes (6) public expenditure on education as a per cent of GDP: quality labour implies quality output. Ostensibly (7) patents, reckoned as the number per million of population, reflect new and better products. *Promptness* strives to capture the speed with which orders are filled. To that end (8) electricity production in thousand kilowatt hours per person comes into play in the belief that electricity generation serves to indicate the speed of communication. Additionally, (9) change in stocks as a per cent of GDP reflects the prevalence of stocks on hand to fill orders. *Reasonable price* is manifested by (10) the CPI inflation rate as a per cent and by (11) the growth rate of labour productivity as a per cent. Productivity growth, of course, affects price through the standard mark-up rule.[5]

Obviously this list contains 11, not 10, series. The extra variable is series 5, gross fixed capital formation which becomes relevant in the next section. For now it can be ignored. What cannot be ignored is the similarity between this ICOM list and the catalogue of international competitiveness measures developed by Bloch and Kenyon in the preceding chapter of this volume. Their measures 1 and 2 revolve around labour productivity and their later remarks stress labour productivity growth, which constitutes series 11 of ICOM. Measure 5 of Bloch and Kenyon is the real exchange rate, and series 4 and 10 of ICOM plainly relate to it. Moreover, their measures 8 and 9 speak about research and development activity, an endeavour closely aligned with patents, series 7 of ICOM. Thus, even though the reasoning of Bloch and Kenyon on the one hand and the thinking behind ICOM on the other start at different points, they tend to come together, and it seems safe to say that ICOM puts into practice ideas offered by Bloch and Kenyon. In the same way, it seems safe to say that ICOM puts into practice ideas advanced earlier by Hopkins and Cabalu (1993, pp. 27–9).

Table 3.2 reports the results for this new version of ICOM based on ten series. As before, the two international variables carry double weights, while the remaining eight factors each have single weight. Years 1975, 1985 and 1995 are historical. For them, the data sources include the International Economic Data Bank from Australian National University, *International Financial Statistics* by the International Monetary Fund, and *Key Indicators of Developing Asian and Pacific Countries* by the Asian Development Bank. They also include *Main Economic Indicators* by the OECD, the Penn World Table Mark 5.5 by Summers and Heston (1993), and the *Statistical Yearbook* by UNESCO. Years 1998 and 1999 in Table 3.2 use forecast data from the *OECD Economic Outlook* which forecasts real GDP growth and the inflation rate. From those two anchors, predictions can be made for labour productivity growth and the unemployment rate, the latter following rough forms of either Okun's Law or the Phillips Curve. Other series are presumed to move accordingly or to exhibit more secular patterns.

As the historical period in Table 3.2 shows, Singapore performs well, ranking first in 1975 and 1995. The United States claims the top spot in

Table 3.2   International competitiveness rankings and scores by ICOM for various years

Rank	1975		1985		1995		1998		1999	
1	Sing	(100.0)	USA	(100.0)	Sing	(100.0)	HK	(100.0)	Sing	(100.0)
2	Chi	(82.5)	Chi	(94.4)	Mal	(90.7)	Sing	(97.9)	HK	(95.3)
3	Indo	(73.1)	HK	(87.9)	HK	(87.4)	USA	(87.3)	Mal	(76.4)
4	Phil	(73.0)	Sing	(82.2)	Thai	(49.6)	Mal	(86.9)	Tai	(68.0)
5	HK	(62.2)	Indo	(76.5)	Jpn	(48.5)	Aus	(80.7)	USA	(64.5)
6	USA	(52.9)	Aus	(64.0)	USA	(44.7)	NZ	(80.7)	Chi	(61.1)
7	Aus	(47.6)	Mal	(44.1)	Indo	(44.0)	Tai	(76.4)	Aus	(58.7)
8	Kor	(43.8)	Jpn	(42.4)	Tai	(42.8)	Phil	(72.3)	NZ	(57.7)
9	Mal	(33.2)	NZ	(41.9)	NZ	(41.7)	Jpn	(66.5)	Phil	(54.2)
10	Thai	(30.1)	Kor	(34.3)	Kor	(38.7)	Chi	(64.8)	Jpn	(40.7)
11	NZ	(24.4)	Thai	(29.0)	Aus	(37.4)	Kor	(34.4)	Thai	(18.1)
12	Jpn	(4.0)	Phil	(11.0)	Phil	(36.8)	Thai	(25.3)	Kor	(17.7)
13	Tai	(0.0)	Tai	(0.0)	Chi	(0.0)	Indo	(0.0)	Indo	(0.0)

Notes: ICOM uses double weights for the trade variables. Parentheses indicate competitiveness scores.

1985, whereas Hong Kong holds third place in 1985 and 1995. Indonesia, too, begins strongly in 1975, being third then, but loses position and drops to last place in 1998 and 1999. The turbulence that Indonesia has been experiencing in the Asian currency crisis costs it dearly in terms of international competitiveness. Much the same can be said for Korea and Thailand, which join Indonesia at the bottom of the scale for 1998 and 1999. The crisis hurts all three nations.

Table 3.3 highlights the country ranks. The overall rankings, derived from the averages of the year-by-year rankings, are instructive. For the historical period 1975–95, Singapore rates first followed in order by Hong Kong and the United States. Indonesia positions itself fourth, Thailand seventh and Korea tenth. For the longer period 1975–99, Singapore, Hong Kong and the United States hold their ranks, but Indonesia erodes to seventh, Thailand to twelfth, and Korea to the bottom. The consequences of the currency crisis are again evident. Australia can be seen in the middle of the pack, where, for the historical setting it ties for seventh, and for the longer time frame it advances to sixth.

Enhancing ICOM

Economic growth in the Asia Pacific region has been the subject of much analysis for quite some time. Work by Gapinski (1997, p. 83; 1999, tables 5.2 and 5.3) indicates that for the East Asian tigers taken as a group, output

Table 3.3   Country ranks by ICOM through time

Country	1975	1985	1995	1998	1999	Overall 1975–95	Overall 1975–99
Hong Kong	5	3	3	1	2	2	2
Korea	8	10	10	11	12	10	13
Singapore	1	4	1	2	1	1	1
Taiwan	13	13	8	7	4	13	10
Indonesia	3	5	7	13	13	4	7
Malaysia	9	7	2	4	3	6	4
Thailand	10	11	3	12	11	7	12
Philippines	4	12	12	8	9	10	10
China	2	2	13	10	6	5	5
Australia	7	6	11	5	7	7	6
Japan	12	8	5	9	10	9	9
New Zealand	11	9	9	6	8	12	8
United States	6	1	6	3	5	3	3

Source: Table 3.2.
Note: The overall scores are based on the average rankings across the relevant years.

growth is determined importantly by international trade and then sequentially by capital quantity, labour quantity, capital quality and – at a considerable distance from trade – labour quality. To bring that finding to bear on ICOM, the index is enhanced in two ways. First, gross fixed capital formation, series 5 in the list given previously, is added to the index increasing to 11 the number of embedded components. Second, double weights are specified for trade, a single weight for physical capital, and half weight for human capital. In arithmetic terms $\alpha_3 = \alpha_4 = \frac{2}{12.5}$, $\alpha_5 = \frac{1}{12.5}$, and $\alpha_6 = \frac{0.5}{12.5}$, the subscripts corresponding to the series number. Each remaining weight equals $\frac{1}{12.5}$.

Table 3.4 presents the results for the Enhanced ICOM. In keeping with its high investment rates, Singapore is now the uniform winner. Hong Kong continues to do well compared against Table 3.2, but the United States, operating with modest investment, slips a bit. Australia remains about the same as before. Again, Korea, Thailand and Indonesia plunge to the bottom of the rating scale for 1998 and 1999. According to either version of ICOM, the international competitiveness of those three countries has been dealt a serious blow by the currency crisis.

Country ranks derived from the enhanced ICOM appear in Table 3.5. Impressively, Singapore ranks first across the board. Overall rankings for the historical period 1975–95 put Singapore at the top with Indonesia second and Hong Kong third. China now jockeys ahead of the United States to fourth,

Table 3.4   International competitiveness rankings and scores by the enhanced ICOM for various years

Rank	1975		1985		1995		1998		1999	
1	Sing	(100.0)	Sing	(100.0)	Sing	(100.0)	Sing	(100.0)	Sing	(100.0)
2	Chi	(58.2)	USA	(91.5)	Mal	(93.7)	HK	(99.0)	HK	(91.7)
3	Indo	(56.0)	Chi	(91.3)	HK	(86.1)	Mal	(88.9)	Mal	(75.4)
4	Phil	(55.5)	Indo	(87.9)	Thai	(55.1)	Chi	(76.5)	Chi	(69.4)
5	HK	(45.0)	HK	(79.2)	Indo	(42.4)	USA	(75.4)	Tai	(60.3)
6	Aus	(34.4)	Aus	(66.7)	Jpn	(41.0)	Tai	(74.3)	USA	(45.2)
7	Kor	(33.5)	Jpn	(53.3)	Kor	(38.6)	Aus	(73.6)	Aus	(44.9)
8	USA	(29.9)	Kor	(46.1)	Tai	(34.5)	NZ	(72.8)	Phil	(43.7)
9	Mal	(14.1)	Mal	(45.2)	Phil	(24.7)	Phil	(66.4)	NZ	(42.7)
10	Thai	(10.1)	NZ	(38.1)	USA	(22.6)	Jpn	(65.6)	Jpn	(39.1)
11	NZ	(9.7)	Thai	(21.1)	NZ	(22.6)	Kor	(37.1)	Thai	(22.4)
12	Jpn	(4.4)	Tai	(7.9)	Aus	(19.9)	Thai	(29.7)	Kor	(17.0)
13	Tai	(0.0)	Phil	(0.0)	Chi	(0.0)	Indo	(0.0)	Indo	(0.0)

Notes: The enhanced ICOM uses double weights for the trade variables, single weight for gross investment, and half weight for education. Parentheses indicate competitiveness scores.

Table 3.5   Country ranks by the enhanced ICOM through time

Country	1975	1985	1995	1998	1999	Overall	
						1975–95	1975–99
Hong Kong	5	5	3	2	2	3	2
Korea	7	8	7	11	12	7	10
Singapore	1	1	1	1	1	1	1
Taiwan	13	12	8	6	5	13	9
Indonesia	3	4	5	13	13	2	6
Malaysia	9	9	2	3	3	6	3
Thailand	10	10	4	12	11	8	12
Philippines	4	13	9	9	8	11	8
China	2	3	13	4	4	4	3
Australia	6	6	12	7	7	8	6
Japan	12	7	6	10	10	10	11
New Zealand	11	10	11	8	9	12	13
United States	8	2	10	5	6	5	5

Source: Table 3.4.
Note: Overall scores are based on the average rankings across the relevant years.

bumping America to fifth. For the broader period 1975–99, the overall rankings still have Singapore at the head of the group; Indonesia drops to sixth while China advances to third. The United States remains fifth. Meanwhile, Australia is placed eighth and sixth respectively in the two periods.

Pictures often reveal what numbers conceal. Figure 3.1 maps out the international competitiveness rankings for the East Asian tigers and the Southeast Asian lions from the enhanced ICOM. Panel (a) which profiles the tigers, highlights the dominance of Singapore and the parallel behaviour of Hong Kong. Those twin success stories of the two city-states mesh nicely with other findings by Gapinski (1998). By contrast, the poor performance of Korea for 1998 and 1999 is manifest. Panel (b), depicting the lions, likewise illustrates the troubled times of Thailand and Indonesia. In fact, Indonesia becomes the horizontal axis.

Figure 3.2(a) shows the strength of the China panda in 1998 and 1999. Panel (b), which sketches the OECD elephants, indicates the United States to be the leader of those metaphorical creatures. Japan, however, plummets from undisputed leader in 1995 to clear trailer in 1998 and 1999 as recession woes gravely impacted its international competitiveness.

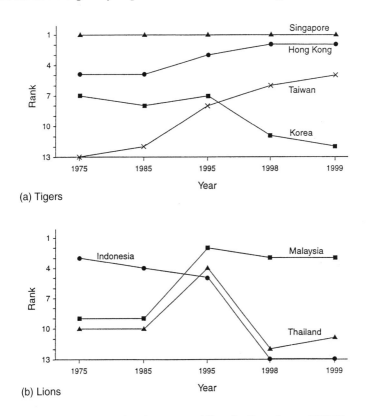

Figure 3.1 Country ranks for the tigers and lions by the enhanced ICOM

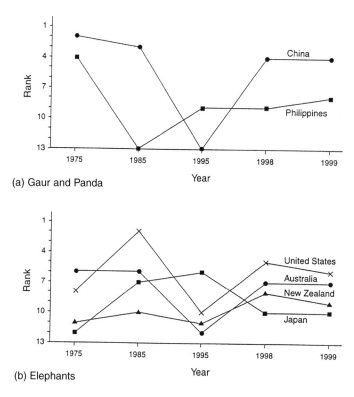

Figure 3.2   Country ranks for a gaur, the panda and elephants by the enhanced ICOM

Concluding thoughts

As modelled here, ICOM ranks country against country. Alternatively, it could be redesigned to focus on industry sectors across countries in the fashion of the productivity analysis for Malaysia by the National Productivity Corporation (1997, pp. 21–2). It could also be tailored to handle individual industries across countries or even individual industries within a given country. In that latter construction the major industries of, say, Australia might be identified and then ranked in terms of their international competitiveness. Of course, the collection of series behind the index might be reselected as the measure becomes more micro-economic in nature.

When rethinking the component series of ICOM either in its global country vs country format or in a more disaggregated industry vs industry form, there may be good reason to consider including information from new survey work. Competitiveness concepts such as quality of product and promptness of delivery are difficult to quantify with data from standard sources. That difficulty could be overcome nicely by specially prepared surveys circulated to appropriate representatives of the government and business communities. Besides, survey data would give ICOM a character of its own; ICOM would become unique.

Finally, it must be remembered that ICOM has a forecasting dimension. Therefore, it can be used as more than just an indicator of international competitiveness. It may be used as a policy guide for countries that are eager to maintain or to expand their presence in the world markets.

Notes

1 Words such as *country* and *nation* are used as loose synonyms for *economy*. Strict legal interpretations are not intended.
2 Since the individual series are denominated in different units, they are normalized to put them on equal footing. The normalization rule is the usual one: subtract the mean and divide by the standard deviation. Mathematically, $z_{ij} = (x_{ij} - \mu_i)/\sigma_i$, where x_{ij} denotes the original series and where μ_i and σ_i are respectively the mean and standard deviation over the 13 countries.
3 Transforming ICOM_j^z into a range from zero to 100 is accomplished by taking ICOM_j^z from expression (1) and calculating $100 \cong [\text{ICOM}_j^z - \min (\text{ICOM}_j^z)]/ [\max (\text{ICOM}_j^z) - \min (\text{ICOM}_j^z)]$.
4 A preferable measure of volatility would be the coefficient of variation. However, requiring a time series, that statistic is beyond reach at least for now.
5 ICOM presumes that a high value for a component series signals high competitiveness, while a low value signifies low competitiveness. Nevertheless, two series by nature tell the opposite story: high is bad whereas low is good. Those two components are series 4, exchange rate volatility, and series 10, the CPI inflation rate. Consequently, they are reversed, prior to any other calculation, by the negative exponential function. In the symbolism of note 2, $x_{4j} = \exp(-x_{4j})$, and $x_{10j} = \exp(-x_{10j}/100)$.

References

Gapinski, J.H. (1997) 'Economic Growth in the Asia Pacific Region', *Asia Pacific Journal of Economics and Business*, vol. 1 (June), pp. 68–91.
— (1998) 'A Tiger's Tale of Two Cities', *Asia Pacific Journal of Economics and Business*, vol. 2 (June), pp. 79–94.
— (1999) *Economic Growth in the Asia Pacific Region*, New York: St Martin's Press.
Hopkins, S. and Cabalu, H. (1993) 'International Competitiveness: A Critical Review of the Concept', Discussion Paper series 93.05, Institute for Research into International Competitiveness, Curtin University of Technology, October.
King, N. Jr. (1998) 'Japan Falls in Rankings; U.S. is No. 1', *Wall Street Journal*, 22 April, p. A16.

Manzur, M. (1996) 'International Competitiveness: Do we have a Good Measure' Discussion Paper series 96.10, Institute for Research into International Competitiveness, Curtin University of Technology, November.

National Productivity Corporation (1997) *Productivity Report 1996*, Petaling Jaya, Malaysia: National Productivity Corporation.

Summers, R. and Heston, A. (1993) *The Penn World Table: Mark 5.5*. Computer materials, National Bureau of Economic Research, Cambridge, Mass., 15 June.

World Economic Forum (1995) *The World Competitiveness Report 1995*, Lausanne: International Institute for Management Development.

Part II

Market Institutions in a Global Economy

4

The Labour Market and International Competitiveness

Peter Dawkins and Peter Kenyon

F13 633
F16 J24
J53

Introduction

One of the more important themes to have emerged in economic policy discussions over the past decade or so is what effect the increased exposure of economies to international trade has had on labour markets and labour market outcomes. Globalization is the term that has emerged to capture the rapid increase in international trade and capital flows that has occurred in the second half of the twentieth century and particularly during and after the 1970s (see Slaughter and Swagel, 1997, table 1 and chart 1).[1]

Increasing globalization has come about due to the easing of policy barriers to trade and factor flows and from technical change. These have lowered the costs of trade and factor flows. For example, tariff rates and the coverage of commodities subject to tariff protection and foreign exchange restrictions have progressively been eased in many countries around the world. This has come about partly as a result of concerted multilateral efforts through the various GATT rounds and, subsequently, the WTO, and partly as a result of a shift in the philosophy underlying economic policy, which has favoured economic liberalization. The lowering of the costs of trade due to such factors as technical change in transportation and communications has bolstered this move from the supply side. With globalization has come concern that not everyone is benefiting from the increasing international integration of markets for goods and services, factors and technology.

Has international competition helped or harmed workers? What affect has the enormous increase in world trade had on wages and jobs? Has globalization contributed to the widening wage dispersion in many countries? Has globalization affected employment opportunities for some groups of workers? What should be the institutional and policy response? In this chapter we will explore these questions.

In the next section we examine the standard economic theory of the relationship between trade and factor markets. We then examine whether this theory can explain developments in labour markets that have occurred concurrently with increased globalization, specifically a widening in the wage distribution between workers with different skill levels and, in some countries, changes in the level and pattern of unemployment. First we examine the effects of trade on prices and wages, and then on the factor content of trade and employment. We then turn to an alternative explanation of labour market developments, and examine whether the bias of technical change can explain recent labour market trends. Following on, we examine institutional and policy responses to the widening wage distribution and the changing patterns of employment and unemployment, and end the chapter with some concluding comments.

International trade theory and the labour market

The standard workhorse model of international trade, Heckscher–Ohlin (H–O) trade theory, suggests that for any country, increased trade increases overall economic welfare (measured as increased consumption possibilities) by increasing specialization in the production of those goods and services which use relatively abundant factors more intensively. By exporting these goods and importing those goods which use relatively scarce factors intensively, an economy will push its consumption possibilities outside its production possibilities. It follows that, in general, increased trade is 'a good thing' and policy ought be designed to assist in increasing, rather than reducing, trade.

However, even basic theory immediately tempers this conclusion with a caveat, which goes something like:

> international trade increases welfare providing that part of the gains from trade are distributed to the country's relatively scarce factors and, also, that the factors which displaced by imports can be immediately redeployed into the sectors that expand as a result of increased trade.

Thus, in the absence of such compensation and smooth adjustment, it is not a universal truth that everyone is necessarily made better off by increased exposure to international trade.

This is because of the Stolper–Samuelson theorem. Increased trade due to a change in relative prices (brought about, say, by reduced tariffs on imported goods or lower trade transactions costs) will affect relative factor incomes. Assume that a country has two types of labour: skilled labour which it has in relative abundance, and unskilled labour which is relatively scarce. It produces some goods, for example computer software and electronics, which are relatively skill-intensive, and other goods such as clothing and footwear which use unskilled labour relatively intensively. The country will export the relatively skill-intensive goods and import goods that use unskilled labour relatively intensively.

Assume that the country reduces the tariff on imported goods. This will lower the price of imports and competing goods will be imported into that country.[2] Production of import competing products will fall, imports will expand and production of skill-intensive goods will expand. Both skilled and unskilled labour will be released on to the labour market from import-competing industries. However, because the import-competing sector utilizes relatively more unskilled than skilled labour, more of the scarce unskilled labour is released from the import competing sector than the exportables sector can absorb at the going relative wage, so this will cause wages to adjust. The relative wage of unskilled labour will fall and that of the relatively abundant factor, skilled labour, will rise. The ratio of unskilled to skilled labour will rise in both industries (which increases the marginal product of the abundant skilled labour and thus their income). There is a tendency for factor incomes to be equalized across countries as a result of trade, so the standard trade model predicts that some factors will see an increase in their incomes as a result of increased international trade and some will see a decrease. Also, some workers displaced from import-competing industries will have to find new employment in the exportables (or non-tradeables) sectors. In actual economies, structural adjustment may not be as smooth and immediate as in the world of the H–O model. It follows that increased exposure to trade may well result in falling living standards for some workers, due to either falling factor incomes or unemployment, as well a widening in the income distribution.[3]

Note that the driving force that leads to changes in relative factor rewards is not increased trade *per se*, but rather increased trade that comes about because of changes in the relative prices of goods and services. It is not sufficient just to observe a contemporaneous increase in trade and a change in relative wages, and then attribute the cause of the change in relative wages to globalization.[4] Note, also, that overall factor intensity in all industries will move in favour of the relatively scarce factor for given factor quantities. These observations are important for assessing the empirical evidence.

The possibility that globalization has affected wages has been studied mostly in the context of the wages for skilled and unskilled workers, particularly in the United States, although there has been some work done for European and other economies as well. We shall comment mostly on the US debate, but make occasional reference to other countries. The idea is that the USA has a *relative* abundance of skilled workers and exports skill-intensive goods and services. Therefore, the wages of its *relatively* scarce unskilled workforce that is concentrated in the import-competing sectors, which use such labour relatively intensively, may have been adversely affected with increases in the traded proportion of US GDP. There are two possibilities: either the demand for skill-intensive goods has risen, increasing their relative prices and the relative wages of skilled workers, and/or the opening of the US market to imports of low-skill-intensive commodities has caused their (domestic) price to fall and so the wages of low-skilled workers to fall as well. Either way, we would expect to see an increase in the skill premium in wages and a widening in wage dispersion between skilled and unskilled labour. Also, if the Stolper–Samuelson theorem is at work, we would expect, for a given skill mix, to see an increase in the relative intensity of the scarce factor, lower skilled labour, across all industries to allow the expansion in skill-intensive industries.

The effect of trade on prices and wages

The first point to be made is that wages for unskilled workers have fallen relative to the wages of skilled workers (and, indeed, may have fallen absolutely over the 1970s and 1980s, see Freeman, 1995). In just about all the ways in which the measurement might be done, there has been a widening in the wage gap in the USA and this widening is related to skill differentials. Although the studies cover different periods, use different wage measures and use different definitions of skill, the results tend to be the same. For example, between 1979 and 1988, the ratio of the average wage of college graduates to the average wage of a high school graduate increased by 20 per cent (Bound and Johnson, 1992). Over the period 1979 to 1987, the ratio of average weekly earnings of males in their forties to the average weekly earnings of men in their twenties rose by 25 per cent (Davis, 1992). In manufacturing, between 1979 and 1989, the ratio of the average annual earnings of non-production workers to those of production workers rose by about 10 per cent (Lawrence and Slaughter, 1993). Finally, Katz and

Murphy (1992), assuming that wages increase with skill over the income distribution, find that the wages of workers at the 90th percentile of the earnings distribution relative to workers at the 10th percentile has increased steadily from the late 1960s to the late 1970s, with a sharp increase since about 1980.

Similarly in other countries, there has been a widening in the wage differential between skilled and unskilled workers. However, significantly, the changes were for the most part not as marked as in the USA (the UK was the exception, giving results more comparable with the USA). It appears that since the 1970s, Australia, Canada, Japan, Spain and Sweden have experienced a modest rise in wage differentials relative to those in the USA and the UK, while France, Germany and Italy had no increase, and the Netherlands a small fall.[5] However, Freeman and Katz (1996) also observe that those countries which only experienced modest or no widening in the wage distribution also tended to experience relatively, higher increases in unemployment and non-participation among less-educated and younger workers. This latter result has been challenged by several researchers who find that unemployment in European countries rose for both skilled and unskilled workers (see Bertola and Ichino, 1995; and Nickell and Bell, 1996). Part of the dispute seems to be over what is meant by 'skilled workers' – see Murphy (1995). In Australia, the evidence appears to be that unemployment has increased among workers with less education, for new entrants to the labour market (youth) and for older males displaced from tariff adjusting industries. Some economists argue that wage rigidity, due to institutional factors, has prevented full wage adjustment to occur, thus shifting the burden to unemployment (see Fahrer and Pease, 1994).

In order for Stolper–Samuelson effects to be present, it is essential that the change in relative wages does not arise from an increase in the relative supply of unskilled workers. However, Katz and Murphy (1992) show that this could not be the case as, relatively the supply of skilled workers increased in the USA over this period and so demand effects must outweigh supply effects. So far, so good for the Stolper–Samuelson effect. What about relative product price changes? Have the prices of skill-intensive commodities risen relative to the prices of commodities which use less-skilled labour intensively? If so, can these price effects be attributed to international trade rather than purely domestic factors?

Here the evidence is not very compelling. Lawrence and Slaughter (1993) examine US manufacturing prices, adjusting for changes in total factor productivity, from 1979 to 1989 and find little evidence of larger price rises in skill-intensive products relative to products which are intensive in less-skilled labour. They find evidence of the opposite, namely that the relative price of products that are intensive in less-skilled labour rose. The authors conclude on the basis of this evidence that trade did not contribute to falling wages for less-skilled labour in the USA. Further analysis by Sachs and Shatz (1994) notes that some adjustment needs to be made for computer prices, given problems in accounting for quality changes in computers. After taking into account the effects of technical change on prices and adjusting for the computer quality problem, Sachs and Shartz find that the relative prices of skill-intensive products increased for some products and for some periods of time. However, for other specifications their findings are similar to Lawrence and Slaughter's results.

Finally, using a computable general equilibrium model of the USA, Krugman (1995, 1996) takes the observed increase in imports from developing countries and calculates the changes in product prices and relative wages that are consistent with the increase in these imports.[6] He finds that the small volume of US imports from developing countries could have led to only small changes in prices and wages and therefore concludes that trade has contributed only marginally, if at all, to a widening of the income distribution.

There is another important anomaly that weighs against a Stolper–Samuelson effect accounting substantially for the relative decline in the incomes of less-skilled US workers. Overall US production did not increase in the intensity with which less-skilled labour was employed over the 1980s (as it would have, if the Stolper–Samuelson theorem was at work, less-skilled labour being the relatively scarce factor). Indeed, the opposite was the case. Berman, Bound and Griliches (1994) find that there was an increase in skill intensity across manufacturing and that when this is decomposed into that part due to a shift in labour demand towards more skill-intensive industries, and that part due to a shift towards greater skill intensity within all industries, over 70 per cent of the increase in skill intensity is explained by within-industry effects rather than across-industry effects. Similarly, Lawrence and Slaughter (1993) find that across all industries, the majority of industries employed a greater proportion of skilled to lesser-skilled workers in the 1980s compared with the 1970s, even though the relative wage of skilled workers had risen (see, also Krugman, 1994a). The Australian evidence, also, is not consistent with Stolper–Samuelson effects in that skill intensity appears to have risen rather than fallen across industry sectors (see Fahrer and Pease, 1994, p. 198).

Of course, the mix between skilled and unskilled workers did not remain fixed over this period, and so there is some scope for slippage from the strict requirement of the Stolper–Samuelson theorem for less-skilled labour intensity to rise. Nevertheless, if trade were driving down the wages of the less-skilled in traded goods sectors and displacing workers from the importables sectors, there would be some overflow into exportables and the non-traded goods sectors. Thus, the ratio of less-skilled to skilled workers would be rising or at least be steady in some industries.

It is not surprising, then, that many economists discount the effects of increased international trade as the major cause of the relative (absolute?) decline in the wages of less-skilled workers in the United States over the past two decades or more. It also appears that trade is not the culprit in explaining the somewhat lesser relative decline in the wages of the less skilled in Europe and elsewhere in the OECD. However, there is less compelling evidence outside the USA. In part, this is simply because there appear to be far fewer studies of the effects of trade on prices and wages (see Slaughter and Swagel, 1997).

Trade, factor content and wages and employment

There is a second set of studies using a different methodology which attempt to ascertain the effects of trade on the labour market. These studies use the so-called 'factor content' method. The idea is simple. When a country imports a commodity, it is implicitly importing the factors which went in to the production of that commodity. Thus, effectively, imports add to a country's endowment of factors in proportion to the factor content of those imports. Exports have the opposite effect. As a result, by affecting effective factor supplies, trade will have an effect on factor prices and on subsequent factor use. If, for example, the USA imports goods with a high proportion of low-skilled labour relative to skilled labour, it is effectively increasing the relative supply of low-skilled labour in the USA through the low-skilled labour embodied in those imports. This would be expected to put pressure on low-skilled workers' wages to fall.

So, using input–output relationships that give the estimates of labour skills used in various sectors, researchers can ascertain how changing trade patterns alter the balance between supply and demand for labour with different skills. Then, using wage elasticities estimated from other studies they can estimate the wage effects of the changes in exports and imports.

Using this methodology, Borjas, Freeman and Katz (1992) find that trade accounted for a modest fall in the employment of low-skilled US workers and about 15 per cent of the increase in wage inequality between 1980 and 1985, but that this effect diminished thereafter. Sachs and Shatz

(1994) analysed trade flows between the USA and less-developed countries and also concluded that imports from these countries had only a modest impact on employment. These and other factor-content studies indicate that trade can account for only 10 to 20 per cent of the overall decrease in labour demand by domestic firms necessary to explain rising wage skill differentials in the USA or unemployment in Europe (see Freeman, 1995). The exception is Wood (1994, 1995) who uses factor-content analysis to show a far greater impact on less-skilled workers. Wood disputes some of the assumptions of the factor-content studies referred to above, asserting that they underestimate the effect of imports on employment of less-skilled workers (for a summary, see Wood, 1995, pp. 64–8). Having made adjustments based on new assumptions, Wood estimates that the demand for unskilled labour in manufacturing in the industrialized countries has fallen by at least 20 per cent. (For critical assessments of Wood's methods, see Freeman, 1995; and Slaughter and Swagel, 1997.)

A major criticism of factor-content analysis, in general, is that it supposedly assumes that wages and prices do not adjust to the changing pattern of trade. There is feedback from trade flows to prices – both commodity and factor prices (see Freeman, 1995). However, Krugman (1996) has shown that this is a misunderstanding of the thought experiment that lies behind the general equilibrium analysis of the effects of changing trade flows on product and factor prices. The question is: what is being compared with what? Krugman's answer is that the correct interpretation is: what is the (comparative static) change in trade volume from, say, the newly-industrializing countries (NICs) necessary to produce the relative changes in product and factor prices that have been observed? He also notes that this trade in goods can just as logically be interpreted as a change in embedded factor content. His answer is that the change in trade volumes (and in embedded factor content) from the NICs is just too small to account for changes in the relative wages of skilled to unskilled workers in the OECD. Nevertheless, he also acknowledges that, ultimately, this is an empirical issue – 'in the end, of course, one must return to the data'.

The fact is that with the exception of Wood's work, the evidence suggests that the effects of trade on less-skilled workers' wages and employment are not great. It appears that increasing globalization and international competitiveness (in the sense of more participants in world markets) cannot explain more than a small amount of the increased income inequality between skilled and less-skilled labour. If increased international trade is not the major, let alone a complete, explanation for increased wage inequality, what is?

Technology, wages and employment

The favoured explanation for the rising ratio of skilled to less-skilled workers and the fall in the rise in the ratio of the wages of skilled labour to those of less-skilled labour is technological progress biased against unskilled workers (see Lawrence and Slaughter, 1993; Krugman, 1994b). Assume, for the moment, that technical innovation is biased against unskilled labour (we will address shortly why this might be so), such technical change increases the desired ratio of skilled to unskilled workers, both in industries that are relatively intensive in skilled workers and in industries that are relatively intensive in unskilled workers. However, the ratio of skilled to unskilled workers will rise by more in the skill-intensive sectors compared with those sectors that use less-skilled labour intensively. As a result, the ratio of wages for skilled labour to the wages of less-skilled labour will rise.

Skill-biased technical progress, for example the rapid development of digital technologies for computing and telecommunications, may have increased the demand for skilled workers relative to unskilled workers. There are two possible reasons, which are not mutually exclusive and may well be working in concert. First, the specific technical change may have increased the relative productivity of skilled workers and so the relative demand for them. Second, the demand for unskilled labour might have fallen due to its inability to adopt and use technologically advanced methods. For example, Bartel and Lichtenberg (1987) show that as new technology is adopted the demand for highly-educated workers increases relative to the demand for less-educated workers. They argue that this is due to the better problem-solving abilities and flexibility of better-educated workers in responding to technical change. Another (and simpler) explanation is that digital technologies are simply unskilled labour-saving, thus replacing less-skilled labour in the performance of many routine tasks (for example the disappearance of typing pools, telephonists and so on).

What is the evidence for the biased technological change story? Again, the data for the USA suggests that there is some evidence for this explanation. As we have seen, there is a huge amount of evidence that shows that virtually no matter how measured, there has been a widening of the skill differential in wages in the USA and that this has come about due to an increase in the relative demand for skilled workers. The evidence for other countries is not quite as compelling. However, in countries where wage inequality based on skill did not rise, there is some evidence that this led to a widening in unemployment experience based on skill

(Freeman and Katz, 1996, p. 4), although this remains controversial (see above, pp. 76–9).

Other studies, for example Bound and Johnson (1992, 1995), argue that the relative increase in the demand for skilled labour triggered by technological change could explain most of the observed change in wage differentials based on skill differentials in the USA during the 1980s. Berman, Bound and Griliches (1994) find that the increased relative demand for skilled labour within US manufacturing over roughly the same period could be linked to investment in computing technology and research and development in general. Krueger (1993) shows that for the second half of the 1980s workers who used computers earned a 10 to 15 per cent wage premium compared with observationally equivalent workers who did not. Autor, Katz and Krueger (1998) examine the effect of skill-biased technological change as measured by computerization on the widening of US educational wage differentials. They find that rapid skill upgrading within industries accounts for most of the growth in the demand for college graduates, particularly since 1970, and that the rate of skill upgrading has been greater in more computer-intensive industries. Similar results are found by Machin and Van Reenen (1998) for seven OECD countries (the USA, Denmark, France, Germany, Japan, Sweden and the UK) except that the measure of technical change is R&D intensity. These authors conclude that skill-biased technical change is a global phenomenon and that it has increased the relative demand for skilled workers.

However, most of the empirical studies on the effects of technological change on wages and employment do not link technological change with trade. Where studies do mix trade explanations with biased technological change, the evidence is mixed – both trade factors and technological change have affected the wage structure, but that technical change may have contributed more to the change. This is the conclusion of Brauer and Hickok (1995) for the USA based on both descriptive and econometric analysis.

In Australia, shift-share analysis, which decomposes changes in employment by industry sector into the respective contributions of trade and productivity effects (and where the trade effects are further decomposed into imports from 'low-wage countries' and 'high-wage countries'), suggests that productivity effects have been the dominant force behind the decline in manufacturing employment between 1981–2 and 1991–2, except for one industry – clothing textiles and footwear. The latter industry is the only one that tends to fit the Stolper–Samuelson stylized facts. Fahrer and Pease (1994) interpret their results as support for an explanation for changed employment patterns based on skill-biased technological change in the presence of wage rigidities.

Feenstra (1998) adds another twist to the 'trade versus technology' debate. He argues that outsourcing of intermediate production from industrialized to industrializing countries also has the effect of reducing the relative demand for unskilled labour in the industrialized countries, with implications for relative wages of unskilled workers in these countries. Thus, globalization may affect the wage structure in the developed economies indirectly through the 'outsourcing' of unskilled jobs. He argues that this is observationally equivalent to skill-biased technical change and, indeed, skill-biased technical change and outsourcing may be complementary in that rapid communications and computerization are necessary for outsourcing to be viable (for example through 'just-in-time' inventory control and the like). Although he finds in another paper (Feenstra and Hanson, 1997) that outsourcing accounts for 20 per cent of the shift in relative employment towards skilled workers in US manufacturing between 1979 and 1990 (with the increased use of computers and other high-technology equipment accounting for a further 30 per cent), the results remain controversial. For example, Autor, Katz and Krueger (1998) find an insignificant role for outsourcing.

In many ways, the biased technological change explanation begs the question, what determines the pattern of technical change? If the skill-biased technical change explanation is to account for recent labour market developments, then it has to be shown that there has been an increase in such technical change in recent decades and that this is linked to international trade. It is plausible to believe that increased exposure to international trade will motivate firms to seek out productivity improvements by introducing technological improvements, and several models exist which show that increased trade openness enhances the transmission of technical knowledge (for example Grossman and Helpman, 1991). And there is some empirical evidence to suggest that this is so (Coe and Helpman, 1995; Eaton and Kortum, 1996; Coe, Helpman and Hoffmaister, 1997).

It is feasible that such technical change could be biased towards one segment of the labour force, such as skilled workers, such that the interaction of trade and technical change would lead to increasing wage dispersion between skilled and unskilled workers. For example, if changes in the terms of trade allow skilled workers to augment human capital at a greater rate than less-skilled workers, because skilled workers are more mobile between sectors (and therefore suffer fewer interruptions to human capital accumulation), then increased exposure to international trade will affect wage differentials based on skill.

Institutional and policy responses to the widening wage distribution

Introduction

The widening earnings distribution as a response to technological change and globalization raises important policy questions. Should the tendency for such widening be facilitated or resisted? If it is to be resisted how should this be done? In some countries there has not been a strong attempt to resist this widening distribution of earnings associated with the increasing differentiation in the labour market. The USA is a classic case. The largely unregulated labour market is associated with a high degree of mobility of labour as indicated in the next chapter by Greenaway, Upward and Wright. This has facilitated the widening distribution of earnings, but low unemployment by international standards has also been experienced.

Most European countries have responded differently. They have resisted labour market deregulation, but have tended to put more effort into raising the education and skill attainment of those who are vulnerable to labour market change. Thus the earnings distribution has not widened as much. Higher unemployment, however, is a common experience.[8] That is not to say, however, that the unemployment is a direct consequence of regulated or centralized wage-setting. There are examples of where a more centralized approach has also produced low unemployment; Austria is a good example. It must be noted, however, that Austria does have a widely dispersed earnings distribution.

Thus the way a country should respond to this environment is a complex question. In the next sub-section we consider what kind of industrial relations and wage-setting systems encourage low unemployment, high productivity and competitiveness, and the ability to adjust to trade and technology shocks. We shall than explore some policy ideas relating to the interface of wages, taxes, social security, education and training in responding to this environment.

Industrial relations and the wage setting-system

There is an extensive literature on the effect of industrial relations and wage determination on productivity, competitiveness and, to a lesser extent, on the ability of the labour market to adjust to trade and technology shocks. Here, we focus on four interrelated issues. First we discuss the role of trade unions; second we discuss the idea that cooperative industrial relations is good for productivity and competitiveness; third we consider the debate about the effect of centralized versus decentralized wages-setting on unemployment and on productivity; and fourth we discuss the ability of the labour market to adjust to trade or technology shocks.

1 *Trade unions* It is sometimes said that there are 'two faces of unions' (Freeman and Medoff, 1994): the monopoly face and the collective voice face. The monopoly face relates to the power that unions can exert in the labour market, either to raise wages or to increase employment and thus reduce productivity through restrictive practices and so on. The collective voice face, on the other hand, can be productivity-enhancing, by causing lower labour turnover and enhanced communications between employees and managers. There has been some empirical support for this productivity-enhancing effect of unions in the USA, but the limited evidence for Australia tends to support the idea that, if anything, unions have a negative effect on productivity (Crockett *et al.*, 1993; Drago and Wooden, 1993). Multiple unions in any single workplace appear to be a particular problem for productivity in Australia.

2 *Cooperative industrial relations* There has been a considerable amount of evidence that cooperative relations between manager and employees can enhance the productivity and competitiveness of enterprises. Crockett *et al.* find evidence of this in Australia, but only in enterprises where unions are not active. This adds weight to the idea that unions in Australia have tended not to provide productivity-enhancing voice effects, but that enterprise-focused employee participation in decision-making can have good voice effects and raise productivity. Perhaps the reason for more evidence of positive union effects on productivity in the USA results from unions having more of an enterprise focus in that country.

3 *Centralized vs decentralized wage-setting* There is a large literature on the costs and benefits of centralized vs decentralized wage determination. The argument for decentralization tends to rest on two main ideas: first, such decentralization, it is argued, enables wages to adjust to the forces of supply and demand more efficiently; and, second, decentralization of wage-setting helps to foster enterprise-based industrial relations with a strong focus on productivity improvement and the benefits to employers and employees of raising productivity.

The argument for centralization rests primarily on the idea that decentralization tends to lead to wage inflation due to the lack of coordination of wage claims and the 'leapfrogging' effect of successive wage claims made to protect wage relativities. Centralization, it is argued, helps to coordinate wage claims and avoid wage bargainers trying to outdo each other. Research that has tried to establish whether centralization or decentralization is best for either productivity or unemployment has tended to be somewhat inconclusive. Probably the most influential work in this area is that of Calmfors and Driffill (1988) who argue that both extreme centralization and extreme decentralization are conducive to real wage restraint, whereas intermediate degrees of centralization are damaging. This is because, at intermediate levels of centralization, organized interests may be strong enough to cause major disruptions but not sufficiently encompassing to bear the social costs of their actions in their own interest (Calmfors and Driffill, 1988, p. 15).

Dowrick (1993) analyses the effect of wage-setting systems on productivity. He argues that a Calmfors and Driffill-type relationship could be expected here as well. The argument is based on the idea that labour-saving productivity growth tends to reduce labour demand when it is inelastic and increase labour demand when it elastic. This suggests that unions are likely to oppose productivity-increasing changes where demand is inelastic and encourage them where demand is elastic. Decentralization of wage-setting, Dowrick suggests, tends to increase the elasticity of demand. While full decentralization might be the preferred situation for productivity, he argues that partial decentralization would be the worst outcome. His cross-country econometric analysis provides support to his hypothesis, finding that radical decentralization is preferred to strong decentralization, and strongly preferred to partial decentralization.

4 *Adjustment to trade or technology shocks*   It is sometimes asked, if the deregulated and decentralized US labour market is such a good model and is the cause of its relatively low unemployment, why did it display higher unemployment than its more regulated European counterparts in the 1960s and 1970s? While the US unemployment rate has been particularly low in the recent past, it has displayed remarkable stability over a 40-year period. In contrast, the OECD average unemployment rate was about 3 per cent in the 1950s and 1960s, and 7 to 8 per cent in the 1980s and 1990s. Is it so clear that the USA has a better system?

Katz (1998) outlines an explanation for this that relies heavily on the proposition that the US economy through the more flexible US labour market responded to international shocks better than other OECD countries. In the USA, a greatly widening wages distribution and avoidance of macro wages problems of the kind experienced, for example, in Australia in 1974–5 helped to keep unemployment down.

Again it has to be repeated that decentralized and deregulated wage-setting is not necessarily the only approach to such successful adjustment to shocks. Austria is also a good example of an economy that showed good micro and macro wage flexibility in a more corporatist and centralized system. Austria has also managed the relationship between wage dispersion and income dispersion by using its social security system to successfully support family incomes. This takes us to some policy ideas about the relationship between wages, taxes and social security and other policy areas.

Wages, tax, social security, education, training, research and development: some policy ideas

Equity is under threat both because of sustained high unemployment in many countries, and because of the widening of pre-tax earnings resulting from technological change and globalization. While deregulating and decentralizing wage-setting and cutting unemployment benefits might be one policy setting to reduce unemployment in this environment, these policies are unlikely to do much for wage inequality in the labour market.

There is, however, a strong argument that this 'diabolical trade-off' between unemployment and wage inequality can be avoided. Greater labour market flexibility to encourage employment might be combined with changes to taxation and social security in a way that improves the distribution of income. This would need to be done in a way that does not have a detrimental effect on work incentives and, ideally, improves them. It is also important to place a strong emphasis on education and training and, arguably, research and development, if full employment and rising productivity and living standards are to be achieved in the long run.

A central feature of this alternative policy is to allow the pre-tax wage distribution to widen (say, by not increasing minimum wage rates), but to institute a system of tax credits at the lower end of the wage distribution for low-wage earners in low-income families. This is a type of wage-tax trade-off. While allowing flexibility in relative wages, so that wages faced by employers adjust, employment for low-income earners is preserved. However, tax credits ensure that after-tax wages for low income workers would not be reduced (and, indeed, would increase). The tax credits are more valuable to low-wage earners than a wage increase because of the avoidance of tax paid on extra wage income and the withdrawal of social security benefits that would result from a straight pay increase. The tax credits would reduce effective marginal tax rates for many people (and increase them for none), thereby increasing the reward to the unemployed who seek out and accept job offers (for a full discussion of this, see Dawkins, 1999).

A feature of such a policy is that it would involve greater integration of public policy across the areas of tax, social security, wage-setting and human resource development. In the long run, there is a strong case for full integration of tax with social security payments in the form of a negative income tax system (see Dawkins *et al.*, 1998). There is also a case for recognizing that the concept of 'social security' should not only involve income transfers. Put another way, passive assistance should increasingly be replaced by active labour market assistance so that as well as a safety net, individuals find that they also have the opportunity to use 'springboards' to help launch them into a more successful participation in the labour market. Training programmes and the continual upgrading of the education system are important features of this. Similarly, income transfers can be used for human capital investment, recognizing the life-cycle dynamics of successful labour market participation and the likely need for lifelong learning (see for example Latham, 1998).

In the long run, increased knowledge embodied in labour, capital or the way in which factors of production are brought together is the source of productivity growth. Education, research and development and policies promoting the openness of the economy, which encourage the acquisition of new knowledge, are the things that raise productivity in the long run (Rogers, 1997). In a free market, individuals might underinvest in education and training because of capital market imperfections and because of risk-aversion especially from those from low-income families. Thus the state has an important role in subsidizing education for efficiency as well as equity reasons.

Conclusions

Over the last two decades, labour market outcomes appear to have altered dramatically in many countries. Although patterns differ between countries, and some countries remain atypical, the following generalizations appear in order. The wage distribution has widened and this appears to be based on skill differentials between workers. In many countries, also, unemployment has risen and, again, the increase in unemployment has impacted more than proportionately on unskilled workers. In this chapter we have examined whether the standard Heckscher–Ohlin trade model working through the Stolper–Samuelson effect can explain these developments in labour markets in recent times.

The evidence suggests that the effects of trade on less-skilled workers' wages and employment are not great. It appears that increasing globalization and international competitiveness (in the sense of more participants in world markets) cannot explain more than a small amount of the increased income inequality between skilled and less-skilled labour.

An alternative explanation for recent labour market developments is that technological progress, which is biased against unskilled workers, has increased over the last several decades. Here, there is compelling evidence that suggests that technical change is capable of explaining a large proportion of the widening wage distribution based on skill differentials. However, most of the empirical studies of the effects of technological change on wages and employment do not link technological change with trade. It is plausible to believe that increased exposure to international trade will motivate firms to seek out productivity improvements by introducing technological improvements. Theory shows that increased trade openness may enhance the transmission of technical knowledge, and there is some empirical evidence to suggest that this is so. Where studies do mix trade explanations with biased technological change, the evidence is mixed – both trade and technological change have affected the wage structure, but technical change may have contributed more to the change.

The final issue considered is whether labour market policy and institutions can ameliorate these effects. This, obviously, is a complex issue. What sort of industrial relations and wage-setting systems are needed to encourage low unemployment, high productivity and competitiveness, and the ability to adjust to trade and technology shocks? It would appear that, first, a union structure that encourages cooperative industrial relations is important. Enterprise unionism that aligns the goals of management and the goals of workers towards higher productivity (and thus higher wages and better conditions) appears to be one way of achieving this outcome.

This suggests very decentralized wage bargaining and industrial relations. However, the evidence here is rather mixed. Either very centralized *or* very decentralized systems appear to promote better outcomes in terms of both productivity growth and wage outcomes that best match productivity growth. The worst arrangements appear to be where the industrial relations and wage determination process is neither centralized nor decentralized. In any case, an institutional environment that promotes cooperative industrial relations appears to be key, whether the system be relatively centralized or relatively decentralized.

Another important factor is the ability of government to manage the relationship between wage dispersion and income dispersion by using its social security system successfully to support family incomes in the face of changes in the external environment, whether these changes are due to trade effects or technology effects. We have concluded with some policy ideas relating to the interface of wages, taxes, social security, education and training, in responding to recent labour market developments. These policy ideas attempt to circumvent the 'diabolical trade-off' between increasing income inequality and persistent unemployment, and it is argued that a systematic approach to labour market programmes, reform of the tax and welfare systems to reduce effective marginal tax rates by moving towards a negative income tax system, and a continual upgrading of the education and training system are the medium-term to long-term ingredients in this strategy.

Notes

1   Although it is salutary to realize that the world volume of international trade did not return to pre-First World War levels until about 1970, and international factor flows in the nineteenth century were, if anything, greater then than they are now, especially international labour flows (Krugman, 1995; Irwin, 1996). Our Victorian ancestors would, perhaps, be bemused by our excitement about globalization.
2   Assuming that the country is sufficiently small that the changes in income cannot change spending patterns sufficiently to change its external terms of trade.
3   There is another major problem in applying the Stolper–Samuelson theorem to actual economies where there are a multitude of factors of production. A clear prediction of the distributional effects of changing product prices then becomes most problematic and depends, among other things, upon relative factor specificity and relative elasticities of factor demands: see Lloyd (1994, p. 228).
4   This point is made by Richardson (1995).
5   The limited evidence for Australia presents a very mixed picture. However, there is no *compelling* evidence for strong Stolper–Samuelson effects (see Fahrer and Pease, 1994, p. 198).
6   Imports from developing countries accounted for about 30 per cent of total US imports in 1995 and about four per cent of US GDP.
7   These authors also find a role for an increase in the capital stock, which represents capital-deepening as well as technical change.
8   This dichotomy should not be taken too far, as there is considerable labour market policy diversity within Europe as well as considerable diversity in labour market outcomes there. Nevertheless, the contrast is still useful as a way of organizing policy ideas.

References

Autor, D.H., Katz, L.F. and Krueger, A.B. (1998) 'Computing Inequality: Have Computers Changed the Labour Market?' *Quarterly Journal of Economics*, vol. 113, pp. 1169–213.

Bartel, A.P. and Lichtenberg, F. (1987) 'The Comparative Advantage of Educated Workers in Implementing New Technology', *Review of Economics and Statistics*, vol. 69, pp. 1–11.

Berman, E., Bound, J. and Griliches, Z. (1994) 'Changes in the Demand for Skilled Labour within U.S. Manufacturing: Evidence from the Annual Survey of Manufactures', *Quarterly Journal of Economics*, vol. 109, pp. 363–679.

Bertola, G. and Ichino, A. (1995) 'Wage Inequality and Unemployment: the United States versus Europe', in the *1995 NBER Macroeconomics Annual*, Cambridge, Mass.: MIT Press.

Borjas, G.J., Freeman, R.B. and Katz, L.F. (1992) 'On the Labour Market Effects of Immigration and Trade', in G.J. Borjas and R.B. Freeman (eds), *Immigration and the Workforce*, Chicago: University of Chicago Press and the NBER.

Bound, J. and Johnson, G. (1992) 'Changes in the Structure of Wages in the 1980s: An Evaluation of Alternative Explanations,' *American Economic Review*, vol. 82, pp. 371–92.

— and — (1995) 'What are the Causes of Rising Wage Inequality in the U.S.?' *Federal Reserve Bank of New York Economic Policy Review* (January).

Brauer, D.A. and Hickok, S. (1995) ''Explaining the Growing Inequality in Wages Across Skill Levels', *Economic Policy Review*, vol. 1, pp. 61–84.

Calmfors, L. and Driffill, J. (1988) 'Centralisation of Wage Bargaining and Macroeconomic Performance', *Economic Policy*, vol. 6 (April), pp. 13–61.

Coe, D. and Helpman, E. (1995) 'International R&D Spillovers', European Economic Review, vol. 39 (May), pp. 134–49.

—, — and Hoffmaister, A. (1997) 'North–South R&D Spillovers', *Economic Journal*, vol. 107 (January), pp. 859–87.

Crockett, G., Dawkins, P., Miller, P. and Mulvey, C. (1993) 'The Impact of Unions on Workplace Productivity', *Australian Bulletin of Labour*, vol. 18, pp. 119–41.

Davis, S.J. (1992) 'Cross-Country Patterns of Changes in Relative Wages', in O. Blanchard and S. Fischer (eds), *1992 NBER Macroeconomics Annual*, Cambridge, Mass.: MIT Press.

Dawkins, P. (1999) 'A Plan to Cut Unemployment in Australia: An Elaboration on the Five Economists' Letter to the Prime Minister, 28th October 1998', *Mercer-Melbourne Institute Quarterly Bulletin of Economic Trends* (Ist Quarter) pp. 48–53.

—, Beer, G., Harding, A., Johnson, D. and Scutella, R. (1998) 'Towards a Negative Income Tax System for Australia', *Australian Economic Review*, vol. 30 (4), pp. 405–17.

Dowrick, S. (1993) 'Wage Bargaining Systems and Productivity Growth in OECD Countries', EPAC Background Paper no. 26, AGPS Canberra.

Drago, R. and Wooden, M. (1993) 'The Australian Workplace Industrial Relations Survey and Workplace Performance', *Australian Bulletin of Labour*, vol. 18, pp. 119–41.

Eaton, J. and Kortum, S. (1996) 'Trade in Ideas: Patenting and Productivity in the OECD', *Journal of International Economics*, vol. 36 (May), pp. 251–78.

Fahrer, J. and Pease, A. (1994) 'International Trade and the Australian Labour Market', in P. Lowe and J. Dwyer (eds), *International Integration of the Australian Economy: Proceedings of a Conference*, Sydney: Reserve Bank of Australia.

Feenstra, R.C. (1998) 'Integration of Trade and Disintegration of Production in the Global Economy', *Journal of Economic Perspectives*, vol. 12, pp. 31–50.

— and Hanson, G.H. (1997) 'Productivity Measurement and the Impact of Trade and Technology on Wages: Evidence for the U.S., 1972–90', *NBER Working Paper*, no. 6052 (June).

Freeman, R.B. (1995) 'Are Your Wages Set in Beijing?' *Journal of Economic Perspectives*, vol. 9, pp. 15–32.
— and Katz, L.F. (1996) 'Introduction and Summary', in R.B. Freeman and L.F. Katz (eds), *Differences and Changes in Wage Structure*, Chicago: Chicago University Press.
— and Medoff, J.L. (1984) *What Do Unions Do?* New York: Basic Books.
Grossman, G.M. and Helpman, E. (1991) *Innovation and Growth in the Global Economy*, Cambridge, Mass.: MIT Press.
Irwin, D.A. (1996) 'The United States in a New Global Economy? A Century's Perspective', *American Economic Review*, vol. 86, pp. 41–6.
Katz, L.F. (1998) 'Reflections on U.S. Labour Market Performance', in G. Debelle and J. Borland (eds), *Unemployment and the Australian Labour Market: Proceedings of a Conference*, Sydney: Reserve Bank of Australia.
— and Murphy, K.M. (1992) 'Changes in Relative Wages, 1963–1987: Supply and Demand Factors', *Quarterly Journal of Economics*, vol. 107, pp. 35–78.
Krueger, A.B. (1993) 'How Computers Have Changed the Wage Structure: Evidence from Microdata, 1984–89,' *Quarterly Journal of Economics*, vol. 108, pp. 33–60.
Krugman, P.R. (1994a) 'Trade, Jobs and Wages', in P. Krugman (1996) *Pop Internationalism*, Cambridge, Mass.: MIT Press.
— (1994b) 'Technology's Revenge', in P. Krugman (1996) *Pop Internationalism*, Cambridge, Mass.: MIT Press.
— (1995) 'Growing World Trade: Causes and Consequences', *Brookings Papers on Economic Activity*, vol. 1, pp. 327–77.
— (1996) 'But For, As If, and So What: Thought Experiments on Trade and Factor Prices', Krugman's web page at http://web.mit.edu/krugman/www/whats-new.html.
Latham, M. (1998) *Civilising Global Capital*, Sydney: Allen & Unwin.
Lawrence, R.Z. and Slaughter, M.J. (1993) 'International Trade and U.S. Wages: Great Sucking Sound or Small Hiccup?' *Brookings Papers on Economic Activity*, vol. 2, pp. 161–226.
Lloyd, P. (1994), 'Discussion', in P. Lowe and J. Dwyer (eds), *International Integration of the Australian Economy: Proceedings of a Conference*, Sydney: Reserve Bank of Australia.
Machin, S. and Van Reenen, J. (1998) 'Technology and Changes in Structure: Evidence from Seven OECD Countries', *Quarterly Journal of Economics*, vol. 113, pp. 1215–44.
Murphy, K. (1995) 'Comment on Bertola and Ichino', in the *1995 NBER Macroeconomics Annual*, Cambridge, Mass.: MIT Press.
Nickell, S. and Bell, B. (1996) 'Changes in the Distribution of Wages and Unemployment in OECD Countries', *American Economic Review: Papers and Proceedings*, vol. 86, pp. 302–08.
Olsen, M (1982) *The Rise and Decline of Nations*, New Haven: Yale University Press.
Richardson, J.D. (1995) 'Income Inequality and Trade: How to Think, What to Conclude', *Journal of Economic Perspectives*, vol. 9, pp. 33–55.
Rogers, M. (1997) 'Knowledge, Technology and Productivity in Australia: Lessons from Overseas', *Mercer-Melbourne Institute Quarterly Bulletin of Economic Trends*, 3rd Quarter, pp. 38–57.
Sachs, J.D. and Shatz, H. (1994) 'Trade and Jobs in U.S. Manufacturing', *Brookings Papers on Economic Activity*, vol. 1, pp. 1–84.

Slaughter, M.J. and Swagel, P. (1997) 'The Effects of Globalisation on Wages in the Advanced Economies', IMF Working Paper no. 9743 (April).

Wood, A. (1994) *North–South Trade, Employment and Inequality: Changing Fortunes in a Skill Driven World*, Oxford: Oxford University Press.

— (1995) 'How Trade Hurt Unskilled Workers', *Journal of Economic Perspectives*, vol. 9, pp. 57–80.

5

Sectoral Mobility in UK and US Labour Markets*

David Greenaway, Richard Upward and Peter Wright

Introduction

The pattern of employment in the United Kingdom has changed rapidly over the past two decades, with perhaps the most dramatic manifestation of this being the shift in the balance between manufacturing and service industries. Between 1975 and 1995 employment in manufacturing fell from 9.6 million to 5.6 million, whilst service employment increased from 12.5 million to over 15 million. Many of these new service sector workers were women, whose activity rates over this period increased from 47.4 to 53.3 per cent. This transition has not been achieved without cost however. Over the 1980s unemployment in the United Kingdom rose rapidly, reaching 3.1 million in 1983 and remaining at over 2 million for much of the 1980s. The period also saw a rapid deterioration in the relative position of unskilled labour, with the less well-educated being more than three times as likely to suffer unemployment (Nickell and Bell, 1996). For those who remained in employment their relative position also worsened, with the wages of blue-collar workers falling rapidly compared with those of white-collar workers (Hine and Wright, 1998).

Similar trends have been observed in the United States, though here the shift in demand away from unskilled workers has manifested itself primarily in increasing wage inequality rather than unemployment. Krugman (1994) attributes this difference to greater levels of wage flexibility in the United States where relativities are less rigid than in the United Kingdom. The reason for these changes remains hotly debated. Wood (1994) argues that the

* Financial assistance from the Leverhulme Trust under Programme Grant F114/BF 'Globalization and Labour Markets' is gratefully acknowledged. The authors are also grateful for comments from participants at seminars at St Andrews University, Stirling University and Curtin University of Technology.

acceleration in the shift away from manufacturing and the decrease in the relative demand for unskilled labour have been caused by an intensification of competition from developing countries. This point of view is challenged by a number of authors who argue that a more credible source of change is skill-biased (Machin and Van Reenen, 1997) or sector-biased technological change (Haskel and Slaughter, 1997).

In this chapter we are not concerned with examining the reasons for these sectoral shifts but rather in how the labour market adjusts in response to them. In considering this issue the mobility of labour between different sectors of the economy will be crucial as this will determine the 'cost' of changing patterns of production, both in terms of lost output and in terms of unemployment. The analysis of micro-level patterns of mobility may also provide valuable insights into the causes of increasing inequality in employment and earnings opportunities between individuals. Finally, from a policy perspective, the speed of adjustment will also influence the willingness of agents to accept change, whether this be technology or trade-based.

We use data on individuals from both the UK and the USA over the 1970s and 1980s to examine the mobility of labour between sectors. This allows us to examine at a micro level the process of structural change and to assess the proposition that the US labour market is more 'flexible' than that of the UK.

The chapter is organized as follows. In the next section we describe the broad structural change and aggregate flows of labour which occurred in the USA and the UK over the 1970s and 1980s. We examine which sectors expanded and which declined, whether it is realistic to characterize the USA and the UK economies as 'similar', and whether the USA and the UK experienced any convergence over this period in terms of employment patterns. We then describe these flows of labour in terms of the movement of individuals between sectors. We then discuss some previous analyses of sectoral mobility, and set out a model of job movement which yields a number of testable predictions at the microeconomic level. An econometric model of the data is specified which estimates transition probabilities as a function of individual and sectoral characteristics. Finally, we provide a more detailed analysis of the determinants of mobility from a 'declining' sector, which includes movements into and out of unemployment.

Sectoral reallocation in the USA and the UK

It is helpful to begin with simple descriptive evidence on the aggregate changes in labour markets in the USA and the UK during the period 1964–93, for several reasons. First, it demonstrates the extent to which changes in patterns of employment are correlated between the USA and the UK. Second, it identifies which sectors can be described as 'declining', 'expanding' or 'static'. Third, it allows us to check the reliability of the data in terms of consistent classifications of sectors across time. The long time-period studied inevitably means that the classification of industries has changed considerably, and so the data have been recoded to be consistent over time and between countries.

Two sources of data are used. The UK *Labour Force Survey* (LFS) is an annual[1] survey of 60 000 households comprising about 120 000 adults (Office for National Statistics, 1998). We use data from 1975 to 1993. In every year of the survey, individuals are asked about their current labour force status (working, unemployed, out of the labour force), and their current occupation and industry if employed. Individuals are then asked about their status, occupation and industry 12 months previously. Therefore, although the LFS is a series of cross-sections, it is possible to construct a set of panels for adjacent years.

The US *Current Population Survey* (CPS) is a monthly survey of about 50 000 households (Bureau of Labour Statistics and Bureau of the Census, 1998). We use annual data from 1964 to 1992, taken from the March survey in each year (National Bureau for Economic Research, 1998). The CPS underrecords the incidence of unemployment in the previous year as, in contrast to the LFS, it records the dominant employment event over the previous 12 months. Since many unemployment spells are of short duration, this causes some problems of comparability.[2]

Aggregate evidence

In Figures 5.1 to 5.3 we plot the annual proportion of the employed workforce in the USA and the UK for 10 broad sectors, using the 1980 UK 1-digit SIC categorization. The USA has a larger proportion of its workforce employed in agriculture, forestry and fishing (SIC 0), distribution (SIC 6), finance and services (SIC 8 and 9), and a smaller proportion in energy (SIC 1), manufacturing (SIC 2, 3 and 4), construction (SIC 5) and transport (SIC 7).

Changes in employment shares are highly correlated between the two countries. Employment in manufacturing declines from the mid-1970s and throughout the 1980s, while employment in finance and services increases rapidly. These diagrams suggest that, broadly speaking, the USA and the UK have experienced similar processes of restructuring. What is interesting from the point of view of this chapter is the way in which labour has adjusted to these similar pressures in the two countries.

75

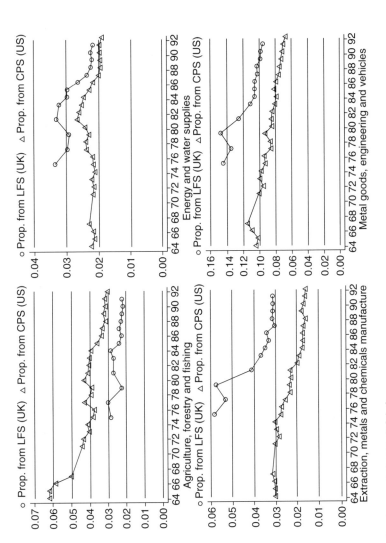

Figure 5.1 Employment shares, *SIC* 0–3

76

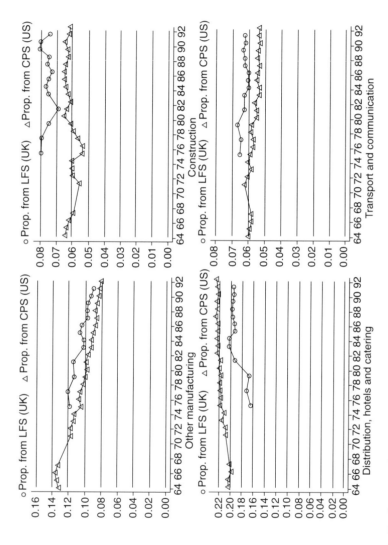

Figure 5.2 Employment shares, *SIC* 4–7

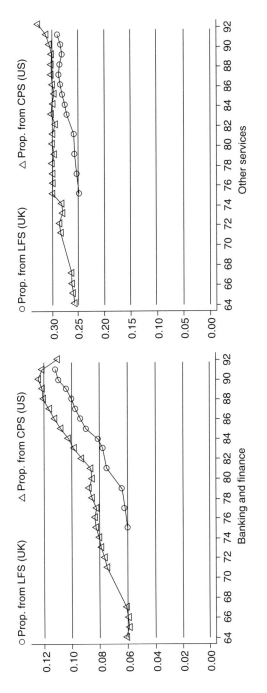

Figure 5.3 Employment shares, *SIC* 8–9

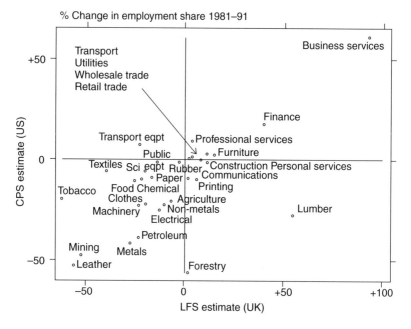

Figure 5.4   Changes in employment shares by detailed sector

To emphasize this point, Figure 5.4 compares the proportionate change in employment shares over the period 1981–91 for a more detailed set of 32 industrial sectors.[3] The correlation between the two countries is positive and high ($\rho = 0.636$), demonstrating that the same industries (at this level of aggregation) experienced increases or decreases in employment shares over this period. It is particularly striking that *every* sector which experienced declines in employment shares in both the USA and the UK (the bottom left-hand quadrant) is in manufacturing. In contrast, the expanding sectors in each country are service sectors. A third group of industries, comprising infrastructure (utilities, distribution, and retail) is essentially static.

These observations suggest a three-way categorization, which may be a convenient simplification. The three manufacturing sectors are grouped together with agriculture to comprise the 'declining sector'; banking and finance and other services are grouped to comprise the 'expanding sector'; and the remainder are classified as the 'static sector'.

$$
\begin{array}{ccc}
& \text{Sector at } t-1 \\
& 1 \quad\ 2 \quad\ 3 \\
\begin{array}{c} 1 \\ \text{Sector at } t \quad 2 \\ 3 \end{array}
&
\begin{array}{ccc}
n_{11} & n_{12} & n_{13} \\
n_{21} & n_{22} & n_{23} \\
n_{31} & n_{32} & n_{33}
\end{array}
\end{array}
$$

Figure 5.5 Job-to-job transition matrix

Individual-level evidence

Using information on employment in the current sector and the previous
year's sector, we can construct the three-by-three transition matrix shown
in Figure 5.5. n_{sr} is the number of individuals in sector s at time t who were
in sector r at time $t-1$.[4] The sample is restricted to those in employment
at both t and $t-1$. Using this notation, the aggregate gross flow between
all three sectors is the total number of people who move from one sector
to another, given by:

$$
\sum_{s=1}^{3}\sum_{r=1}^{3} n_{sr}, \quad j \neq k, \tag{1}
$$

the sum of the off-diagonal elements in Figure 5.5. The estimated
probability of moving between any two sectors is $\Pr(s \neq r)$, which is given
by aggregate gross flows divided by the total stock.[5] Inflows and outflows
to and from a particular sector are subsets of relation (1). For example,
inflows to sector 1 are $(\sum_{r=2,3} n_{1r}$, while outflows from sector 1 are
$(\sum_{r=2,3} n_{1r}$. Inflows and outflows can be normalized by the stock in any
sector at time t, or at time $t-1$.[6]

The three sectors are defined as before: manufacturing (declining);
business, finance and other services (expanding); and construction,
distribution and transport (static). Figures 5.6 and 5.7 plot proportionate
inflows and outflows for sectors 1 and 2. Inflows and outflows for both
countries are procyclical. In the USA, for example, we can see peaks in
inflows and outflows in 1966, 1974, 1980 and 1989, and each of these
years is at or near the peak of a cycle as measured by unemployment. But
overlaid on top of these cycles there appears to be a longer-term decline
from 1966 to 1986 in the USA, with flow rates falling from around 13 per
cent in the 1960s to around 6 per cent in the 1980s, before jumping again
to nearly 10 per cent in at the beginning of the 1990s. The dramatic

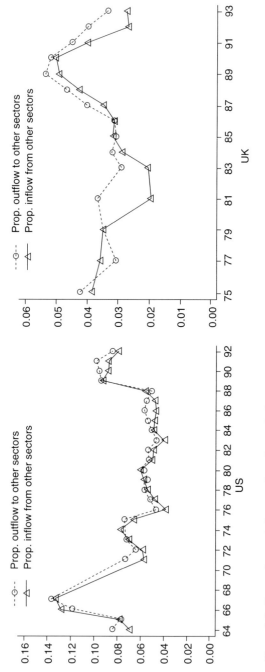

Figure 5.6 Proportionate inflows and outflows: declining sector (manufacturing)

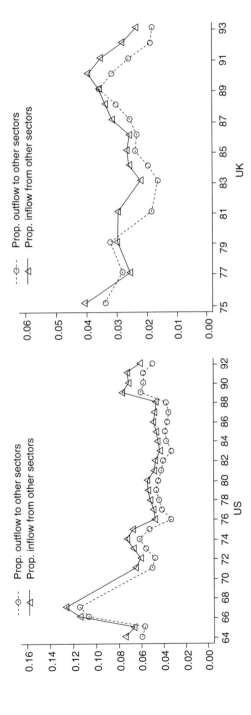

Figure 5.7 Proportionate inflows and outflows: expanding sector (services)

decline from the 1960s to the 1980s in the USA was noted by Jovanovic and Moffitt (1990, table 1), but Figures 5.6 and 5.7 suggest that this decline has been sharply reversed. Unfortunately, the shorter time period for the UK does not enable us to identify whether a similar decline occurred in the UK. However, there has clearly been a similar increase in flow rates in the mid- to late-1980s.

We can recall that the measure of a sector at $t - 1$ was likely to be an underestimate for the USA because it refers to the major activity over the last 12 months. Despite this, and despite the great variability in flow rates, the USA has consistently higher inflows and outflows by a factor of around 2.

The next feature to note is that inflows and outflows are of a similar magnitude. Outflows tend to be higher than inflows in the declining sector, and vice versa for the expanding sector, but in general the difference is less than 1 per cent of stocks. This implies that net flows (the relative change in the size of a sector) are small compared to gross flows. The major exception to this is in the UK in the period 1979–83, when there were some quite dramatic declines in the manufacturing sector, a proportion of which appear to have been 'mopped up' in the service sector. However, for a more complete picture of this period we also need to refer to unemployment, as we shall see later.

What proportion of changes are *within* rather than between sectors? If job moves are primarily a response to changing patterns of labour demand between sectors, then we would expect that only a small proportion of moves would occur within sectors. However, many job-to-job moves are within the same sector. This is illustrated in Figure 5.8. We can estimate within-sector moves for the UK because the LFS contains a specific question: 'are you working for the same firm as 12 months ago?' If an individual has not changed sector, but is also not working for the same firm, they must have moved jobs within sectors.

The left-hand panel of Figure 5.8 shows within- and between-sector flows for our three aggregate sectors. Both within- and between-sector moves are procyclical, but within-sector flows are about one-third more frequent. Of course, whether a flow is counted as 'within' or 'between' depends on how finely the sectors are disaggregated. At the finest level of disaggregation (the firm), by definition all flows are between sectors. As the level of aggregation increases, so the proportion of flows that are between sectors decreases. This is illustrated in the right-hand panel of Figure 5.8. Redefining sectors according to UK 1980 1-digit SIC codes, so that there are 10 sectors rather than three, we can see that between-sector flows are now of a similar magnitude to within-sector flows.

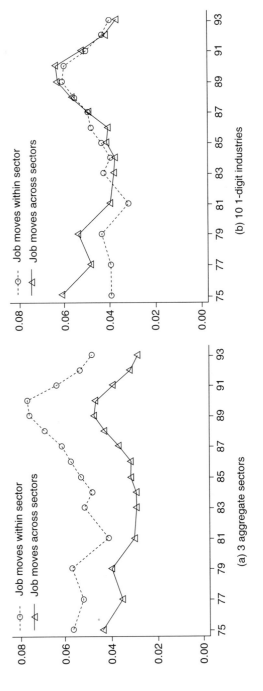

Figure 5.8 Within and between flows, UK

Because of this aggregation problem, it is difficult to compare within and between flows and draw a firm conclusion about the relative importance of sectoral demand shifts on the movement of individuals between jobs. A more useful comparison is between net and gross flows. If flows between sectors are a result of exogenous shocks to labour demand, then we would expect net flows (that is, flows in one direction which are not 'cancelled out' by flows in the other direction) to be a high proportion of all flows. However, if flows are a result of continuous search processes between workers and firms, then gross flows will tend to be much higher than net flows.

In the most extreme case where all flows are due to sectoral shifts in demand, the declining sector has inflows of zero and the expanding sector has outflows of zero. Net flows will equal gross flows. At the other extreme, where sectors do not change in size at all, all inflows are cancelled out by outflows and net flows are zero. The ratio of net flows to gross flows may vary from zero (where all flows from r to s are 'cancelled out' by flows in the reverse direction, and sectors remain the same size) to one (where none of the movement from r to s is cancelled out by return flows).

Proportionate gross flows are given by equation (1) divided by the total stock. Proportionate net flows are defined as the sum of the changes in stocks, divided by the total stock.[7] Figure 5.9 plots gross and net flows for the two countries, and the left-hand panel shows again that flows tend to be higher in the USA. The procyclical pattern is also clear. The right-hand panel reveals how small net flows are compared to gross flows. This could also have been deduced from Figures 5.6 and 5.7, since inflows and outflows to each sector were generally so close together. What was not clear from the earlier diagrams is (a) how volatile net flows are, and (b) how different the pattern of net flows is between the USA and the UK. The USA has tended to have higher net flows, except for the period 1979–83 when the severe manufacturing recession compounded by Dutch Disease effects in the UK forced a relatively large number of people to move out of manufacturing with no corresponding inflow.

What role does unemployment and dropping out of the labour market play in the flows of individuals between sectors? Previous work on sectoral mobility has focused on movements directly between sectors, which involves analysing only those individuals who remain in employment at times t and $t-1$. But unemployment may be a crucial part of the restructuring process if individuals who leave a declining sector cannot find work elsewhere. Unemployment is the most visible evidence of the costs of adjustment. Similarly, individuals may leave the labour market altogether, or enter jobs in an expanding sector from out

85

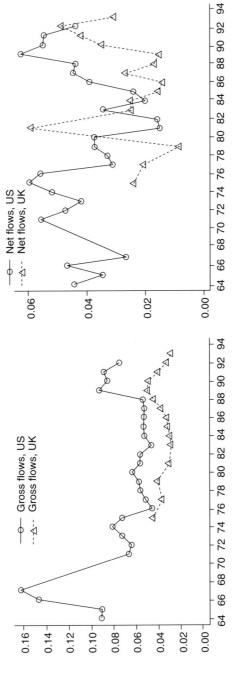

Figure 5.9 Gross and net flows, US and UK

of the labour market. Figures 5.10 and 5.11 plot inflows and outflows between sectors 1 and 2, unemployment and 'not in the labour force' (NILF) for the UK.

Looking first at the declining sector, it is unsurprising to see that outflows into unemployment are counter-cyclical and inflows from unemployment are pro-cyclical. The dramatic effects of the 1979–83 period are again clear, and it is also clear that flows between the declining manufacturing sector and both unemployment and NILF are higher than flows with other sectors: compare Figure 5.10 with Figures 5.6 and 5.7 for the UK. For example, during the 1979–83 period a larger number of people in manufacturing became unemployed than managed to find employment in either of the other two sectors. The expanding sector (Figure 5.11) shows a different pattern. Inflows and outflows with unemployment are small, but we can see from the right-hand panel how the increase in the size of this sector has been driven by entrants from out of the labour force. Indeed, this is the only case where net flows (represented as the distance between inflows and outflows) are a large proportion of gross flows.

Figures 5.10 and 5.11 show how important it is to include flows with unemployment and NILF in any analysis of mobility patterns. They suggest that in the UK the restructuring process, and in particular the recession of the early 1980s, was associated with large inflows into unemployment and large outflows from NILF. The process of expansion and contraction of sectors occurs via movements of labour into and out of unemployment and NILF.

Previous work on sectoral mobility

One approach to explaining the sectoral mobility of labour is to emphasize sectoral shifts in demand which occur as a result of sector-specific shocks. In these models, a significant proportion of unemployment is frictional, and there is a substantial labour economics literature which works from this perspective. Interestingly, this is also the natural starting point from a neo-classical trade perspective. Stolper–Samuelson-type adjustment essentially works through the consequences of a sector-specific shock and, particularly in a specific factors context associates unemployment with frictions which frustrate the transfer of labour from one sector to another. Lilien (1982) concludes that 'at least half of the variance of unemployment over the post-war period may be attributed to ... slow adjustment of labour to shifts of employment demand between sectors of the economy' (p. 778). One implication of these models is that

87

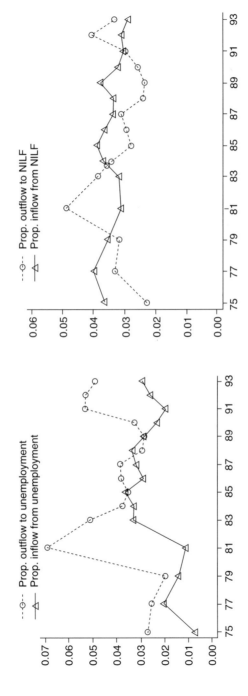

Figure 5.10 Flows into and out of unemployment and NILF, declining sector

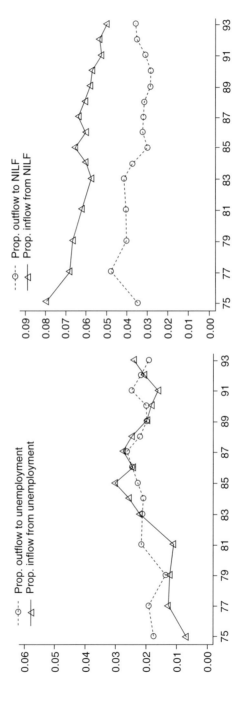

Figure 5.11 Flows into and out of employment and NILF, expanding sector

the 'flexibility' of the labour force is a crucially important determinant of aggregate unemployment.

However, the fact that gross flows dominate net flows to such a large extent, as illustrated in the previous section, may suggest that intersectoral flows of labour occur for other reasons as well. Search models, such as that formalized by Jovanovic (1979), suggest that the world is characterized by incomplete information and that the majority of worker movements can be explained within a framework where workers and firms are searching for their most suitable job match. These models imply that authors such as Lilien (1982) may be misinterpreting the impact of demand shifts, since many observed job changes may be for matching reasons rather than because the sector in which they are working has been subject to an external shock.

It may also be the case that external shocks are associated with *intra*sectoral movement. As Figure 5.8 showed, intrasectoral flows within three aggregate sectors are rather higher than intersectoral flows. The prevalence of intraindustry trade is well-documented (see for example Greenaway, Hine and Milner, 1995; Greenaway and Torstensson, 1997). A sector-specific shock in this setting can change the composition of output within a sector, triggering 'within' rather than 'between' job movements. A further key feature to have emerged from US studies of labour mobility is that gross flows have declined secularly over the 1970s and 1980s (Murphy and Topel, 1987; Jovanovic and Moffitt, 1990), and that this has coincided with an increase in the unemployment rate. This may have occurred because workers with high levels of sector-specific human capital are unwilling to change sector, even at the expense of longer periods of unemployment (Thomas, 1996).[8]

In the UK, the focus of econometric work has tended to be on the issue of regional mobility, which is closely related to sectoral mobility (Pissarides and Wadsworth, 1989; Jackman and Savouri, 1992; McCormick, 1997). A particular issue, which has attracted attention in the UK, is the relationship between housing tenure and mobility. Several authors have argued that rigidities in the housing market contribute to the immobility of labour, although for various different reasons (Hughes and McCormick, 1981; Oswald, 1996; Henley, 1998).

A model of job movement

Our approach is to adapt and develop a model of intersectoral movement from Jovanovic and Moffitt (1990), allowing us to analyse gross as well as net labour movements. Assume there are N sectors in the economy, each with a constant number of identical price-taking firms, normalized to unity. Each firm is assumed to have a production function of the form:

$$y_{st} = f^s(x_{st}, z_{st}) \tag{2}$$

where y_{st} is the output of sector s at time t; $f^s(x_{st}, z_{st})$ is the production function of sector s at time t, x_{st} is total labour in efficiency units; and z_{st} is a sector-specific shock.

On the demand side, each firm is assumed to choose the amount of labour in efficiency units which will maximize profits:

$$\max_x [p_{st} f^s(x, z_{st}) - w_{st} x]. \tag{3}$$

where p_{st} is the output price in sector s at time t and w_{st} is the price per efficiency unit of labour in sector s at time t. Thus employment is chosen so that the marginal revenue product of efficiency units equals the wage, which implies a derived demand for labour of the form:

$$x_{st} = \Psi^s \left[\frac{w_{st}}{p_{st}}, z_{st} \right] \tag{4}$$

where Ψ^s is the inverse marginal product function in sector s.

The productivity of the firm's workforce depends on how well the characteristics of its workers match with those of the firm. A worker's productivity is assumed to be randomly drawn from a normal distribution and is specific for each worker–firm match. Workers and firms only discover the quality of the match once the appointment has been made:

$$F(m) \sim N(\overline{m}, \sigma^2) = \Phi \left[\frac{m - \overline{m}}{\sigma} \right]. \tag{5}$$

Individual workers are paid according to the quality of the match that they achieve with the firm. That is, they are paid their own marginal revenue product:

$$w_{ist} = m_i p_{st} f^{s\prime}(x, z_{st}) = m_i w_{st} \tag{6}$$

where w_{ist} is the wage per worker and m_i is the worker-specific match. This structure is important because it determines the mobility of individuals. Poorly-suited individuals receive a wage lower than the mean, whilst well-suited individuals obtain a wage above the mean. If a worker is poorly paid, then in the next period they may decide to move job in the hope of improving their situation. In deciding whether or not to move, individuals compare the quality of their existing match and the expected benefit of moving.

Consider an individual who is considering a move from sector r to sector s. Their expected second-period earnings are $w_{st}\bar{m}$, because workers new to a sector are randomly matched with a firm and so on average they achieve the mean value of a prospective match, $\bar{m}$. So if the cost of moving is c, the expected benefit of moving is $w_{st}\bar{m} - c$. This implies that the minimum acceptable alternative wage is one which is just high enough to compensate them for the cost of moving, that is:

$$w_{rt}m_i = w_{st}\bar{m} - c. \tag{7}$$

Hence the quality of the current match below which movement will be induced is given by:

$$m = \bar{m}\frac{w_{st}}{w_{rt}} - \frac{c}{w_{rt}}. \tag{8}$$

The probability of a given individual moving from r to s is thus the probability that the match is less than this level. Since the distribution of matches is defined by $F(\ )$:

$$q_{s|r,t} = F(\bar{m}\frac{w_{st}}{w_{rt}} - \frac{c}{w_{rt}}) \tag{9}$$

where $q_{s|rt}$ is the probability of an individual moving from sector r to s in period t. This movement of workers from sectors with low wages per efficiency unit to those with high wages serves to equalize rewards per efficiency unit across sectors. This is the process by which net flows are generated. Note, however, that even if payments per efficiency unit are equalized across sectors, movements of individuals will still occur between sectors. Some workers will still find themselves badly matched in their current job and will find it beneficial to move.

This model seems to accord with the patterns of labour movement that we observed earlier for the USA and the UK. Gross flows are generated by individuals' positions in the matching distribution, and occur even in the absence of shocks. Moreover, flows may occur from an expanding to a declining sector as a result of this process. The model predicts that individual mobility will be decreasing with the quality of the firm–worker match, and with the costs of moving between sectors.

Net flows are generated by differences in the wage per efficiency unit across sectors, which result from sector-specific shocks. An increase in the return to efficiency units in another sector (a beneficial shock in another sector) will induce movements as individuals are now on average paid better in this sector. This will serve to increase supplies of labour where there have been beneficial sectoral shocks and lead to equalization of payments per efficiency units across sectors.

At a more aggregate level, if it is assumed that the marginal product of efficiency units is procyclical, then booms lead to a rightward shift in demand. By stimulating an increase in the wage per efficiency unit, this increases the separation rate. The prospective rewards of moving have increased relative to the costs, and hence we would expect to find gross flows to be procyclical which is the pattern observed in the left-hand panel of Figure 5.9. Further, if it is the case that declining sectors contract relatively more quickly in recessions, then net flows will be counter-cyclical. This is the pattern found for the UK in the right-hand panel of Figure 5.9, although not for the USA.

Of course, this is not a complete characterization of labour movements, because we have assumed that (a) all separations are voluntary, and (b) individuals do not move between employment and non-employment; as we have seen, flows between employment and non-employment are significant. In the econometric analysis below we therefore allow for non-employment as an additional state.

An econometric analysis of sectoral mobility

The matching model provides a framework for modelling the determinants of labour mobility, and yields a number of testable predictions. We estimate the probability of changing from sector r at time $t - 1$ to sector s at t, given by equation (9). The key question is: what determines the transition probabilities $q_{s|r}$? The model set out in the previous section allows us to identify these as:

1 The quality of the match, m. This is expected to be a function of job-specific and general skills, as suggested by Grossman and Shapiro (1982). Job-specific skills are expected to increase the value of the existing match, whilst general skills raise the quality of all matches.
2 The costs of movement, c. These are expected to be affected by housing (ownership status, region) and family circumstances (marital status, age and sex).
3 Sector specific shocks, z_{st}, which reflect themselves in differences in the wage per efficiency unit, w_{st}.

In this chapter we estimate transition probabilities as a function of items (1) and (2), and Table 5.1 describes the variables used to proxy these items.

Table 5.1   Independent variables

	USA		UK	
	Mean	S.D.	Mean	S.D.
Log age	3.545	(0.346)	3.590	(0.334)
Log age squared	12.685	(2.434)	12.997	(2.363)
Female	0.421	(0.494)	0.407	(0.491)
Married	0.654	(0.476)	0.733	(0.443)
Completed high school[a]	0.749	(0.434)	0.272	(0.445)
Manual occupation	0.330[c]	(0.470)	0.383	(0.486)
Skilled occupation	0.452[c]	(0.498)	0.470	(0.499)
Dependent children[b]	0.669	(0.471)	0.570[d]	(0.495)
Housing owned outright			0.124[d]	(0.329)
Housing being bought			0.475[d]	(0.499)
Housing private rented			0.058[d]	(0.235)
Sample size	1 397 961		960 116	
Time period	1964–92		1975–93	

Notes:
[a] Not an equivalent measure for the USA and the UK. The US figure refers to the proportion of the sample who complete high school, whilst the UK figure refers to the proportion who leave school after the age of 16.
[b] US figure refers to children under 18, UK under 16.
[c] Only available 1971–92.
[d] Only available 1983–93.

There are two restrictions which make the choice of variables difficult. First, for time-varying information we require information from $t-1$ rather than t, and only a small proportion of questions in the LFS refer to 12 months previously. Thus, for example, we are prevented from including employment tenure as a regressor, since this is only known at time t. Those who move sectors will therefore always have tenure of less than 12 months. Second, we require variables which are consistently defined over a long period of time.

We estimate the transition probabilities using a multinomial Logit model. This assumes that the probability of an individual being in sector s at time t conditional on being in sector r at time t is given by:

$$q_{s|r,t} = \frac{\exp(\mathbf{x}_i' \beta_{s|r})}{\sum_{j=1}^{4} \exp(\mathbf{x}_i' \beta_{j|r})}, s = 1, ..., 4, r = 1, ..., 4 \quad (12)$$

where $\mathbf{x}_i$ is the vector of characteristics of individual i. We define movement probabilities relative to the probability of staying in the same sector, which allows us to normalize the coefficient vector $\beta_{s|r} = 0$ when $s = r$. Equation (12) is estimated separately for each sector at $t - 1$, allowing the estimates of β to vary across r. In the most basic specification x_i contains age, gender, marital status, education and occupation indicators. Each estimate includes a set of year dummies to control for the business cycle effects, which are so pronounced in Figures 5.6 and 5.7. Tables 5.2 and 5.3 therefore give the marginal impacts of individual characteristics on the probability of moving sector. That is, the impact of age, gender and so on the off-diagonal elements in the three-by-three transition matrix shown in Figure 5.5.

For each element in the transition matrix we also report the baseline probability of a move. As we would expect, the probability of moving out of the declining sector is higher than the probability of entering. For example, the probability of entering manufacturing in the USA is 0.0399 (0.0149 + 0.0250), while the probability of leaving is 0.0642 (0.0268 + 0.0374). The reverse is true of the expanding sector. Note that the baseline probabilities for the US estimates are everywhere greater than those for the UK: this confirms that, on average, movements are more likely in the US data for all sectors and for both inflows and outflows.

We concentrate on describing the characteristics of those who leave the declining sector, and those who enter the expanding sector. Those individuals who leave the declining sector and enter the expanding sector are in both these groups.

What are the characteristics of individuals who leave the declining sector? These are given by the top panels of Tables 5.2 and 5.3. In the USA, the probability of entering both the expanding and the static sector from the declining sector declines with age, but this effect diminishes with age-squared; younger individuals are more mobile. This result does not hold for the UK: age is insignificantly related to movements into services, and positively related to movements into the static sector. The absolute size of the age effect is also much greater in the USA than in the UK. Females are more likely to leave the declining sector to enter services in both countries, and the effect is of similar size. We find that workers in manual and in skilled occupations are less likely to enter services in both countries. Note that the size of the marginal effects in the USA is nearly always larger, indicating that the difference in movement probability between different types of individual is greater in the USA.

What are the characteristics of individuals who enter the expanding sector? In the USA, mobility into the expanding sector from the declining sector declines with age (top left panel), but mobility from the static sector increases with age (lower right panel). In the UK both flows into the

Table 5.2 Multinomial Logit estimates of inflow and outflow characteristics, USA[a]

	$\Pr(s_t = 2 \mid s_{t-1} = 1)$		$\Pr(s_t = 3 \mid s_{t-1} = 1)$	
	Marg. eff.	*P*-value	Marg. eff.	*P*-value
Log age	−0.1183	[0.000]	−0.1707	[0.000]
Log age squared	0.0136	[0.000]	0.0179	[0.000]
Female	0.0138	[0.000]	−0.0125	[0.000]
Married	−0.0071	[0.000]	−0.0051	[0.000]
Completed high school	−0.0064	[0.000]	−0.0055	[0.000]
Manual occupation	−0.0100	[0.000]	0.0019	[0.004]
Skilled occupation	−0.0044	[0.000]	−0.0082	[0.000]
Baseline probability	0.0268		0.0374	

	$\Pr(s_t = 1 \mid s_{t-1} = 2)$		$\Pr(s_t = 3 \mid s_{t-1} = 2)$	
	Marg. eff.	*P*-value	Marg. eff.	*P*-value
Log age	−0.0375	[0.000]	−0.2035	[0.000]
Log age squared	0.0033	[0.008]	0.0233	[0.000]
Female	−0.0063	[0.000]	−0.0112	[0.000]
Married	−0.0016	[0.000]	−0.0043	[0.000]
Completed high school	0.0019	[0.000]	−0.0018	[0.000]
Manual occupation	0.0097	[0.000]	0.0149	[0.000]
Skilled occupation	−0.0058	[0.000]	−0.0132	[0.000]
Baseline probability	0.0149		0.0341	

	$\Pr(s_t = 1 \mid s_{t-1} = 3)$		$\Pr(s_t = 3 \mid s_{t-1} = 3)$	
	Marg. eff.	*P*-value	Marg. eff.	*P*-value
Log age	0.0028	[0.809]	0.0821	[0.000]
Log age squared	−0.0040	[0.016]	−0.0169	[0.000]
Female	−0.0048	[0.000]	0.0211	[0.000]
Married	−0.0011	[0.021]	−0.0101	[0.000]
Completed high school	0.0041	[0.000]	−0.0042	[0.000]
Manual occupation	0.0099	[0.000]	−0.0106	[0.000]
Skilled occupation	−0.0065	[0.000]	−0.0092	[0.000]
Baseline probability	0.0250		0.0439	

Note: [a]Estimates of equation (12). All estimates include year dummies 1971–92.

expanding sector are increasing with age. Females are more likely to enter the expanding sector than males in both countries. Once again, it is noticeable that entrants to the service sector are less likely to be skilled or manual, suggesting that new jobs in the service sector are more likely to be in unskilled non-manual occupations.

Table 5.3   Multinomial Logit estimates of inflow and outflow characteristics, UK[a]

	$\Pr(s_t = 2\|s_{t-1} = 1)$		$\Pr(s_t = 3\|s_{t-1} = 1)$	
	Marg. eff.	P-value	Marg. eff.	P-value
Log age	0.0172	[0.163]	0.0914	[0.000]
Log age squared	−0.0044	[0.012]	−0.0180	[0.000]
Female	0.0114	[0.000]	0.0007	[0.216]
Married	0.0013	[0.006]	0.0030	[0.000]
Completed high school	0.0064	[0.000]	−0.0014	[0.034]
Manual occupation	−0.0057	[0.000]	0.0004	[0.457]
Skilled occupation	−0.0031	[0.000]	−0.0078	[0.000]
Baseline probability	0.0164		0.0241	

	$\Pr(s_t = 2z\|s_{t-1} = 1)$		$\Pr(s_t = 3\|s_{t-1} = 2)$	
	Marg. eff.	P-value	Marg. eff.	P-value
Log age	−0.0060	[0.498]	0.0118	[0.300]
Log age squared	−0.0014	[0.256]	−0.0055	[0.001]
Female	−0.0023	[0.000]	−0.0022	[0.000]
Married	−0.0000	[0.898]	−0.0001	[0.823]
Completed high school	−0.0027	[0.000]	−0.0059	[0.000]
Manual occupation	0.0044	[0.000]	0.0061	[0.000]
Skilled occupation	−0.0031	[0.000]	−0.0079	[0.000]
Baseline probability	0.0107		0.0178	

	$\Pr(s_t = 1\|s_{t-1} = 3)$		$\Pr(s_t = 2\|s_{t-1} = 3)$	
	Marg. eff.	P-value	Marg. eff.	P-value
Log age	0.0097	[0.468]	0.0222	[0.084]
Log age squared	−0.0058	[0.002]	−0.0057	[0.002]
Female	−0.0007	[0.241]	0.0139	[0.000]
Married	0.0025	[0.000]	−0.0009	[0.073]
Completed high school	−0.0004	[0.442]	0.0079	[0.000]
Manual occupation	0.0024	[0.000]	−0.0030	[0.000]
Skilled occupation	−0.0061	[0.000]	−0.0065	[0.000]
Baseline probability	0.0204		0.0216	

Note: [a]Estimates of (12). All estimates include year dummies 1975–1993.

There are clearly systematic differences in (a) the characteristics of movers between different sectors, and (b) the characteristics of movers between the USA and the UK. Even characteristics in which there are no definitional problems between the two countries, such as age and sex, have different coefficient values for the USA and the UK. Although the aggregate picture suggests that the USA and the UK are experiencing similar restructuring in terms of declining and expanding sectors, it appears that it is not the same type of individuals who are moving between sectors.

Table 5.4 reports estimates of equation (12) where the vector of characteristics includes information about housing tenure and dependent children. This information is available only for the UK. It has been suggested that housing tenure is a key characteristic in determining labour market flexibility because owner-occupation makes it more difficult for individuals to relocate (Oswald, 1996). However, estimates of unemployment propensity at the individual level show that, for obvious reasons, owner-occupiers are *less* likely to experience unemployment.

Every panel in Table 5.4 shows that individuals who own or who are buying their accommodation are less likely to move than those in public-rented accommodation (the base category) and private-rented accommodation. Indeed, in almost every case the mobility probabilities can be ordered in the same way: private renters are the most likely to switch sectors, followed by public-sector renters, those with a mortgage, and the least likely to move are those who own outright.

One important drawback with the interpretation of these results is that we have ignored the possibility of unemployment. The samples comprise only those who are in employment in both years. Thus it is difficult to ascertain whether those individuals who are 'mobile' are more or less likely to suffer from unemployment. One should not therefore equate higher movement probabilities with individual 'success'. In the next section we utilize information on employment status for the UK to include those who move into and out of employment.

The determinants of mobility from the declining sector

Why do so many people in the UK move via the unemployment pool to other sectors, rather than directly from job to job? Using the LFS data for the UK, we can construct a five-way transition matrix, consisting of the three sectors defined earlier (Figure 5.5), plus unemployment and 'not in the labour force' (NILF). Instead of estimating five five-way multinomial Logits, we concentrate only on movements where $r = 1$: that is, movements out of the declining manufacturing sector. To simplify further, we have collapsed the five possible outcomes down to four by adding together flows into either of the other two sectors. The four outcomes are then: $s = 1$ (stay in sector 1), $s = 2, 3$ (find a job in another sector), $s = 4$ (enter unemployment), or $s = 5$ (enter NILF).

Table 5.4 Multinomial Logit estimates of inflow and outflow characteristics, UK, preferred specification[a]

	$\Pr(s_t = 2 \mid s_{t-1} = 1)$		$\Pr(s_t = 3 \mid s_{t-1} = 1)$	
	Marg. eff.	P-value	Marg. eff.	P-value
Log age	−0.0152	[0.386]	0.0248	[0.246]
Log age squared	0.0002	[0.923]	−0.0079	[0.010]
Female	0.0115	[0.000]	0.0030	[0.000]
Married	0.0007	[0.310]	0.0000	[0.959]
Completed high school	0.0067	[0.000]	−0.0011	[0.175]
Manual occupation	−0.0079	[0.000]	−0.0015	[0.032]
Skilled occupation	−0.0035	[0.000]	−0.0075	[0.000]
Dependent children	0.0014	[0.010]	0.0017	[0.019]
Housing owned outright	−0.0026	[0.007]	−0.0042	[0.000]
Housing being bought	−0.0007	[0.341]	−0.0006	[0.453]
Housing private rented	0.0057	[0.000]	0.0065	[0.000]
Baseline probability	0.0177		0.0241	

	$\Pr(s_t = 1 \mid s_{t-1} = 2)$		$\Pr(s_t = 3 \mid s_{t-1} = 2)$	
	Marg. eff.	P-value	Marg. eff.	P-value
Log age	−0.0266	[0.012]	−0.0257	[0.067]
Log age squared	0.0018	[0.234]	0.0002	[0.936]
Female	−0.0020	[0.000]	−0.0010	[0.014]
Married	−0.0003	[0.458]	−0.0009	[0.092]
Completed high school	−0.0018	[0.000]	−0.0051	[0.000]
Manual occupation	0.0046	[0.000]	0.0062	[0.000]
Skilled occupation	−0.0026	[0.000]	−0.0074	[0.000]
Dependent children	−0.0004	[0.196]	0.0026	[0.000]
Housing owned outright	−0.0020	[0.001]	−0.0027	[0.000]
Housing being bought	−0.0011	[0.014]	−0.0026	[0.000]
Housing private rented	0.0013	[0.030]	0.0020	[0.009]
Baseline probability	0.0107		0.0178	

	$\Pr(s_t = 1 \mid s_{t-1} = 3)$		$\Pr(s_t = 2 \mid s_{t-1} = 3)$	
	Marg. eff.	P-value	Marg. eff.	P-value
Log age	0.0050	[0.764]	−0.0194	[0.276]
Log age squared	−0.0047	[0.050]	0.0003	[0.918]
Female	−0.0003	[0.606]	0.0156	[0.000]
Married	0.0015	[0.026]	−0.0016	[0.022]
Completed high school	−0.0004	[0.510]	0.0085	[0.000]
Manual occupation	0.0016	[0.005]	−0.0036	[0.000]
Skilled occupation	−0.0046	[0.000]	−0.0066	[0.000]
Dependent children	−0.0004	[0.422]	0.0023	[0.000]
Housing owned outright	−0.0033	[0.000]	−0.0031	[0.001]

Table 5.4   (*continued.*)

	$\Pr(s_t = 1 \mid s_{t-1} = 3)$		$\Pr(s_t = 2 \mid s_{t-1} = 3)$	
	Marg. eff.	*P*-value	Marg. eff.	*P*-value
Housing being bought	−0.0012	[0.050]	−0.0002	[0.803]
Housing private rented	0.0028	[0.005]	0.0072	[0.000]
Baseline probability	0.0204		0.0216	

Note: ᵃEstimates of equation (12). All estimates include year dummies 1983–93.

Table 5.5   Business cycle effects on outcomes from the declining sector, UK

	$\Pr(s_t = j \mid s_{t-1} = 1)$			
	j = 0 No move	*j* = 1 Another sector	*j* = 2 Unemp.	*j* = 3 NILF
1975	0.9084	0.0419	0.0271	0.0226
1977	0.9180	0.0317	0.0261	0.0243
1979	0.9204	0.0369	0.0201	0.0226
1981	0.8716	0.0353	0.0636	0.0295
1983	0.8844	0.0301	0.0553	0.0302
1984	0.8950	0.0283	0.0407	0.0360
1985	0.9041	0.0315	0.0358	0.0286
1986	0.9016	0.0310	0.0381	0.0293
1987	0.8914	0.0399	0.0381	0.0306
1988	0.8983	0.0476	0.0297	0.0244
1989	0.8938	0.0545	0.0282	0.0235
1990	0.8906	0.0514	0.0324	0.0255
1991	0.8750	0.0410	0.0542	0.0298
1992	0.8602	0.0367	0.0566	0.0465
1993	0.8764	0.0316	0.0534	0.0386
All years	0.8958	0.0378	0.0382	0.0282

Table 5.5 displays the relative proportions of the outcome for each year from 1975 to 1993. Notice how the proportion that enters another sector relative to unemployment runs counter-cyclically. Table 5.6 shows estimates of marginal effects calculated from equation (12). Marginal effects sum to zero across rows, since outcome probabilities are mutually exclusive. The results seem intuitively sensible. Older workers are more likely to remain in the same sector or to find work in another sector, and less likely to enter unemployment, and these effects are declining with age (the coefficient on age-squared has the opposite sign in every case). It is well-established that mobility is declining in age, although a large part of this effect is due to declining mobility with job tenure (Mincer and Jovanovic, 1981).

Table 5.6 Multinomial Logit estimates of outcomes from the declining sector, UK[a]

	$\Pr(s_t = j\|s_{t-1} = 1)$							
	$j = 0$ No move		$j = 1$ Another sector		$j = 2$ Unemp.		$j = 3$ NILF	
Log age	1.085	[0.000]	0.027	[0.316]	-0.347	[0.000]	-0.764	[0.000]
Log age squared	-0.145	[0.000]	-0.010	[0.011]	0.046	[0.000]	0.109	[0.000]
Female	-0.041	[0.000]	0.014	[0.000]	-0.000	[0.631]	0.028	[0.000]
Married	-0.005	[0.006]	-0.000	[0.984]	-0.006	[0.000]	0.011	[0.000]
Completed high school	-0.007	[0.000]	0.007	[0.000]	-0.004	[0.003]	0.004	[0.000]
Manual occupation	-0.002	[0.151]	-0.010	[0.000]	-0.004	[0.003]	0.002	[0.003]
Skilled occupation	0.020	[0.000]	-0.011	[0.000]	0.010	[0.000]	0.002	[0.003]
Dependent children	-0.024	[0.000]	-0.011	[0.000]	-0.007	[0.000]	-0.003	[0.000]
Housing owned outright	0.030	[0.000]	0.002	[0.042]	0.008	[0.000]	0.014	[0.000]
Housing being bought	0.040	[0.000]	-0.005	[0.000]	-0.020	[0.000]	-0.005	[0.000]
Housing private rented	-0.004	[0.120]	0.000	[0.915]	-0.026	[0.000]	-0.014	[0.000]
Baseline probability	0.896		0.012	[0.000]	-0.008	[0.000]	0.001	[0.544]
			0.038		0.038		0.028	

Note: [a] Estimates of equation (12). Estimates include year dummies 1983–93. p-values in square brackets.

Females are more likely to enter another sector or NILF, but less likely to remain in the same sector. This illustrates how much more useful it is to examine a model which includes unemployment as an outcome. We can see that although females are more mobile between sectors (as the earlier results also showed), they are not correspondingly more likely to suffer unemployment.

It is interesting to compare the results on housing tenure and mobility from the model that includes unemployment with the model estimated only for job-to-job moves. The earlier results showed that private renters were the most likely to switch sectors, and owner-occupiers the least likely. Table 5.6 shows that although owner-occupiers are less mobile between sectors, they are less likely to enter unemployment than either category that are in rented accommodation. Those in public-rented accommodation are the most likely to enter unemployment, but both renting groups are more likely to move sector than those who own their accommodation outright. These results suggest that it is important to include the possibility of moving out of the labour market or into unemployment when assessing the relative mobility of different individuals.

Summary and conclusions

Shifts in employment patterns in the USA and the UK are well-established at the aggregate level, but less is known about how this restructuring has taken place at the micro level. This paper is a first attempt to compare the restructuring process between the USA and the UK. We have shown that:

- Both the USA and the UK have experienced similar long-run shifts in employment shares, but the UK has experienced far higher increases in unemployment.
- Gross outflows and inflows are procyclical; individuals are more likely to switch jobs when times are good. This is true of both manufacturing and services.
- Gross outflows and inflows are higher in the USA for all sectors and for almost all time periods: individuals are more likely to switch sectors in the USA.
- Net flows are tiny compared to gross flows, even when employment restructuring is significant. This suggests that (a) most job-to-job moves can be explained by search and matching models, and (b) employment restructuring is driven by movements into and out of unemployment and the labour force.

• For the UK, changes in the size of the manufacturing and services sector have been facilitated by individuals in manufacturing entering unemployment, and individuals entering services from out of the labour market.

• The characteristics of those individuals who are more likely to move between sectors differ between the USA and the UK. It is interesting to note that even characteristics that are unambiguously defined between the USA and the UK do not have the same correlations with the probability of moving between sectors. Perhaps surprisingly, individuals are more likely to leave the declining sector as they get older in the UK, but less likely in the USA. This shows that the process of restructuring in the two countries has not affected the same types of individuals in the same way.

• There is some evidence for the UK that housing tenure is an important determinant of sectoral mobility. Those in private-rented accommodation are more likely to change sectors than other groups.

• It is misleading to only look at job-to-job moves in determining the way in which industrial restructuring affects individuals, because unemployment is as likely to occur as moving sector.

This chapter presents only an initial analysis of a large topic, and there are several directions in which the analysis could be developed. First, we need to be able to make a consistent comparison of flows into and out of the labour market for the USA and the UK. This will help to establish whether the higher job-to-job flows in the USA correspond to lower flows into unemployment, or possibly shorter unemployment durations. Second, we need a more detailed examination of the reasons why the effect of individual characteristics varies so much between the USA and the UK. In particular, we would like to be able to include better measures of education and skill. It is often suggested that education is the key to a flexible workforce: 'The very high levels of education and training embodied in the German labour force enables them to respond in a flexible manner to demand shifts' (Nickell and Bell, 1996, p. 306).

As well as investigating the relationship between individual characteristics and mobility patterns, we would also like to be able to explore the role of external factors. How important are shocks in determining the flow of workers? It is clear that the UK experienced a dramatic combination of recession and restructuring in the early 1980s. How precisely were these events related to the flow of workers? We have ignored the fact that some movements are voluntary ('quits') and some are involuntary ('layoffs').

We might expect that external shocks have a differential effect on quits and layoffs.

A more disaggregated approach to external shocks might also be fruitful. The sectoral definitions in this chapter have been very broad, but given the large sample sizes it should be possible to focus on particular sectors, and particular policy-changes that affect those sectors. For example, we can identify changes in trade policy at various points during the sample period, which affect certain well-defined sectors.

Finally, it would be useful to extend the analysis to labour markets in other countries. As has been noted, some countries, such as Germany, have responded far more successfully to the process of restructuring than others, such as the UK. Is it the case that we can identify the source of successful responses to structural adjustment in the additional flexibility of labour force movements between sectors?

Notes

1 Biennial from 1973 to 1983; quarterly from 1992 onwards.
2 For this reason we focus on job-to-job moves in this section.
3 The time period was chosen so that consistent industry definitions could be matched between country and over time.
4 We discuss the flows between employment and non-employment in later (pp. 118–19).
5 The total stock is constant between t and $t-1$ because this is a series of balanced 2-year panels.
6 In practice the stock in a particular sector at t is usually close to the stock at $t-1$, and so this makes little difference.
7 Net flows are also divided by two to avoid double counting (see Jovanovic and Moffitt, 1990, p. 830).
8 Grossman and Shapiro (1982) develop a model relating investments in general and specific human capital to factor mobility.

References

Bureau of Labor Statistics and Bureau of the Census (1998) *Current Population Survey*, homepage at http://www.bls.census.gov/cps/cpsmain.htm, 2 July 1998.
Greenaway, D., Hine, R. and Milner, C. (1995) 'Vertical and Horizontal Intra-Industry Trade: A Cross Industry Analysis for the United Kingdom', *The Economic Journal*, vol. 105, pp. 1505–18.
— and Torstensson, J. (1997) 'Back to the Future: Taking Stock on Intra-Industry Trade', *Weltwirtschaftliches Archiv*, vol. 133, pp. 249–69.
Grossman, G. and Shapiro, C. (1982) 'A Theory of Factor Mobility', *Journal of Political Economy*, vol. 90, pp. 1054–69.
Haskel, J. and Slaughter, M. (1997) 'Does the Sector Bias of Skill-Biased Technological Change explain Changing Wage Inequality?', mimeo, Queen Mary and Westfield College, London.
Henley, A. (1998) 'Residential Mobility, Housing Equity and the Labour Market', *The Economic Journal*, vol. 108, pp. 414–27.

Hine, R. and Wright, P. (1998) 'Trade with Low-Wage Economies, Employment and Productivity in the UK', *The Economic Journal*, vol. 108, pp. 633–47.

Hughes, G. and McCormick, B. (1981) 'Do Council House Policies Reduce Migration Between Regions?', *The Economic Journal*, vol. 91, pp. 919–37.

Jackman, R. and Savouri, S. (1992) 'Regional Migration in Britain: An Analysis of Gross Flows using NHS Central Register Data', *The Economic Journal*, vol. 102, pp. 1433–50.

Jovanovic, B. (1979) 'Job Matching and the Theory of Turnover', *Journal of Political Economy*, vol. 87, pp. 972–90.

— and Moffitt, R. (1990) 'An Estimate of a Sectoral Model of Labor Mobility', *Journal of Political Economy*, vol. 98, pp. 827–52.

Krugman, P. (1994) 'Past and Prospective Causes of High Unemployment', in *Reducing Unemployment: Current Issues and Policy Options*, Federal Reserve Bank of Kansas City, pp. 68–81.

Lilien, D.M. (1982) 'Sectoral Shifts and Cyclical Unemployment', *Journal of Political Economy*, vol. 90, pp. 777–93.

Machin, S. and Van Reenen, J. (1998) 'Technology and Changes in Skill Structure: Evidence from Seven OECD Countries', *Quarterly Journal of Economics*, vol. 113, pp. 1215–44.

McCormick, B. (1997) 'Regional Unemployment and Labour Mobility in the UK', *European Economic Review*, vol. 41, pp. 581–9.

Mincer, J. and Jovanovic, B. (1981) 'Labour Mobility and Wages', in S. Rosen (ed.), *Studies in Labor Markets*, Chicago, Ill.: University of Chicago Press.

Murphy, K. and Topel, R. (1987) 'The Evolution of Unemployment in the United States 1968–1985', in S. Fischer (ed.), *NBER Macroeconomics Annual*, Cambridge Mass.: MIT Press.

National Bureau for Economic Research (1998) 'Uniform March CPS Extracts', available at http://www.nber.org/data_index.html.

Nickell, S. and Bell, B. (1996) 'Changes in the Distribution of Wages and Unemployment in OECD Countries', *American Economic Review*, Papers and Proceedings, vol. 86, pp. 303–8.

Office for National Statistics (1998) *Labour Force Survey*, homepage at http://www.ons.gov.uk/ons_f.htm.

Oswald, A. (1996) 'A Conjecture on the Explanation for High Unemployment in the Industrialized Nations: Part I', mimeo, Department of Economics, University of Warwick, England.

Pissarides, C. and Wadsworth, J. (1989) 'Unemployment and the Inter- Regional Mobility of Labour', *The Economic Journal*, vol. 99, pp. 739–55.

Thomas, J. (1996) 'An Empirical Model of Sectoral Movements by Unemployed Workers', *Journal of Labor Economics*, vol. 14, pp. 126–53.

Wood, A. (1994) *North–South Trade, Employment and Inequality*, Oxford: Clarendon Press.

6
Market Power and Foreign Trade: Implications for Competition Policy

Harry Bloch*

F11 L40

F41 L13

Introduction

Competition policy deals with the control of market power, and two approaches have been dominant. First, there have been policies designed to limit market structures that could lead to the exercise of market power, such as the restrictions on monopolization in the US Sherman Anti-Trust Act. Second, there have been policies designed to limit the abuse of market power, such as government controls on the prices set by public utilities and restrictions on certain anti-competitive business practices (for example, the prohibition of price discrimination).

Foreign trade can be viewed as an alternative to competition policy in terms of both reducing market concentration and restraining the abuse of market power. The number of firms selling into any market can expand when there are both foreign and domestic competitors. Perhaps more important is the alternative potential supply that occurs when there are foreign producers who redirect their output among countries in response to market opportunities. This alternative supply may be expected to respond to prices that are set above costs by domestic producers, thereby limiting the abuse of market power.[1]

The issue addressed in this chapter is whether foreign trade provides a sufficiently effective constraint on the abuse of market power to undermine the case for competition policy. Critics of competition policy argue that the rise in international trade strengthens the efficacy of

* Helpful comments on the version of this paper presented at the conference on Creating an Internationally Competitive Economy were received from my discussant, Gavin Wood, and from other participants, particularly Tim Hazledine and Michael Olive. Responsibility for errors or omissions remains with the author.

markets through introducing additional competition, removing the need for government intervention.[2] Further, they argue that there are potentially adverse consequences for a country's trading position from government intervention that restricts business practices.

We review some essential elements of models of imperfect competition with international trade in the next section, and then examine the implications of these models for the conditions under which trade restrains the abuse of domestic market power. A central role is identified for the degree of integration of national markets into a single global market as well as for the extent of market power that foreign producers hold in the domestic market. Key findings from empirical literature relating to the impact of foreign trade on domestic producers are the reviewed, and the final section summarizes the analysis and evidence, concluding that the balance of argument supports the continued need for effective domestic competition policy in an era of increasing trade.

Models of international competition

Economic analysis of international trade is increasingly focused on the role of imperfect competition. Dornbusch (1987) shows that with imperfect competition, the impact of foreign competition on domestic prices, and hence on domestic economic performance, varies with demand conditions, market structure and the relative sizes of domestic and foreign markets. Subsequent theoretical developments have not been successful in restricting the range of possible outcomes. However, these models still play a key role in guiding empirical studies and, especially, in interpreting the implications of empirical findings.

Three important categories of models can be distinguished. Firstly, there are models designed for small open economies, in which prices charged by overseas competitors are treated as independent of the behaviour of domestic producers. Second are models of international oligopoly, in which domestic and foreign firms interact in both the domestic market and foreign markets. Finally, there are models of foreign monopoly, in which the domestic producer is a monopolist in a foreign market. These categories of models are taken up in turn below.

Small open economy models

One approach to analysing imperfect competition with international trade has been to examine the behaviour of a single domestic producer or group of producers acting as a monopoly when faced with a given price for competing imports. The price of foreign products is assumed to be unaffected by behaviour of domestic producers because they are small relative to the world economy. It is appropriate to refer to this model as the Canadian model because of its extensive application in empirical studies of the Canadian economy and also because of the prominence of Canadian economists in developing the model.

An early contribution to the development of the Canadian model is that of Eastman and Stykolt (1967). They focus on the implications of tariff protection for both pricing and productivity when there is a monopoly domestic producer or collusive group of domestic producers operating behind a tariff wall. The products of the domestic producers are homogenous and are perfect substitutes for foreign products. The analysis leads to a general prediction that domestic producers will sell solely in the domestic market by 'pricing up to the tariff'. This implies a price above marginal cost as well as an inefficiently small scale in domestic production.

A general equilibrium version of the Canadian model with, alternatively, 'pricing up to the tariff' and monopolistic pricing, is developed and applied by Harris (1984) and Harris and Cox (1984). They close the model using the assumptions from monopolistic competition of symmetric product differentiation, identical cost structures and free entry and exit, so that firms earn zero profits in long-run equilibrium. Simulations of the model show potentially very large gains, in terms of reduced domestic prices and costs, are derived from trade liberalization. Much of the predicted gains come from an increased scale of operation for domestic producers that remain in operation after liberalization. Hence, this analysis strongly supports the argument that foreign competition can achieve the type of economic performance that would otherwise be the objective of domestic competition policy.

While the key focus of the Canadian model is on import competition, there is a symmetric treatment of prices in export markets. Prices charged by other sellers in the destination market are assumed to be unaffected by the exporter's price. In the Eastman and Stykolt (1967) analysis it is assumed that domestic products and foreign products are perfect substitutes, leading to a sharp distinction between the behaviour of exporters and that of firms operating solely in the domestic market. Exporters operate with price equal to marginal cost and are large enough to produce at outputs beyond the minimum efficient scale. Thus, access to foreign markets can induce competitive and efficient behaviour from domestic firms, providing further support for the argument that trade serves as a substitute for domestic competition policy.

The Harris version of the Canadian model does not provide the sharp difference in behaviour between exporters and other firms. Here, differentiated products are assumed, so domestic producers generally have both exports and domestic sales. Still, simulations of the model show that the multilateral free trade case, with improved access to foreign markets combined with improved foreign access to domestic markets, generates more competitive and efficient outcomes than does the unilateral free trade case, with only improved foreign access to domestic markets.

Oligopoly models

Interaction between domestic producers and their foreign competitors in either domestic or foreign markets is the specific focus of models of international oligopoly. In many world markets, the number of dominant producers is small enough to suggest interdependence in behaviour in all markets where the dominant producers interact. An obvious example is the market for commercial jet passenger aircraft, where Boeing and Airbus interact in the home market of each as well as in markets where both are exporters. There are many other industries for which concentration of production is at a high level even when measured on a worldwide basis. The model is generally presented in its simplest form, with all firms as producing in a single plant in the home country. However, extensions to multi-plant and multinational operations are possible.

A simple symmetric model of homogenous product duopoly is used to demonstrate many of the results from the analysis of international oligopoly. In particular, the pro-competitive effect of trade is demonstrated by comparing price and output for a particular model of international oligopoly to that from each producer operating as a separate domestic monopolist. The results generally show price is lower and output higher with trade than without (see Krugman, 1989, appendix A.2, for a demonstration in the case of a Cournot oligopoly model).

Contrasting the results from the simple duopoly model to those from the Eastman and Stykolt version of the Canadian model suggests that the impact of trade is generally less pro-competitive with duopoly. Models of symmetric homogenous product duopoly generate prices exceeding marginal costs for the domestic producer in both home and foreign markets. This is true even in the limit when trade is costless and there are no government-imposed barriers to trade. Thus, the efficacy of trade in preventing the exploitation of domestic market power is lessened when domestic producers interact with foreign producers rather than take foreign prices as exogenously determined.[3]

The simplest version of an international oligopoly model with product differentiation involves Bertrand–Nash equilibrium between domestic and foreign producers. Producers in each country take prices of all domestic and foreign competitors as unaffected by their own behaviour, but exogenous changes affecting only a single firm, such as a cost change, lead to price changes in the same direction by all firms in the market when firms have upward-sloping reaction curves.[4]

The effect of trade in the simple model of Bertrand–Nash equilibrium is to increase the number of sellers in each market. For the usual demand function assumptions, this leads to each seller facing a more elastic demand for its product. The profit-maximizing mark-up of price on marginal cost falls, so trade has a pro-competitive effect as in the Canadian model with product differentiation. Indeed, aside from the effects consequent on equilibrium price adjustments by rivals, the impact of trade in the Bertrand–Nash equilibrium model is identical to that of the Canadian model with product differentiation.[5] As the price-adjustment effects encourage higher price–cost margins, the effect of accounting for international oligopoly is to somewhat lessen the pro-competitive impact of trade. Other models of oligopoly would tend to generate results closer to a collusive outcome, further reducing the pro-competitive effects of trade.

Foreign monopoly models

When there is no competing production in the destination market, exporters are able to exploit a monopoly position in that market. This type of market structure has been analysed extensively, particularly in terms of the impact of trade policy by the government of the destination economy on rent-shifting between countries (see Helpman and Krugman, 1989, chapter 4). If an exporter is required to charge the same price for exports as for domestic production, a price is chosen to maximize profits over total world sales. The availability of a foreign market can lead to a price that is lower, higher or the same as the price in the home market without trade. Thus, the ability to exploit a monopoly position in foreign markets may have a pro-competitive, anti-competitive or nil impact on the behaviour of domestic producers in their home market.

The foreign monopolist earns higher profits if it is not constrained to charge the same price at home and abroad, but can rather price discriminate between the home market and foreign markets. Here, there is a separate demand facing the seller in each market. The mark-up of price on marginal cost that maximizes profit is inversely related to the price elasticity of demand in that market. This leads to the phenomenon of 'pricing to market'. The only opportunity for trade to impact on the profit maximizing price for the home market then is limited to impacts on production costs, such as through economies of scale.

The possibility of 'pricing to market' can also be included in the analysis oligopoly (see Krugman, 1987) and the Canadian model of small open economies.[6] Here, also, the link is broken between trade and the mark-up of price over cost in an exporter's home market. Thus, the ability to price-discriminate between markets can remove any impact of competition in foreign markets on price determination in a producer's home market.[7]

Foreign market power, integration of national markets and the abuse of domestic market power

The primary distinction made among the models of the previous section is in terms of the degree of foreign market power held by domestic producers. In the Eastman and Stykolt version of the Canadian model, there is no foreign market power for domestic producers as they face horizontal demand curves for their products in foreign markets. In the Harris version of the Canadian model, there is a limited degree of foreign market power for domestic producers. Domestic producers face downward-sloping demand for differentiated products in foreign markets, but they have no strategic interaction in these markets with foreign producers. Models of international oligopoly emphasize strategic interaction with either homogenous or differentiated products, leading domestic producers to generally set prices above marginal costs for their products in foreign markets. Finally, the market power of domestic producers in foreign markets is unconstrained by competitors in the models of foreign monopoly.

Generally, those models in which domestic producers have little foreign market power are also models in which foreign competition restrains the abuse of market power by domestic producers in the home market. At one extreme we have the Canadian model, with little or no foreign market power for domestic producers and a powerful restraining influence of trade on domestic producers in their home market. At the other extreme we have the foreign monopoly model, with domestic producers having monopoly positions in foreign markets and potentially raising the domestic mark-up of price on marginal cost to better exploit their overseas monopoly position. Models of international oligopoly do not generate unambiguous equilibrium outcomes for either foreign market power or abuse of domestic market power. However, a common approach is to treat the outcomes for both foreign market power and abuse of domestic market power as intermediate between the more competitive and more monopolistic models.

In addition to the degree of foreign market power, the impact of foreign competition in the models of the previous section depends on the degree to which buyers at home or abroad switch between domestic and foreign products. A high elasticity of substitution combines with the absence of natural and artificial trade impediments to enhance competition both at home and abroad. Full integration of national markets into a global market occurs when 'geography or nationality do not have systematic effects on transaction prices for otherwise identical products' (Goldberg and Knetter, 1997, p. 1245). In a world of fluctuating exchange rates and differing national rates of inflation, such integration is likely to be approximated only when there is a minimal degree of differentiation among competing products, low transport costs and low barriers to trade. Otherwise, varying degrees of segmentation of national markets are likely to occur, such that product prices differ across countries.

When national markets are fully integrated, foreign competition can have a powerful restraining influence on the abuse of domestic market power. This is well-illustrated in the Eastman and Stykolt version of the Canadian model. Here, full integration of national markets leads to perfectly competitive behaviour by domestic producers, even though these producers are assumed to have a joint monopoly position in the domestic market. Full integration implies that the landed price of imports and the export price are identical. With the assumption that domestic producers are price-takers with respect to foreign prices, the domestic producers face a horizontal demand at the foreign price measured in domestic currency. They then maximize profit by operating with marginal cost equal to price. Further, if there is free entry and exit in the domestic market, each producer will operate at minimum average cost output in the long run.

Segmentation of national markets occurs in the Eastman and Stykolt version of the Canadian model when there are transport costs, tariffs or other impediments to trade. This leads to the abuse of market power in the domestic market with 'pricing up to the tariff' and also to the inefficiently small production units that is the focus of concern in Eastman and Stykolt (1967). Comparison of these outcomes to those with an integrated global market provides a clear illustration of an inverse association between the abuse of domestic market power and the degree of integration of national markets. An inverse association is also demonstrated in the Harris version of the Canadian model in terms of the simulation results for the applied general equilibrium model in Harris (1984) and Harris and Cox (1984).

In models of international oligopoly with an integrated global market, the prices set by domestic producers and foreign producers are identical. Further, each price is greater than marginal cost for most models of oligopoly behaviour. Also, achievement of production at minimum average cost is not assured. Thus, full integration is not sufficient to lead to fully competitive behaviour by domestic producers when those producers operate in international oligopolies.

The ambiguous results for the mark-up of price over cost in models of international oligopoly eliminates the possibility of universal predictions regarding the impact of an integrated global market. However, as suggested in the previous section, there will generally be some pro-competitive effect on domestic producer behaviour associated with the trade flows, and it is noted that this pro-competitive effect is undermined when there is price discrimination between domestic and foreign markets. Such price discrimination is associated with segmented national markets. Thus, it is reasonable to expect a reduction in the pro-competitive effect of trade on domestic producer behaviour whenever the global market is segmented rather than integrated.

In summary, consideration of the various models suggests a tendency for the pro-competitive impact of trade to decline with both the degree of foreign market power and the degree of segmentation of the global market. This is problematic for the proposition that trade can be expected to restrain the abuse of market power by domestic producers. It is those domestic producers who exercise considerable power in the domestic market that are most likely to have foreign market power or to operate in segmented markets. For example, commercial jet aircraft producers have market power both at home and abroad, while regional industries, such as cement, bricks, milk and bread, often have highly concentrated local production and operate in markets that are segmented both nationally and internationally.

Evidence

Three types of relevant evidence can be distinguished in empirical studies of international competition. First, there are studies that examine the association between some proxy measure of foreign competition, most often import share, and some proxy measure of domestic economic performance, most often the gross profit margin. These studies sometimes make reference to a particular model of market competition, but do not estimate the model directly. Second, there are studies that examine the degree of integration or the degree of foreign market power by domestic producers, thereby providing evidence on the conditions required for foreign competition to limit the abuse of domestic market power. Finally and most recently, there are studies that fit models of international oligopoly, thereby providing the specific information on parameter values that allows the direct assessment of the efficacy of foreign competition in limiting the abuse of domestic market power.

Trade and profitability

There have been a large number of studies that estimate the determinants of industries' gross profit margins, including foreign trade shares among the determinants. These studies have been carried out for a wide variety of countries, over many different time periods and using many different econometric specifications. The most consistent finding concerning trade is a negative coefficient on import share. Further, it is noted that the negative impact of import share interacts with domestic market concentration. In particular, Caves (1985, p. 378) notes that:

> Empirical studies reach consensus that the larger is imports' share of the domestic sales, the smaller is the effect of concentration of domestic producers on the profits earned by those producers.

These results are interpreted as providing evidence that imports impose discipline on the exploitation of domestic market power.

Our review above of the various models raises doubts about the above interpretation. There certainly are models in which import share is negatively related to the mark-up of price over marginal cost (see, for example, the international oligopoly model of Lyons, 1981), but there are no imports in the Eastman and Stykolt version of the Canadian model even though foreign competition has a substantial constraining influence on the abuse of domestic power. More generally, the level of imports is affected by a wide variety of influences, including consumer preferences where products are differentiated, so that the level of imports is at best a very imperfect indicator of the degree of exposure to foreign competition. Finally, we should note that there is a general problem with cross-section regression studies of determinants of profit margins, namely that they estimate reduced-form relationships without allowing for the simultaneous causation associated with market equilibrium (see Clarke and Davies, 1982).[8]

Levinsohn (1993) provides a somewhat more direct test of the import-as-market-discipline hypothesis, without using import share as an explanatory variable or the gross profit margin as the dependent variable. He examines changes in the mark-up of price over marginal cost for Turkish manufacturing firms before and after a substantial import liberalization, finding that price–cost margins are reduced in those industries characterized by price above marginal cost prior to a reduction in their level of protection. By relating the mark-up of price over marginal cost to a direct measure of the degree of exposure to foreign competition, Levinsohn is able to avoid the potential ambiguity associated with using import share as a proxy for this exposure. Also, there is perhaps more confidence that the changes in protection experienced by the Turkish manufacturing industries are not influenced by the height of price–cost margins of domestic producers, in contrast to the high likelihood that import shares are influenced by domestic margins.

Hazledine (1980) also studies the relationship between price–cost margins and protection. He uses data for a cross-section of import-competing Canadian manufacturing industries to examine the determinants of the ratio of domestic price to the price for the corresponding US industry (used as a proxy for the world price). This price ratio is found to increase with the height of the Canadian tariff on imports, especially when the tariff rate interacts with a measure of the concentration of sales among the Canadian producers. These results provide support for the Eastman and Stykolt version of the Canadian model, in which unrestricted exposure to foreign competition provides an effective restraint on abuse of domestic market power.[9]

Integration and foreign market power

There are now a very large number of studies that examine evidence of integration and foreign market power in global markets. The analysis of the previous section suggests that these two features of international markets are important to determining the efficacy of foreign trade in restraining the abuse of market power by domestic producers. As noted there, foreign trade is most effective in inducing competitive behaviour from domestic producers who have little or no market power in foreign markets. Also, the restraining influence of foreign trade may be greater when domestic and foreign markets are integrated into a global market rather than segmented as national markets.

The degree to which international markets are integrated into a global market is examined in studies of the validity of the 'law of one price' and its aggregate counterpart, purchasing power parity. In a competitive world, arbitrage across national markets would ensure that prices were equalized, providing there were no transport costs or other impediments to trade. In a recent review article, Rogoff (1996, p. 654) notes that:

> Overall, it is hard to read the empirical evidence without concluding that outside a fairly small range of homogenous goods, short-run interna-

tional arbitrage has only a limited effect on equating international goods market prices.

This leads to the conclusion that (Rogoff, 1996, p. 665):

> International goods markets, though becoming more integrated all the time, remain quite segmented, with large trading frictions across a broad range of goods.

A similar view is expressed in Goldberg and Knetter (1997, p. 1270), who close a survey of the literature on goods prices and exchange rates by noting that:

> the conclusion from this research that ought to affect the way we think is this: National markets for goods are better viewed as segmented than integrated.

The consensus seems clear, namely, that integrated global markets are a rarity rather than the expected norm.

One of the factors cited by Goldberg and Knetter in explaining the pervasive lack of integration is the practice of international price discrimination. Price discrimination requires market power, so price discrimination as revealed in the practice of 'pricing to market' provides evidence of the existence of foreign market power, and Goldberg and Knetter cite a number of studies that find evidence of 'pricing to market'. Knetter's (1989) own pioneering study provides evidence of variations in price relative to marginal cost across destination markets for a variety of US exports and German exports.

Estimation of oligopoly models

There is a tradition of using models of international competition, particularly oligopoly models, as the foundation for empirical studies of the impact of foreign trade. However, it has only been relatively recently that empirical studies have been applied to estimating the parameters of the underlying models. These estimates are used to test the applicability of the particular oligopoly model. Here, we are more interested in using the estimates to determine the impact of increased exposure to foreign trade on the mark-up of price over marginal cost for producers operating in their domestic market.

Stållhammar (1991) estimates a model of oligopoly with firms having separate conjectures for quantity responses from domestic and foreign rivals. He uses cross-section firm data for 67 Swedish manufacturing industries to determine an estimate of the degree of implicit collusion (the conjectural elasticity) for each industry. He finds that 32 estimated values are statistically significant and lie between zero and one, the range of values consistent with conjectures ranging from Cournot to full implicit collusion. His regression equation also includes an import share variable which has a positive and statistically significant coefficient. This implies that domestic firms expect more collusion from foreign firms than from their domestic rivals, so that the greater is the exposure to foreign competition, as measured by the import share, the greater is the average degree of implicit collusion in the market. There is some offset in the form of a negative estimated coefficient of import share in explaining the degree of implicit collusion among domestic firms. However, the general thrust of the results does not support the view that foreign trade disciplines the abuse of market power by domestic producers in their home sales.

Allen (1998) uses times-series data, aggregated at the industry level, to estimate a model of oligopoly with price conjectures for each of a sample of US manufacturing industries. His model allows for different conjectures by domestic firms and foreign firms, but assumes that firms within each group have the same conjecture for each rival firm whether foreign or domestic. His estimates of the price conjectural elasticity cover almost the full range from minus infinity to plus one, although with the conjectures for foreign firms always being more negative than for domestic firms in the same industry. This suggests that a rise in import share negatively influences the average degree of collusion in the domestic market. However, in only two industries do foreign firms appear to behave as a competitive fringe and in one industry there is clear evidence of jointly collusive behaviour between domestic and foreign firms.

Verboven (1996) estimates a Bertrand oligopoly model for the motor vehicle markets in five European countries, Belgium, France, Germany, Italy and the UK. Domestic and foreign suppliers are included in his model for each country. His results support the use of the Bertrand model for Belgium, France and Italy, but an alternative model of collusive behaviour cannot be rejected for Germany and the UK. More important from the viewpoint of this chapter are the results concerning foreign competition. First, the results suggest that foreign producers charge prices above marginal cost, so they are exploiting market power on their own. Second, the cross-elasticities of demand between foreign and domestic models are lower than among the group of domestic models. Finally, foreign and domestic cars tend to dominate in different size, prestige and use categories, with low cross-elasticities of demand across categories. Thus, there is little support for the notion that foreign trade acts as an important restraint on the exercise of market power by domestic producers.[10]

Conclusions and policy implications

A reasoned assessment of the theory and evidence reviewed above raises serious doubts about the proposition that foreign trade provides an effective restraint on the abuse of market power by domestic producers. If forced to provide a simple yes or no response to the validity of this proposition, my clear choice would be no. If allowed some leeway for exceptional cases in terms of particular countries and industries, my response would be not generally.

The evidence on the lack of integration of national markets into a global market features prominently in my reasoning for doubting the efficacy of foreign trade in restraining the abuse of market power. It is difficult to see how foreign trade can be successful in this task unless foreign products are good substitutes for domestic products and their producers or inter-mediaries are willing and able to engage in international arbitrage in response to price differentials. The evidence against such arbitrage is very powerful.

A further important worry is the ample evidence on the existence of foreign market power. It seems reasonably clear that domestic producers generally do not behave as perfect competitors in exporting to foreign markets. Setting price above cost in the foreign market allows the domestic producer to do likewise in the domestic market.

Evidence that favours a restraining influence on the abuse of domestic market power due to foreign trade is very limited and, perhaps not surprisingly, much of the supporting evidence comes from studies of Canada.[11] Even prior to entering a free-trade agreement with the USA, the Canadian and US economies were reasonably well-integrated. High tariffs were isolated to particular industries, and transport costs between US and Canadian markets have often been lower than between adjacent Canadian markets. Further, the US economy is generally considered to have the most structurally competitive markets in the world. Finally, US firms are constrained from exploiting market power in Canada by the opportunity for consumers to engage in personal arbitrage through cross-border shopping.

Verboven's (1996) study of the European car market reveals a more common situation in which foreign trade has little restraining influence on the abuse of domestic market power. Here, foreign suppliers are found to exercise at least some, and often considerable, market power in each country in which they operate and domestic buyers generally do not treat domestic and foreign models as good substitutes. Even with the ongoing removal of national barriers against the movement of goods, workers and investment in Europe, the various national markets remain segmented and lacking in competitive discipline. Thus, the rationale for a vigorous competition policy remains strong, even with free trade.

Before closing it is worth noting that my consideration of the implications of foreign trade for competition policy is based on a narrow interpretation of the purpose of competition policy. I have examined competition policy only as a means of restraining the abuse of market power, particularly keeping prices from exceeding marginal cost. Competition policy can have many other objectives. In particular, Lloyd (1998, p. 182) argues that 'the development of pro-competitive competition policies leads to more international trade and international production'.[12] Also, Anderson and Khosla (1995, p. 11), in reviewing Canadian competition policy, note the view that 'competition policy has an important bearing on productivity growth and competitiveness'. Assessment as to whether foreign trade can substitute for domestic competition policy in the achievement of these other objectives is clearly a worthy topic for further research.

Notes

1 This alternative supply may in general take the form of either imports or international production through the establishment of subsidiaries in the domestic market by foreign producers. Much of the discussion that follows can be applied equally well to either the impact of international trade or of international production. However, the literature reviewed generally deals explicitly only with the impact of international trade and in some cases does not easily extend to cover international production.

2 For example, the Australian Competition and Consumer Commission has generally not opposed mergers of domestic producers in markets where the share of imports exceeds 10 per cent, including a recent merger of whitegoods manufacturers that produced a domestic duopoly for some appliances.

3 A related point is made by Hazledine (1991, p. 46), noting that, 'the pro-competitive impact of a tariff cut is inversely related to the complexity of the model, in the sense of the range of factors taken to be endogenous'.

4 The impact of a firm's own price change on the profit-maximizing prices of its rivals depends on the convexity of the demand function (see Bloch, 1992). With constant elasticity demand, a price change by a firm leaves the profit maximizing mark-up for the rivals unaffected and the resulting price change depends only on whether marginal cost is increasing or decreasing with output. However, when demand is less convex than constant elasticity, the

profit maximizing mark-up for rivals moves in the same direction as the original price change.

5　The Bertrand model of assumption that rivals maintain constant prices is similar to the Canadian model assumption that foreign prices are exogenously determined. Thus, it is not surprising that the pro-competitive effect of trade in a Bertrand model is related to that of the Canadian model.

6　A primary empirical application of the 'pricing-to-market' analysis has been by American economists explaining why prices of exports to the USA failed to reflect the substantial depreciation of the US dollar during the 1980s. Here, an assumption that prices of other sellers in the destination market are unaffected by exporter behaviour is justified by the large size of the US market relative to the sales of most exporters. Thus, it is tempting to refer to this type of 'pricing-to-market' analysis as the 'American' model, just as we use 'Canadian' model to refer to the analysis of small open economies.

7　Ironically, it has been foreign governments that have done the most to ensure a link between domestic and foreign prices through anti-dumping legislation. If domestic firms are prevented by foreign governments from charging a lower price abroad than at home, they are faced with having to lower their domestic price to achieve their desired price in the foreign market. Of course, it is foreign producers who are responsible for initiating anti-dumping prosecutions to protect their own domestic market power (see the contribution by Feaver and Wilson, in this volume).

8　Lopez and Lopez (1996) explain the variety of findings on the relationship by pointing to the ambiguity of the predicted relationship between import share and the mark-up of price over marginal cost in a conjectural variation model of international oligopoly, once imports are treated as endogenously determined. Another possibility, noted by Bloch and Kenyon in Chapter 2 of this volume, is that a domestic industry with relatively high productivity by international standards can achieve high profits together with a relatively attractive (internationally competitive) product in terms of price and quality.

9　It should be noted that Karikari (1988) examines the same issue using data for both the early 1970s (overlapping the 1972 annual data used by Hazledine) and the late 1970s, whilst allowing for import prices to be endogenous as in the 'pricing-to-market' models. He finds evidence that supports the use of the Eastman and Stykolt version of the Canadian model in the earlier period, but not in the latter period.

10　Goldberg (1995) finds a similar pattern of results in a study of the US automobile market. Specifically, she estimates that both foreign and domestic sellers charge prices above their respective marginal costs when maximizing profit. Further, the cross-elasticity of demand between foreign and domestic models within each vehicle category is estimated to be quite low.

11　Bloch and Olive (1998) estimate price equations for samples of manufacturing industries in seven major industrialized countries; Canada, Germany, Japan, Korea, Sweden, the United Kingdom and the United States. Only the results for Canada are fully consistent with the predictions of the Canadian model of the impact of foreign competition, with foreign prices having a restraining influence on domestic prices that increases with the level of concentration in domestic production. Evidence of a restraining influence is also found in

Germany, Sweden and the USA, but the influence in each of these countries is less powerful than in Canada.

12 Lloyd (1998) considers the impact of enhanced international production through multinational companies as well as the impact of enhanced international trade, concluding that, 'openness with respect to borders is not sufficient for market contestability' (Lloyd, 1998, p. 181). He then goes on to suggest that, 'strengthened competition law or its stricter enforcement on the one hand and international supply through both international trade in goods and services and international production reinforce each other' (Lloyd, 1998, p. 182).

References

Allen, C. (1998) 'An Empirical Model of Pricing, Market Share and Market Conduct: An Application to Import Competition in US Manufacturing', *Manchester School*, vol. 66, pp. 196–221.

Anderson, R.D. and Khosla, S.D. (1995) *Competition Policy as a Dimension of Economic Policy: A Comparative Perspective*, Occasional Paper no. 7, Ottawa: Industry Canada.

Bloch, H. (1992) 'Pricing in Australian Manufacturing', *Economic Record*, vol. 68, pp. 365–76.

— and Olive, M. (1998) 'Pass-through Elasticities for Production Costs and Competing Foreign Products: Evidence from Manufacturing Prices in Seven Countries', in E. Bairam (ed.), *Production and Cost Functions: Specification, Measurement and Applications*, Aldershot, UK: Ashgate, pp. 106–24.

Caves, R.E. (1985) 'International Trade and Industrial Organization: Problems, Solved and Unsolved', *European Economic Review*, vol. 28, pp. 377–95.

Clarke, R. and Davies, S.W. (1982) 'Market Structure and Price–Cost Margins', *Economica*, vol. 49, pp. 277–87.

Dornbusch, R. (1987) 'Exchange Rates and Prices', *American Economic Review*, vol. 77, pp. 93–105.

Eastman, H.C. and Stykolt, S. (1967) *The Tariff and Competition in Canada*, Toronto: University of Toronto Press.

Goldberg, P.K. (1995) 'Product Differentiation and Oligopoly in International Markets: The Case of the U.S. Automobile Industry', *Econometrica*, vol. 63, pp. 891–951.

— and Knetter, M.M. (1997) 'Goods Prices and Exchange Rates: What have we Learned?', *Journal of Economic Literature*, vol. 35, pp. 1243–72.

Harris, R. (1984) 'Applied General Equilibrium Analysis of Small Open Economies with Scale Economies and Imperfect Competition', *American Economic Review*, vol. 74, pp. 1016–32.

— and Cox, D. (1984) *Trade, Industrial Policy and Canadian Manufacturing*, Toronto: University of Toronto Press.

Hazledine, T. (1980) 'Testing Two Models of Pricing and Protection with Canada/United States Data', *Journal of Industrial Economics*, vol. 29, pp. 145–54.

— (1991) 'Trade Policy as Competition Policy', in R.S. Khemani and W.T. Stanbury (eds), *Canadian Competition Law and Policy at the Centenary*, Halifax: Institute for Research on Public Policy, pp. 45–60.

Helpman, E. and Krugman, P.R. (1989) *Trade Policy and Market Structure*, Cambridge, Mass, MIT Press.

Karikari, J.A. (1988) 'International Competitiveness and Industry Pricing in Canadian Manufacturing Industry', *Canadian Journal of Economics*, vol. 21, pp. 410–26.

Knetter, M.M. (1989) 'Price Discrimination by U.S. and German Exporters', *American Economic Review*, vol. 79, pp. 198–210.

Krugman, P.R. (1987) 'Pricing to Market when the Exchange Rate Changes', in S.W. Arndt and J.D. Richardson (eds), *Real-Financial Linkages among Open Economies*, Cambridge, Mass. MIT Press, pp. 49–70.

— (1989) 'Industrial Organization and International Trade', in R. Schmalensee and R. Willig, (eds), *Handbook of Industrial Organization*, Vol. 2, Amsterdam: North-Holland, pp. 1179–233.

Levinsohn, J. (1993) 'Testing the Imports-as-Market-Discipline Hypothesis', *Journal of International Economics*, vol. 35, pp. 1–22.

Lloyd, P.J. (1998) 'Globalisation and Competition Policies', *Welwirtschaftliches Archiv*, vol. 134, pp. 161–85.

Lopez, E. and Lopez, R.A. (1996) 'Market Structure and the Impact of Imports on Price Cost Margins', *Review of Industrial Organization*, vol. 11, pp. 107–13.

Lyons, B. (1981) 'Price-Cost Margins, Market Structure and International Trade', in D. Currie, D. Peel and W. Peters (eds), *Microeconomic Analysis*, London: Croom Helm, pp. 276–95.

Rogoff, K. (1996) 'The Purchasing Power Parity Puzzle', *Journal of Economic Literature*, vol. 34, pp. 647–68.

Stållhammar, N.-O. (1991) 'Domestic Market Power and Foreign Trade', *International Journal of Industrial Organization*, vol. 9, pp. 407–24.

Verboven, F. (1996) 'International Price Discrimination in the European Car Market', *Rand Journal of Economics*, vol. 27, pp. 240–68.

7

Investment, Imports and Productivity Growth in the US Cement Industry

*David Prentice**

L6| L11

F14

Introduction

In many industries, the competitiveness of a firm is still ultimately determined by its productivity. And the firm's survival depends on its achieving a rate of productivity growth at least as great as that of its competitors. Improvements in productivity at the firm level, including those resulting from innovation, typically require investment. There is a popular belief that more-competitive industries achieve more rapid productivity growth through competition-driven innovation and the elimination of inefficient firms. The opening up of an economy is, then, commonly thought to result in increased productivity. Existing firms either become internationally competitive or they exit the industry. However, writers, following Schumpeter (1950), have argued that investment in innovation flourishes only with the prospect of economic profits. Theory, then, does not provide a conclusive effect of the extent of competition, including import competition, on productivity growth.

In this chapter the effects of domestic and import competition on investment and competitiveness are investigated through a case study of the US Portland cement industry. Over the postwar period, the cement industry has achieved substantial factor productivity growth, experienced considerable investment and disinvestment, and falling effective protection. First, it is argued that for certain industries, such as Portland cement, physical investment and innovation are directly linked. Competitiveness and productivity growth can then be driven by the forces that drive

*   I would to thank Harry Bloch, Micheal Olive, Lou Will, Xiangkang Yin and participants at the Creating an Internationally Competitive Economy conference for many useful comments. All errors remain my own responsibility.

innovation, or strategic considerations as highlighted in the industrial organization literature. Then the experience of the industry is outlined and the roles of import competition and both strategic and innovation-driven investment are examined statistically.

Both import competition and domestic competition are found, in general, not to have significant effects on investment and disinvestment. There exists some evidence of strategic disinvestment by multiplant firms, but it appears that the combination of long-run demand and plant-cost characteristics seem to drive investment, entry and exit decisions.

Though these results are for just one industry, the suitability of this industry for such a case study makes them of broader interest. The Portland cement industry provides a particularly clean case for analysis for several reasons. First, Portland cement is homogeneous, its technology relatively simple and there have been relatively few substantial innovations in the last few decades. Hence, there is a clear and direct set of links between investment, changes in productivity and competitiveness. Second, relatively high transport costs have resulted in the industry featuring a set of regional oligopolies, which vary from effective monopolies to being substantially competitive. With a common macro-economic and regulatory environment the differences in regional experiences are particularly revealing of the effects of differences in competition. Finally, over the period of interest, the industry has gone from being effectively protected from international competition by substantial transport costs to experiencing a substantial national import share, peaking at nearly 20 per cent. Hence, the US Portland cement industry provides an excellent opportunity to examine the links between competition, investment, productivity growth and competitiveness.

This chapter will proceed as follows. In the next section the theoretical literature on innovation, strategic investment and exit is reviewed to extract a set of relationships between domestic competition, import competition and investment for a stylized manufacturing industry. The Portland cement industry is then introduced along with the data, and a case study is performed using, in the main, chi-squared tests of homogeneity. Finally, the results from the case study are discussed.

Competition, investment and productivity growth

In this section, the links between innovation, investment and competition are examined for a stylized industry with features common to many of the large process-based intermediate materials industries. The stylized industry is characterized by the following assumptions:

1 Domestic and foreign firms produce a single product that is homogeneous.
2 Investment in capacity is lumpy putty clay, substantially sunk and finitely lived. There is increasing returns to scale in construction.
3 Innovation is, solely, embodied in the relevant factor.
4 Domestic and foreign firms could be a monopolist, Cournot competitors, or price-takers depending on the size of the domestic market, entry and transportation costs.
5 Demand can be growing, constant or declining.

Assumptions 1 to 3 restrict the discussion to industries, like Portland cement, where there is a direct link between investment, productivity and competitiveness. Investment increases plant and industry productivity; disinvestment typically increases industry productivity. Assumption 3 implies investment is similar to the costly adoption of a process innovation which is a private rather than a public good.

Assumptions 4 and 5 provide a framework in which three cases – monopoly, oligopoly and a price-taking industry – can be considered. If transportation and entry costs are high enough, the industry is best characterized as a set of regional markets. If demand is small enough relative to scale, the domestic firm will be a monopolist. With a somewhat larger market, substantial transport costs and lumpy putty clay capacity, domestic competition is best characterized as a Cournot oligopoly with potential entrants. And if transport costs and trade barriers are low enough, then all firms are price-takers.

Entry, investment, exit and import competition in each industry is determined, not only by long-run demand, as framed by assumption 5, and costs, but both incentives similar to those for innovation and strategic incentives. These are discussed in the following sub-sections.

Monopoly

If entry is not blockaded, then the incumbent monopolist, faced with potential entry, invests to preempt the entrant; that is, to deter or accommodate entry. Tirole (1988) argues that if the incumbent, through investment, can maintain the monopoly, the monopolist would do so as the return to a monopoly exceeds its return in a post-entry duopoly. Entry deterrence requires preemptive investment in a larger capacity (in a static model such as Dixit, 1980) or in an earlier period (in a dynamic model such as Gilbert and Harris, 1984). In addition, as Vives (1988) argues, the greater the number of potential entrants, the greater the return to entry-deterring investment. On the other hand, if the monopolist decides to accommodate, upon entry, industry investment will be greater as total capacity increases over monopoly capacity. Hence, whether there is entry deterrence or accommodation, industry investment is greater than when entry is blockaded.

Oligopoly

There are two broad groups of models of investment in an oligopoly. The first group is for the case, with constant marginal cost, where demand is constant or increasing. The set of strategies and effects relevant for the incumbent oligopolist is as just outlined for the monopolist facing potential entry, with one important qualification. There is a tendency for the oligopolists, as a group, to underinvest in entry deterrence. This occurs because investment in entry deterrence by any one firm has a positive pecuniary externality for the other incumbents which is not accounted for (Tirole, 1988). Hence the incentives for preemptive investment decline as the market becomes less concentrated. This is consistent with the relatively weak empirical evidence for effective preemptive investment (Gilbert and Lieberman, 1987, for chemicals; Johnson and Parkman, 1983, for cement).

However, the prospect of a monopoly provides greater incentives to innovate for current oligopolists or price-takers than for monopolists, as the marginal gain to innovation is greater (this is referred to as the replacement effect in Tirole, 1988). The incentive for such investment, hereafter referred to as competitive investment, increases as concentration falls and pre-innovation profits decline. Hence, the relationship between concentration and investment is not clear.

The second group of models is for the case where demand is declining or it is constant but with marginal cost increasing over time. The oligopolists must decide how and when to disinvest and exit. The theoretical literature has focused on the relationship between plant or firm size and the order of exit. If capacity cannot shrink, high fixed-cost (larger) plants exit first due to the greater profitability of smaller plants under declining demand (Ghemawat and Nalebuff, 1985), and, similarly, if capacity can shrink, large firms will disinvest first until they are the size of small firms (Ghemawat and Nalebuff, 1990). While there is empirical evidence that plants of multiplant firms are more likely to close (Gibson and Harris, 1996), an increase in the size of the plant is found to increase the probability of survival (Lieberman, 1990; Deily, 1991; Gibson and Harris, 1996).

Price taking

Under assumptions 1–3, units of different productivity can survive in a price-taking equilibrium, sunk costs deterring low-cost entrants from entering to eliminate older higher-cost units (Salter, 1966). When demand grows such that the return from investment exceeds current sunk investment costs, low-cost entry/investment occurs. When demand declines, plants exit on order of their costs. Hence (competitive rather than preemptive) investment and disinvestment results in higher industry factor productivity.

Import competition

If opening up an economy creates a price-taking market, then the discussion of the previous section holds. However, if after trade barriers fall and the market remains, at most, an oligopoly, importing oligopolists will provide less-forceful competition than additional domestic competitors for three reasons.

First, in the absence of other advantages, the importing oligopolist has effectively higher marginal costs because of per unit transportation costs. Second, the sunk costs upon entry are different. An importer does not have to incur sunk costs to produce as these have already been sunk for the foreign market. However, the importer still incurs other sunk costs such as setting up distribution facilities and learning about the domestic market (see for example, Ait-Sahalia, 1994). The third difference is that the importer is, in essence, a multimarket oligopolist. Bulow *et al.* (1985) note that a multimarket oligopolist in such a market is a less-aggressive competitor if their other markets are booming. In addition, it is argued that firms that compete in multiple markets can more easily tacitly collude (Rosenbaum and Yans, 1993 for cement).

The US Portland cement industry: overview and data

This section is composed of three parts. First, it is demonstrated that the Portland cement industry matches up closely with the stylized industry presented in the previous section. Then the data are presented. Finally, we present an overview of the experience of the industry.

The nature of the Portland cement industry

Cement is the powder that, when mixed with water, sand and aggregate, forms concrete. Most cement is Portland cement and, though there are a few types of it, over 90 per cent of Portland cement shipments are of types I and II, Both of which and most of the remaining types having similar prices. There is little difference between Portland cements produced across manufacturers, domestic or foreign.

Cement production requires a small number of transformations using primarily limestone, fuel, electricity and labour. Limestone is ground into a raw mix which is baked in a large kiln producing an intermediate product, clinker. Clinker is ground and mixed with gypsum to produce Portland cement. There are increasing returns to scale in construction of the kiln (Kohanowski, 1966). Once a kiln is installed, the quantities of each input required to produce at capacity are substantially fixed (Førsund and Hjalmarsson, 1983; Das, 1991). Fuel and electricity requirements across kilns vary systematically with their size, type (process) and vintage, and a typical plant operates a small number of kilns that may vary in their vintage and, less frequently, their process. Other equipment is scaled around the kiln(s).

Kilns differ, then, by process and vintage. In order of fuel requirements, the wet process features the highest, followed by the dry process and then the preheater/precalciner process. Older kilns tend to feature greater fuel consumption because of embodied small innovations and depreciation resulting in increased fuel requirements rather than less production (Das, 1992; Rosenbaum, 1994). By the early 1960s, a series of small advances and changes made it possible to construct much larger kilns featuring higher fuel and labour productivity (Kohanowski, 1966). In addition, some problems with raw materials in the use of preheater kilns, after their introduction in the 1950s, were overcome by the 1970s. Hence, investment takes the form of installing a new kiln(s) and investment is also the (primary form of) adoption of a process innovation. Even if production capacity is not altered, the competitiveness of the plant has increased.

Finally, as land transportation costs are high relative to cement's value, cement markets typically distribute within just 200 miles of the plant (Bureau of the Census, 1979). Hence, the industry can be characterized as a set of regional oligopolies with, in practice, different degrees of competition depending on the size of the regional market. Furthermore, plants located inland will be effectively insulated from import competition providing the opportunity to make comparisons at each point as well as over time. Hereafter, a plant is classified as coastal if it is within 200 miles of a customs district ocean or border main point of entry (hereafter referred to as ports).[1] Otherwise a plant is classified as being inland.

The data

In this section, the original sources and the details of the construction of the data used in this study will be presented. A more detailed account is presented in chapter 4 of Prentice (1997), though some of the series used there have been updated and extended.

There are two broad groups of data. First, there is a set of aggregate statistics compiled mainly from the Cement chapter in the *Minerals*

Yearbook of the Bureau of Mines (various years, a). Second, there is qualitative and quantitative data on plant characteristics obtained from the Plant Information Summaries for 1974–91 (Portland Cement Association, 1974–91) and the Bureau of Mines (various years a & b). A complete set of data on characteristics is only available, though, for 1974–90, for earlier years only an incomplete account, with various selection biases, is obtainable from the Portland Cement Association, trade journals and company annual reports. The main sets of data used in this chapter are presented in Table 7.1.

Table 7.1   Data

Variable	Nature	Notes	Source
Output	Annual domestic clinker production by short ton		Bureau of Mines (various years, a)
Employment	Annual production workers employed		Bureau of Labor Statistics (various years)
Fuel consumption	Fuels consumed million BTU per short ton of clinker	Weighted, by BTU content, sum of fuels consumed	Bureau of Mines (various years, a)
Cement consumption	Annual domestic cement consumption	National and state, used for demand	Bureau of Mines (various years, a)
Plant operations: (1) clinker production (2) cement production	For each year: (1) was clinker produced at a plant or not (2) was cement produced at a plant or not	Used to compile entry and exit statistics	Portland Cement Association (1974–91), Bureau of Mines (various years, a & b), trade journals and company annual reports
Plant operations: Qualitative data	Location, ownership, process of kilns	Used for vintage, investment and number of competitors data	as above
Plant scale	Output divided by number of plants	Number of plants according to plant operations (1) above	Bureau of Mines (various years, a & b) as above
Import share	Imports of cement and clinker as a share of domestic consumption by state		Bureau of Mines (various years, a)

For the statistical analysis, two series are constructed using the above data: growth in plant demand and total number of competitors. To calculate growth in plant demand we first estimate cement consumption within plant-specific markets.[2] US and plant-specific demand growth rates are then estimated using semi-log regressions on a time trend. To calculate the number of competitors faced by a plant in each year we first select the set of plants operating within 200 miles of the relevant plant. Plants owned by the same company as the plant of interest are eliminated, and, likewise, multiple plants operated by a competitor are counted as one plant. This leaves the total number of competitors. Finally, firms that were among the 10 largest, by capacity in 1947, 1969 and 1981 are classified as the top 10 for the relevant period.

Experience of the industry

In Table 7.2 the experience of the industry over the period 1948–90 is presented. The period ends in 1990 since after 1991 the industry remained largely stable. Statistics are given for the whole period and a series of sub-periods divided by peaks of the business cycles, according to NBER dating, excluding the short cycle in 1980–81. For 1949–90, output and consumption of the cement industry grew relatively slowly compared with manufacturing.[3] However, both labour and fuel productivity grew more rapidly than for manufacturing as a whole.

Turning to the sub-periods, after 1973 there appears to have been a slowdown in the rate of growth of cement consumption. And production in the industry appears to have slown down even earlier – perhaps from 1970. Labour productivity grew rapidly up to 1970, slumped and then grew even more rapidly after 1981. Fuel productivity growth also accelerated after 1973. Output per plant (scale) grew rapidly during the pre-oil shock period and, especially since 1981.

Before discussing the change in import patterns, it is worthwhile noting three substantial supply-side shocks that occurred during this period: increased environmental regulation, energy price shocks and the collapse of a previously strong labour union. First, the *Clean Air Act* of 1970 required substantial investments to enable the dust-intensive cement plants to meet the requirements of environmental authorities. In concurrent Bureau of Mines reports several plants are stated to have closed rather than incur the cost of installing pollution control equipment. Furthermore, several plants, as a result of other environmental legislation, had to change their source of raw materials. Such regulation increased both the capital and operating costs of cement production.

Table 7.2 Industry experience

Period	Consumption growth (1)	Output growth	Labour productivity growth	Fuel productivity growth	Growth of scale (2)	No. enter	No. exit	Max. import share (3)
1948–90	2.015	1.423	3.774	1.922	2.086	67	101	
1948–53	5.266	4.892	5.002	1.792	3.943	8	0	0.630
1953–57	2.659	3.454	2.950	0.913	2.163	8	0	1.629
1957–60	2.664	2.142	3.626	1.834	−0.477	15	4	1.464
1960–69	2.914	2.386	5.185	1.114	2.258	21	19	2.166
1970–73	3.447	0.84	3.421	0.438	2.627	3	13	7.533
1973–81	−2.582	−1.80	−1.22	2.344	−0.587	10	36	11.268
1981–90	2.256	0.517	6.697	3.563	3.84	2	30	19.729

Notes: (1) Growth rates are exponential. (2) Scale is measured as average output per plant. (3) Maximum annual import share of national cement consumption during the period.
Sources: As for Table 7.1.

Second, the two energy price shocks increased costs in this fuel-intensive industry. The US industry was relatively disadvantaged by these shocks as it had committed substantially to the relatively fuel-intensive wet process – the combination of relatively low fuel costs and the chemical composition of the raw materials resulted in firms preferring to invest in large wet-process kilns rather than the smaller fuel-efficient preheater, and then precalciner kilns. A third shock occurred in the early 1980s when the formerly powerful labour union in the industry effectively lost its power (Northrup, 1989). Northrup argues, though, that one of the reasons for the loss of power was increased import competition.

Over the period examined, the maximum share of imports during each cycle has increased substantially. Examining Figure 7.1, depicting the annual import share for 1948–92, reveals hysteresis in the share as well. Because of high transport costs, it is not unreasonable to assume that imported cement is consumed in the state in which it lands.[4] During the whole period there are considerable regional variations in import shares. Before 1970, only Florida, Hawaii and New England experienced state import shares greater than 10 per cent; 11 more states experienced such shares during the 1970s; and during the period 1982–90, of those states with clinker producing plants, only Georgia, Illinois, North Carolina and Ohio experienced state import shares of less than 10 per cent.

Several reasons appear to be behind such a dramatic increase. First, over the period 1967–72, the relatively small tariff was removed on imports of

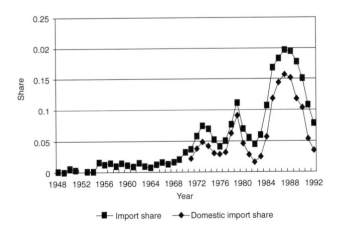

Figure 7.1 Import share of Portland cement consumption, 1948–92.
Domestic import share refers to the share of cement consumed imported by domestic producers. See Prentice (1997) for more details.

cement from free list countries. Perhaps more significantly, ocean transportation costs fell from the early 1970s for several reasons. Cement is best shipped by specialized cement carriers, and during the early 1970s the size of the cement carrier fleet increased and the size of the carriers themselves increased. In addition, floating trans-shipment terminals were increasingly used (Drewry Shipping, 1983). The increase in the size of ships and the use of terminals increased the convenience and flexibility in the supply of imported cement – factors also suggested as important in imported steel (Jondrow *et al.*, 1982). Two short-run influences further reduced the cost disadvantage experienced by imports during the mid-1980s: first, the charter shipping market was in a relatively depressed state (Price, 1987), and, second, there was a substantial appreciation of the US$ against several currencies.

One possible explanation of the patterns of import competition and productivity growth is based primarily on a competitive-type analysis, with demand growth encouraging entry and investment and then high fuel prices leading to the closure of small older fuel-intensive kilns and their replacement with larger kilns with both higher fuel and labour productivity. However, with declining trade barriers, rising import shares, and an industry of regionalized oligopolies, import competition and the extent of strategic competition might be expected to have some effect on investment decisions and therefore productivity growth.

A statistical analysis of the links between import competition, domestic competition, investment and productivity growth

In this section, the effects of import and domestic competition on investment and therefore competitiveness are analysed. First, after introducing the statistical tools, the importance of long-run demand growth for investment decisions is determined. Then we test the effect of domestic and import competition on entry and exit (the most substantial forms of investment and disinvestment).[5]

Methodology and the role of long-run demand growth

A statistical case study is the preferred approach because of data limitations and other problems that make an econometric analysis problematic. A series of hypotheses suggested earlier (p. 153 ff) are tested using chi-squared tests of homogeneity or goodness of fit as follows. First, each plant is classified according to investment or disinvestment decisions taken during the period of interest. Then each plant is additionally classified as suggested by an economic hypothesis to be tested. For example, plants can be classified as to whether each experiences above or below average growth. Each combination of classifications is then enumerated and tabulated yielding a series of cells, each containing the number of plants with the appropriate combination. Then a null hypothesis for the distribution of the sample across the cells is specified, for example to capture the hypothesis that demand growth makes no difference, the number in each demand-growth cell is kept constant. Then the test statistic is calculated and compared with the critical value from the chi-squared distribution (Ben-Horim and Levy, 1984, chapter 15). For the example, failure to reject the null hypothesis is interpreted as concluding that demand growth does not matter in determining investment or disinvestment. If the null hypothesis is rejected, the sample distribution is examined to determine if the pattern responsible for rejection is consistent or contrary to the economic hypothesis. To continue the example, we then check if investment is positively or negatively correlated with demand growth.

The main problem in performing these tests is that they are valid only if the expected number of observations for each cell is at least five. Hence, cells in tables presented in the text will need to be aggregated to perform a test and, in some cases, insufficient observations will be available to perform the test at all. Second, investment decisions, for example, are influenced by more than one factor.

So, to simplify the analysis, the importance of demand growth in determining investment decisions, as described in the example, will be considered first. Statistics on entry and exit are presented in Table 7.3, where the null hypothesis that demand does not matter is captured by assuming symmetry of the distribution of plant numbers around the US growth rate of 1.47 per cent.

Table 7.3 Entry, exit and growth rates

Growth rate	Entry: 1948–90	Exit: 1948–90	Exit: 1948–69	Exit: 1970–81	Exit: 1982–90
4–6.5%	3	1	1	0	0
3–4 %	9	3	0	0	3
2–3 %	18	20	1	8	11
1.5–2%	14	18	3	10	5
1–1.5%	5	9	3	3	3
–0.01–1%	18	51	15	28	8
Total	67	102	23	49	30
Test statistic	6.58	2.22	5.26	3.45	2.13

Symmetry is rejected at 5 per cent for entry for the whole period, but not exit. Because of the supply shocks in the 1970s and increased import exposure in the 1980s, tests are performed separately for each of three sub-periods with respect to exit. For the sub-period 1948–69, symmetry is rejected. However, for the 1970–81 and 1982–90 sub-periods symmetry is not rejected. Entry and exit are not independent of demand growth and inspection suggests a positive relationship between investment and demand growth. This finding is positive in that a positive relationship between investment and demand is hypothesized for all market structures. In addition, subsequent hypothesis tests regarding entry and exit (that is investment and disinvestment) for the sub-period 1948–69, are made conditional on whether plant demand growth was above or below the US average.

The effects of import competition on entry, investment and exit

Import competition could affect investment, so as to create productivity growth, in two ways. First, through a greater rate of exit of high-cost plants, and, second, through encouraging competitive investment. Existing firms invest in new kilns to obtain a cost advantage and economic profits over imported cement and other high-cost firms. To focus the analysis, only plants within 200 miles of customs district main entry ports in states where the maximum import share for the period exceeded 10 per cent are counted as coastal. All other plants will be considered as inland.

First, the effect on exit will be considered. For the period 1970–81 there is anecdotal evidence of importing influencing plant exit decisions, but environmental and energy price shocks may make separating out the influence of import competition difficult. In Table 7.4 exit outcomes for plants operating at the start of 1970 are classified by vintage, process of the most recently constructed kiln, and location. Vintage and process is taken at the start of 1970.

Table 7.4   Exit, 1970–81

Classification	Exit: coastal	Exit: inland	Survive: coastal	Survive: inland
Wet – pre-1946	6	7	1	4
Wet – 1946–59	8	10	14	18
Wet – 1960–69	6	0	18	16
Dry – pre-1946	1	2	3	2
Dry – 1946–59	2	5	4	18
Dry – 1959–69	1	1	9	16
Total	24	25	49	74

Note: Dry includes preheater kilns built before 1970.

Plants with older kilns and wet-process kilns were more likely to close, which most likely drove the rapid fuel productivity growth during this period. However, it is not obvious from the table that plants in regions experiencing imports are more likely to exit. In none of the tests for total plants, wet plants, wet plants with first kilns built after 1945, and plants with kilns built pre-1946, 1946–59 and 1946–69 is the null hypothesis of homogeneity across regions rejected. With a common pattern of closures across both inland and coastal regions, input price shocks seem to dominate the exit decision.

Next, the period 1982–90 is considered; this period saw the highest, to date, import share of national consumption. Furthermore, anti- dumping cases were initiated against Mexican and Venezuelan producers importing into the southern states from Florida around to California. Again, plants are classified according to the vintage and process of their newest kiln, and the exit data are summarized in Table 7.5.

Homogeneity tests are performed for wet-process plants, dry-process plants, 1950s and post-1960 plants. Surprisingly, the null hypothesis of homogeneity across regions is not rejected in any of the cases. Plants were exiting in coastal areas but similar plants were closing inland. Hence, exposure to import competition has no distinctive effect on exit patterns. Further improvements in productivity, once again, appear to be driven by the closure of high-cost plants regardless of location.

Import competition, though, may encourage competitive investment also resulting in productivity growth. Plants are classified as having invested (I) if a new kiln was built in this period, or not invested (NI) if no new kilns were built in the period. Because investment is likely, like entry, to be driven by demand expectations, plants, again, are also classified as to

Table 7.5 Exit, 1982–90

Plant characteristics	Exit: coastal	Exit: inland	Survive: coastal	Survive: inland
Wet – pre-1946	0	1	0	1
Wet – 1950s	6	5	3	5
Wet – 1960s	4	2	10	10
Wet – 1970s	1	1	7	5
Dry – pre-1946	2	0	1	2
Dry – 1950s	3	2	2	1
Dry – 1960s	2	1	4	7
Dry – 1970s	0	0	3	6
Preheater – 1970s	1	0	19	20

Note: The three preheater plants from before the 1960s are included with dry 1950s.

whether they experience above or below average (AA or BA) growth. The investment data is summarized in Table 7.6.

Tests of homogeneity, for both below and above-average demand cases, were performed for wet-process plants and plants built after 1945. Once again, homogeneity is not rejected in any of these cases, suggesting that import exposure did not systematically affect investment decisions during this period. For the period 1982–90, only eight investments in new kilns occurred, mostly in coastal areas suggesting import competition is unlikely to have caused the overall decline in investment. These findings can be interpreted in two ways. First, either domestic markets behave as though competitive, so import competition provides no additional competition. Alternatively, as suggested, earlier (p. 156), competition by importer oligopolists is relatively weak compared with that of domestic oligopolists. The weak, if any, effect of import exposure on investment, entry and exit is surprising but is consistent with earlier empirical work (Deily, 1991).

The effect of domestic competition on productivity growth

Next, the effect of domestic competition on investment decisions will be considered. The period 1948–69 provides an excellent period for testing for strategic behaviour as demand grew fairly continuously and there were no substantial supply-side shocks. Analysing investment after 1970 is severely complicated by supply shocks. Data limitations restrict the analysis to entry and exit decisions for the whole period and investment decisions after 1970.

Table 7.6   Investment, 1970–81

Plant class	Demand	Inland – I	Inland – NI	Coastal – I	Coastal – NI
Wet – pre-1946	BA	0	1	1	0
	AA	2	1	0	0
Wet – 1950s	BA	4	5	2	2
	AA	3	6	4	6
Wet – 1960	BA	0	8	1	10
	AA	4	4	3	4
Dry – pre-1946	BA	0	1	0	2
	AA	1	0	0	0
Dry – 1950s	BA	8	4	0	0
	AA	3	3	2	2
Dry – 1960s	BA	6	5	2	2
	AA	2	3	1	4

First, entry decisions are examined for strategic decision-making. The null hypothesis is that new plants are distributed randomly according to the distribution of plants at the start of the period. If preemption is effective, or competitive investment important, then in regions of growing demand, entry would be concentrated in relatively competitive regions. If preemption is ineffective or competitive investment relatively unimportant, then entry would be concentrated in relatively concentrated regions. Table 7.7 summarizes the distribution of the number of competitors faced by plants operating at the start of 1948, and the average number of competitors faced by plants that entered from 1948 till 1969 from the date of entry to the end of 1969. A dividing line is drawn at 3.13 as a recent paper by Azzam, Rosenbaum and Weliwita (1996) demonstrates; 32 per cent is a critical concentration ratio between perfectly and imperfectly competitive outcomes in the cement industry. A test of goodness of fit between the distribution of incumbents in 1948 and entrants over 1948–69 is performed, for both above-average and below-average demand cases.[6]

In the above average demand case the numbers are suggestive. However, in neither demand case is the null hypothesis of the distributions of incumbents in 1948 and entrants being identical rejected. This outcome may be due to either a compounding of preemptive and competitive investment or that local markets are effectively competitive. While the numbers are not suggestive either way, the lack of evidence for strategic investment is notable.

Next, all forms of investment (entry or kiln construction) for the period 1970–90 were considered. Plants were classified by demand, process, vintage and as to whether they faced more than four competitors or not at the end of 1990. Because of the relatively low number of investments made during this period it was not possible to perform formal statistical tests. The results, though, were again consistent with greater returns driving investment rather than strategic considerations.

Table 7.7 Entry decisions

Number of competitors	Above average demand		Below average demand	
	1948	Entrants	1948	Entrants
0–1	11	11	4	3
2–3	13	10	6	2
4–5	14	6	9	3
6–9	10	8	19	4
10+	2	0	54	9
Test statistic	6.01		1.76	

Two sets of tests were then performed for preemptive entry. First, for each entrant it can be determined if entry was followed by exit, and in Table 7.8 the number of competitors faced by a plant upon entry is compared with the number of plants at the end of 1969. Plants that entered after 1964 are excluded to allow time for changes to work through (in nearly all of these cases, there was no change).

In both above and below-average growth regions, most entry is followed by no change in plant numbers. It is relatively rare that entry was followed by a decline in numbers, particularly if demand was growing above average. Where growth is below average there is some exit.[7] With the number of entrants followed by zero change in numbers, it cannot be concluded that preemptive investment does not occur but it also cannot be stated with confidence that it is important. This is consistent with the conclusion that the incentive for preemptive investment is weaker in an oligopoly.

A second form of preemption is for incumbents to build plants near other plants they own, taking advantage of the efficiency effect. For both periods (1948–69) and 1970–90 it was determined if new plants were built within 200 or 300 miles of another plant owned by the same company or not. The results are summarized in Table 7.9.

Table 7.8   Preemption?

Change in competitors	Below average growth	Above average growth
–2	1	0
–1	3	1
0	9	17
1	2	7
2	1	3
3	0	2
4	0	2
5	0	0

Table 7.9   Spatial preemption

	1948–69				1970–90	
	AA – top 10	AA – other	BA – top 10	BA – other	Top 10	Other
New firm	0	10	0	8	0	4
< 200 mls	2	3	4	5	2	2
200–300 mls	5	3	0	0	1	1
> 300 mls	4	4	2	2	1	4

Though the numbers are suggestive the null hypothesis that plants are evenly divided between regions within 300 miles and regions more than 300 miles distant is not rejected for either above or below-average growth groups of plants. The number of entrants post-1970 is too small to make any definite conclusions. The relatively weak results on preemption are broadly consistent with the work of Johnson and Parkman (1983) on the cement industry and the theoretical conclusion that the incentive for preemptive investment in an oligopoly is relatively weak.

Finally, the occurrences of strategic exit will be examined. In particular, for all three periods exiting plants are classified as to whether they are within 200 or 300 miles of another plant owned by the same firm, and the results are summarized in Tables 7.10 and 7.11.

For the first two periods, the null hypothesis of equal distribution across regions within and outside 300 miles of their plants is rejected. This provides additional evidence supporting the work of Ghemawat and Nalebuff (1990). For the most recent period, the null hypothesis of random distribution is not rejected.

In summary, though some numbers are suggestive there is no definite evidence of strategic considerations influencing entry decisions and therefore productivity growth. Likewise, the evidence for strategic considerations influencing investment during 1970–90 is also not strong. Domestic and import competition do not seem to provide additional influences (beyond long-run demand and cost conditions) on investment

Table 7.10 Strategic exit, 1948–69

	BA – top 10	BA – other	AA – top 10	AA – other
Single plants	0	2	0	0
Within 200 mls	13	2	2	0
200–300 mls	0	0	3	0
> 300 mls	0	0	1	0

Table 7.11 Strategic exit, 1970–81 and 1982–90

	1970–81: top 10	1970–81: other	1982–90: top 10	1982–90: other
Single plants	0	6	0	3
Within 200 mls	14	6	4	5
200–300 mls	5	4	5	2
> 300 mls	7	2	9	1

Note: In 1970–81 and 1982–90 five and one plants were not classified as they were part of a mass closure by two different firms.

decisions. For the two periods up to 1981, there is evidence that strategic considerations did influence exit decisions. While it cannot automatically be inferred that exit patterns were not efficient, resulting in slower than optimum productivity growth, the possibility does exist.

Conclusions

For a process-based intermediate materials industry, there is a direct link between investment, productivity growth and competitiveness. Hence, the literature on innovation and strategic investment can be drawn on to hypothesize a set of relationships between domestic and import competition and investment. The Portland cement industry is argued to be a particularly suitable industry for examining these relationships. The experience of the industry has been reviewed, highlighting the substantial factor productivity growth, investment, disinvestment, entry and exit and increased import competition. Then, a set of statistical tests were performed to determine if significant relationships exist between import competition and investment, and the type of domestic competition and investment. Surprisingly, import competition is found not to significantly affect exit or investment. Data availability limits the work that could be done with domestic competition, but there is, again, surprisingly little definite evidence of strategic investment. Strategic exit is in evidence up until the 1980s.

Long-run demand and plant cost characteristics seem to be the dominant determinants of plant investment and exit decisions in the cement industry. However, the data-set and statistical techniques used are limited so import competition and strategic investment cannot be conclusively ruled out as determinants of investment, productivity growth and competitiveness. Hence, further research with more complete data and more sophisticated techniques may yet discover if strategic investment and import competition are determinants of productivity growth and competitiveness.

Notes

1 There are approximately 36 of these comprehensively covering the borders and coasts of the US.
2 Cement consumption rather than construction is used because a complete construction series is not available for the whole period and demand is believed to be relatively price inelastic. See Prentice (1997) for further details on construction.
3 Manufacturing data was obtained from the BLS Data home page at http:// stats.bls.gov/datahome.htm on 9 December 1998.

4 The main exception to this is Louisiana where there is considerable anecdotal evidence of imported cement travelling up the Mississippi during the 1980s. However, an anti-dumping inquiry on Mexican cement suggests the share was probably not great; International Trade Commission (1990).
5 Statistics on investment for 1974–90 were also considered but as these did not yield strong results, they have been ommitted from this discussion.
6 To perform the tests, different aggregations had to be used–AA: (0–1), (2–3), (4–5), (6+); and BA: (0–7), (8–12), (13+).
7 One of these cases is unlikely to be preemption as the plant was less than half the size of a typical plant, entered into one of the most competitive markets, and it exited four years later.

References

Ait-Sahalia, Y. (1994) 'Entry–Exit Decisions of Foreign Firms and Import Prices', *Annales D'Economie et de Statistique*, vol. 34, pp. 219–44.
Azzam, A.M., Rosenbaum, D.I. and Weliwita, A. (1996) 'Is There More Than One Critical Concentration Ratio? An Empirical Test for the Portland Cement Industry', *Applied Economics*, vol. 28, pp. 673–8.
Ben-Horim, M. and Levy, H. (1984) *Statistics*, 2nd edn, New York: Random House.
Bulow, J., Geanakoplos, J. and Klemperer, P. (1985) 'Multimarket Oligopoly: Strategic Substitutes and Complements', *Journal of Political Economy*, vol. 93, pp. 488–511.
Bureau of Labour Statistics (various years) *Employment, Hours and Earnings*, Bureau of Labor Statistics, US Department of Labor, GPO Washington DC.
Bureau of the Census (1979) *1977 Census of Transportation*, US GPO.
Bureau of Mines (various years, a) *Minerals Yearbook*, chapters on cement, US Department of the Interior, GPO Washington DC (1948–92).
—(various years, b), *Minerals Yearbook*, state chapters, US Department of the Interior, GPO Washington DC.
Das, S. (1991) 'A Semiparametric Structural Analysis of the Idling of Cement Kilns', *Journal of Econometrics*, vol. 50, 235–56.
— (1992) 'A Microeconometric Model of Capital Utilization and Retirement: The Case of the U.S. Cement Industry', *Review of Economic Studies*, vol. 59, pp. 277–97.
Deily, M.E. (1991) 'Exit Strategies and Plant-Closing Decisions: The Case of Steel', *RAND Journal of Economics*, vol. 22, pp. 250–63.
Dixit, A. (1980) 'The Role of Investment in Entry Deterrence', *Economic Journal*, vol. 90, pp. 95–106.
Drewry Shipping (1983) *World Seaborne Cement Trade, Transport and Handling*, London: Drewry Shipping Consultants Ltd.
Førsund, F.R. and Hjalmarsson, L. (1983) 'Technical Progress and Structural Change in the Swedish Cement Industry 1955– 1979', *Econometrica*, vol. 51, pp. 1449–67.
Ghemawat, P. and Nalebuff, B. (1985) 'Exit', *RAND Journal of Economics*, vol. 16, pp. 184–94.
— and — (1990) 'The Devolution of Declining Industries', *Quarterly Journal of Economics*, vol. 18, 17–33.
Gibson, J.K., and Harris, R.I.D. (1996) 'Trade Liberalization and Plant Exit in New Zealand Manufacturing', *Review of Economics and Statistics*, vol. 78, pp. 521–9.

Gilbert, R.J. and Harris, R.G. (1984) 'Competition with Lumpy Investment', *RAND Journal of Economics*, vol. 15(2), pp. 197–212.

— and Lieberman, M. (1987) 'Investment and Coordination in Oligopolistic Industries', *RAND Journal of Economics*, vol. 18(1), pp. 17–33.

International Trade Commission (1990) 'Grey Portland Cement and Cement Clinker from Mexico', US International Trade Commission, Determination of the Commission Investigation no. 731-TA-451, August.

Johnson, R.N. and Parkman, A. (1983) 'Spatial Monopoly, Non-Zero Profits and Entry Deterrence: The Case of Cement', *Review of Economics and Statistics*, vol. 63(5), pp. 431–9.

Jondrow, J.M., Chase, D.E. and Gamble, C.L. (1982) 'The Price Differential between Domestic and Imported Steel', *Journal of Business*, vol. 55, pp. 383–99.

Kohanowski, F.I. (1966) 'Trends in Cement Plant Kiln Size', *Pit and Quarry*, vol. 59(1), pp. 112–20, 140.

Lieberman, M.B. (1990) 'Exit from Declining Industries: "Shakeout" or "Stakeout"?', *RAND Journal of Economics*, vol. 21, pp. 538–54.

Northrup, H.R. (1989) 'From Union Hegemony to Union Disintegration: Collective Bargaining in Cement and Related Industries', *Journal of Labor Research*, vol. 10, pp. 339–76.

Portland Cement Association (various years, 1974–92) 'US and Canadian Portland Cement Industry: Plant Information Summary', Portland Cement Association, Skokie, Ill.

Prentice, D. (1997) 'Import Competition in the U.S. Portland Cement Industry', PhD thesis, Yale University.

Price, E. (1987) 'General Trend in World Cement Trade to Continue Down', *World Cement*, 18 (June), pp. 204–7.

Rosenbaum, D.I. (1994) 'Efficiency v. Collusion: Evidence Cast in Cement', *Review of Industrial Organization*, vol. 9, pp. 379–92.

— and Yans, I. (1993) 'Multimarket Contact and Collusive Pricing: Evidence from the U.S. Cement Industry', mimeo, University of Nebraska-Lincoln.

Salter, W.E.G. (1966) 'Productivity and Technical Change', University of Cambridge, Department of Applied Economics Monograph no. 6, Cambridge University Press.

Schumpeter, J. (1950) *Capitalism, Socialism and Democracy*, New York: Harper.

Tirole, J. (1988) *The Theory of Industrial Organization*, Cambridge, Mass.: The MIT Press.

Vives, X. (1988) 'Sequential Entry, Industry Structure and Welfare', *European Economic Review*, vol. 32, pp. 1671–87.

Part III

Government Policy in a Global Economy

8
Trade and Communication

Don Lamberton

In the Feiwel interview, Arrow (1987a, p. 213) took the view that the usual general equilibrium theory tends to predict convergence, noting that convergence might be very slow because all countries have very different capital structures. Elsewhere, he mentioned 'an inextricable mixture of individual differences and productivity effects' and warned against the assumption of homogeneous agents: 'If agents are all alike, there is really no room for trade' (Arrow, 1987b, p. 205). This mind-set leads towards a stable future in which new information is unwanted: towards a vision of a 'world [that] has been made safe for optimisation, and hostile to innovation' (Davies, 1967, p. 320). To counter this, we need to look closely at the homogeneity assumption and consider carefully what is included in capital structures.

Diversity: a necessary condition

The 'tides among nations' are diverse. International communication is the international dimension of the information economy: letters, phone calls and e-mail messages; the flow of goods and services with associated transport activities; movements of money and capital; the movement of people as visitors, guest workers and migrants; relocations of head offices. In all such cases, information flows are involved along with complementary efforts to modify the state of readiness of those who might wish to make use of the information (Lamberton, 1998a).

It is, of course, easy to marvel at the changes that have occurred in the underlying technologies, especially in recent decades, and to focus on the speed of satellites circling the globe and the growth rate of the number of Internet messages being transmitted. However, to do so is misleading in several ways. We are offered reassurance that these new technologies are benign and encouraged to focus on their enabling potential, but the enabling effects are offset, to an unknown extent. First, while we should take account of the diffusion of Internet access, we should not ignore the Internet dropouts (Katz and Aspden, 1998). Second, information and information technology facilitate control, but the ways in which control is exercised will depend upon the objectives being pursued. Private versus public gain issues arise; and as Veblen pointed out long ago, profit can be made by hindering as well as aiding production – an early OECD report labelled some of the actors on the economic stage as 'embezzlers of knowledge' (OECD, 1971). This can range from simple industrial espionage (Harris, 1997) to activity on a much grander scale as in CoCom, the US effort over many years to deny the Soviet Union access to technology of supposed military significance (Macdonald, 1998). Or it can be interwoven with organizational change. A recent paper investigates information concealment in the theory of vertical integration (Choi, 1998).

A third kind of offset arises when it turns out that needed inputs, coordination or behaviour patterns are not available or not operative. Babbage's computer was long-delayed. The market is an enormous information system but information is never complete and always costly. Furthermore, the wishes of many economists notwithstanding, there are awkward attitudes, with associated outcomes, such as those captured through such concepts as organizational obsolescence, lock-in and cognitive dissonance; attitudes that cause relevant information to be ignored.

The seemingly easy way out, the path indicated by 'rational expectations and all the rest of that devil's trap' (Arrow, 1987a, p. 231) has to be rejected. Arrow is correct when he argues that you cannot really have rational expectations – they can only be rational given the information at hand, and not taking account of all one might know. In practical terms, cost effectiveness is the best that might be achieved and optimization remains a mirage. This knowledge gap opens up a wide range of possibilities as additional information – discrete pieces, batches or flows – becomes available with the passage of time or through deliberate action (Lamberton, 1999). Here is a major source of diversity, amongst different contemplated futures, that can even work as a stabilizing influence.

The information intensity of the dynamic reality leads some commentators to try to set aside considerations of scale and scope that have been so important in mainstream thinking. They tend to reason that both small and large firms have access to the new technologies and to infer that small firms will have the same chances of survival as the large ones. Presumably, the world is safe for those who think 'small is beautiful' and an era of cooperation, with a reduced role for the state, is ensured. However, the basic combination of economic characteristics possessed by information, especially its indivisibility, means the cost of information is independent of its use. It pays large firms, domestic and international, and governments to acquire more and better information than small firms. It is difficult to separate information from information-handling forms of organization including software (Baetjer, 1998), but it would appear that networks, for example, also bring scale benefits. The result is that the information-intensive economy looks set to be a fertile field for large organizations, with plenty of scope for departures from the competitive model (Lamberton, 1998b).

International competition can no longer be viewed as turning on strength of individual firms; now, the strength of the firm depends first on its own networking capability, and second on the infrastructure provided by development generally and by its national government. In a sense governments compete in terms of the provision of infrastructure, not just in telecommunications equipment but also computers in elementary schools and sophisticated equipment for research – from street information services telling tourists 'You are here' to comprehensive international business intelligence. All this might be seen as simply a modernization of the wisdom that led some governments to give high priority to education.

The role of the state has been extended in significant ways in the global information economy. As Rodrik (1998) has argued recently, the more open economies may well have been obliged to have larger government because of the need for coordinated action in terms of risk reduction. In fact, the firm, no longer to be conceived of as a mathematical point, has become a network that involves linkages across industry and national boundaries and extends to elements of the state. Such firms could then find new ways to cooperate with the state and new ways to capture regulatory mechanisms.

Just as the sovereignty of states is coming under attack, so is the identity of industries. Industrial classifications, even if they have been internationally agreed upon, remain to a large extent arbitrary. Each industry in such a classification is part of a broader structure so that changes recorded within any one category may have been initiated elsewhere or may themselves set off reactions spreading in a complex way through the entire structure. The network character of the industry may be more important than any clearly defined production technology or product, such as for example in the case of tourism. In such circumstances it helps little to use the convergence label if everything is supposedly converging with everything else. For example, we have been told that:

what are converging are not simply different media nor different industries, but at least three quite different paradigms, each with its own history, its own cast of characters. Each paradigm also is marked by a distinctive industry structure, legal and regulatory framework, and assumptions about human behavior. The three paradigms are the Communications Paradigm, the Information Paradigm. and the Entertainment Paradigm. (Institute of Information Studies, 1995, p. xv).

What is needed is a charting of the processes and awareness of both the domestic and international dimensions of these patterns of change. Domestic policy and the trade interests of individual countries may well be shifting more and more onto the international stage, but there is a distinct possibility that old localized or regional patterns may be strengthened and new ones may be emerging. A recent study comparing bilateral telephone traffic with trade patterns in the Asia-Pacific region reported progressive Asian integration (Madden, 1999). This research supported the view that '*regionalization* frequently appears a better description of world market evolution than globalization' (Lamberton, 1993).

Capital structures

These considerations take us back to the problem of defining capital structures. A recent paper on real investment trends (Kirova and Lipsey, 1998) points out that much investment is missing from national accounts where the emphasis is on physical capital – plant and equipment, infrastructure narrowly defined, and housing. Missing elements identified were education, R&D, consumer durables and military spending. *The Economist* (1998a) added computer software. And a case can be made for spending on information and on information production, handling and using capabilities that are not caught in the education net. Conceptually, there is overlap with spending that creates organizational capital.

Kirova and Lipsey found that the USA had invested more than the average for rich countries – a conclusion strengthened when adjustment is made for investment goods being cheaper in the USA than elsewhere. One might well ask whether this difference has more to do with the relative performance of the US economy than do certain market flexibilities that have been targeted for emulation elsewhere.

If economies are viewed from this wider perspective, with firms being complex organizations rather than the mathematical points of theory; communication being an integral part of inquiring, communicating and deciding; and information being complex, interwoven and structured batches and flows rather than the discrete pieces envisaged by Arrow in his seminal 1962 paper, there are major, interrelated implications for both theory and policy.

Consider, first, the contention that competition policy so overlaps with trade policy that it belongs at the World Trade Organization (*The Economist*, 1998b). Alliances, as in the telecommunications industry, attract special attention, but there does not seem to be a good theory of alliances. It appears that a useful theory will need to combine the information perspective with new ideas from industry organization and organization science, and, as suggested above, a new interpretation of state regulatory efforts.

There would seem to be several major obstacles. First, can such policy be extended to every organizational and informational nook and cranny of the entire business sector as the wider perspective would require in the information economy? Second, the wider perspective opens the way for non-market forms of power. Capture-theory terminology seems to have fallen into disfavour and to have been replaced by endogenous regulation (Reiter, 1996), but the practical outcomes seem unchanged. Industry influence remains a major consideration in domestic policy and there seems little reason to believe it absent or less important in the processes taking place in international forums.

The not-so-simple economics of intellectual property is a case in point. Strong support can be given for the proposition that the patent system works in favour of those countries selling technology rather than the buyers of technology; and these are categories that tend to fit with 'advanced countries' where convergence is taking place, on the one hand, and 'the other set of countries' with 'the mixed record of take offs, stalls and nose dives' (Pritchett, 1998, pp. 3–4). From an Australian perspective or from the perspective of other small or developing countries, participation in these international processes should be approached not in the warm glow of hopes of unlimited gains from free trade, but in terms of the hard reality that explains how 'one country, the US, was able to persuade more than 100 countries that they, the importers of technological and cultural information, should pay more for the importation of that information' (Drahos, 1995, p. 7).

As international economics has merged with industrial economics, analysis of the workings of international agreements and negotiations should take into account the size distribution of companies, their balance of trade in technology, and their competence in these international processes of information-handling and reaching agreement. Radio spectrum policy is an excellent illustration where developing countries have lacked the expertise and resources and/or the bargaining strength to play a significant role in standards-setting or allocation processes (Smythe, 1987).

Economics of language

Another element of capital structures – or alternatively of information infrastructures – is language; and the economics of language is sadly neglected. An integrated society, be it one nation or many, is much dependent upon the natural complementarity amongst people because no one has all the information (Arrow, 1973). In the functioning of such a society, communication and language, spoken and written, are major instruments and at times weapons in conflicts. The role of language of all kinds – natural, corporate, machine and silent – is therefore of great economic significance. It is a matter fit to be explored as part of economics, belonging in 'the search for optimality in fields extending beyond, though including, the production and distribution of marketable goods' (Marschak, 1965, p. 523). The learning of language and the provision of translation capacity absorb resources, and language as a labour skill affects exploitation and absorption of immigants and is reflected in earnings (Chiswick and Miller, 1995). A second or third language is a bankable skill.

Language has become a policy matter and there is now, especially with current Internet practice, a good deal of debate about English as the global language. The focus of debate seems to have shifted from resistance to standardization, and cultural loss towards coordination with trade matters (Lamberton, 1998c).

In a pioneering paper, Snow (1998) has examined economic, statistical and linguistic factors affecting success in the test of English as a foreign language (TOEFL). Adults' success in learning English, as measured by TOEFL scores, was regressed as a function of GNP per capita (proxying instructional effort); share of foreign trade in GNP (proxying everyday exposure to English); percentage of speakers taking the TOEFL (for comparability of populations); and the relatedness of English to one's native language, indicated by the Indoeuropean language tree. All four regressors were significant.

Another study (Marschan *et al.*, 1997) argues that language needs to be considered as an important element in the management of multinational firms because it permeates virtually every aspect of their business activities. A shared company language is inadequate because of the demands of operating in multiple foreign language environments. An in-depth case study of a Finnish multinational – one of the world's leading companies in the elevator industry – demonstrated the pervasive impact of language, the range of individual responses and the potential cost implications.

International organizations

The information perspective has yet another implication. The extent to which new forms of international organizations have proliferated in recent decades has not attracted much attention amongst economists (Wolfe, 1977). The new forms range through joint private efforts as in alliances, non-government bodies, specific-purpose regulatory schemes and, especially in the UN context, organizations that aim at a mixture of coordination and regulation. Just as the design of efficient forms of domestic business organization may be in its infancy, so too may be the design of alternative forms of international cooperation. Those responsible for policy might benefit from reading Tinbergen's (1978) provocative essay in which he compared alternative forms in terms of their efficiency. Such a design effort would be a good complement to future debate about what a level playing field means in the 'global' information economy.

Conclusion

The wider perspective on the information infrastructure and the communication process suggests there are many opportunities for building competitive strength that seem to lie outside traditional approaches, for example intellectual property, disclosure or conceal-ment of information as appropriate, and language. More generally, payoff from the organization of capabilities (Loasby, 1998) would seem to hold greater promise than the unhesitating rush to adopt the latest IT. First, government and industry needs to be reminded of both Marshall's warning to the businessman about competitive supply that would follow quickly on his heels, and Schumpeter's 'swarm of innovators'. New technology that is readily available to all competitors is likely to be less advantageous than the use of that technology in further innovation. One might well wonder about the competitive implications of communications developments when, as would seem to be the case in Australia, the dominant firm looks to a future relying on off-the-shelf technology supplied by major producing countries. The prospect of this strategy has already evoked in political quarters the suggestion that Australia may be destined for a 'rich slave' role, paying a high price for its technology.

Preoccupation with the marvels of technology and wishes to make the market a level playing field have obscured many influences that together play a vital part in trade competitiveness. The objective of this chapter has been to suggest that many of these influences are bound up with the role of information, and adoption of this information perspective is a major step with significant implications:

- It is consistent with an evolutionary modelling that might bring us closer to an economic dynamics that captures rather more of the real world processes with which consumers, business and governments are having to cope.
- It places what happens in organizations on an equal footing with what happens in markets.
- It recognizes the political economy nature of those dynamics.
- It pleads a case for a much wider concept of capital and infrastructure.
- And it poses some very important questions about the resource base of future development.

These questions deserve elaboration, which can best be achieved by two quotations:

> What will retain value, is what computers cannot produce: that most intangible and elusive of economic goods – the creative output of the human mind. (Jonscher, 1999, p. 285)

> What information consumes is rather obvious: it consumes the attention of its recipients. Hence a wealth of information creates a poverty of attention and a need to allocate that efficiently among the overabundance of information sources that might consume it. (Simon, as quoted in Hardin, 1999, p. 13)

The preoccupation with technology has led us to devote too much of our efforts to information supply and far too little to information demand. Most firms and governments suffer, in greater or lesser degree, from organizational obsolescence. They favour change but only change that is within their current vision, and that vision is a product of their experience (Macdonald, 1998, ch. 12). Perhaps there is a need to give attention to the agent/principal problem rather than the principal/agent problem, so facilitating radical thinking and listening. Decision and policy processes both need to be redesigned so that organizational obsolescence or lock-in can be challenged. There needs to be recognition that the greatest productivity gains may come from subversiveness.

References

Arrow, K.J. (1962) 'Economic Welfare and the Allocation of Resources for Invention', in National Bureau of Economic Research, *The Rate and Direction of Innovative Activity: Economic and Social Factors*, Princeton: Princeton University Press.
— (1973) 'Some Ordinalist-Utilitarian Notes on Rawls' Theory of Justice', *The Journal of Philosophy*, vol. LXX, (9), pp. 245–63.
— (1987a) 'Oral History I: An Interview', in G.R. Feiwel (ed.), *Arrow and the Ascent of Modern Economic Theory*, London: Macmillan.
— (1987b) 'Rationality of Self and Others in an Economic System', in R.M. Hogarth and M.W. Reder (eds), *Rational Choice: The Contrast between Economics and Psychology*, London: University of Chicago Press, pp. 201–15.
Baetjer, H. Jr (1998) *Software as Capital: An Economic Perspective on Software Engineering*, IEEE Computer Society.
Chiswick, B. and Miller, P. (1995) 'Language and Earnings', *Journal of Labor Economics*, vol. 13, pp. 246–88.
Choi, J.P. (1998) 'Information Concealment in the Theory of Vertical Integration', *Journal of Economic Behavior and Organization*, vol. 35, pp. 117–31.
Davies, D. (1967) 'A Scarce Resource called Curiosity', in D.M. Lamberton (ed.), *Economics of Information and Knowledge*, Harmondsworth, UK: Penguin.
Drahos, P. (1995) 'Global Property Rights in Information: The Story of TRIPS at the GATT', *Prometheus*, vol. 13, pp. 6–19.
The Economist (1998a) 'Co-operate on Competition', 4 July, p. 14.
— (1998b) 'The Borders of Competition', 4 July, pp. 77–8.
— (1998c) 'Investigating Investment', 18 July, p. 82.
Hardin, S. (1999) 'Human Work in a Computer Age', *Bulletin of the American Society for Information Science*, vol. 25, pp. 13–15.
Harris, J. (1997) *Industrial Espionage and Technology Transfer Britain and France in the 18th Century*, Aldershot, UK: Ashgate.
Institute of Information Studies (1995) *Crossroads on the Information Highway: Convergence and Diversity in Communications Technologies*, Queenstown, Md: Institute of Information Studies.
Johnscher, C. (1999) 'The Economics of Cyberspace', in A. Leer (ed.), *Masters of the Wired World*, London: Financial Times/Pitman, pp. 278–85.
Katz, J.E. and Aspden, P. (1998) 'Internet Dropouts in the USA. The Invisible Group', *Telecommunications Policy*, vol. 22 (May/June), pp. 327–39.
Kirova, M. and Lipsey, R. (1998) *Measuring Real Investment. Trends in the United States and International Comparisons*, National Bureau of Economic Research, Working Paper no. 6404.
Lamberton, D.M. (1993) 'Globaloney: The Impact of Regions on the Future of Emerging Markets in Information Technology and Trade', *Pacific Telecommunications Review*, vol. 14, pp. 3–10.
— (ed.) (1998a) *Communication and Trade. Essays in Honor of Meheroo Jussawalla*, Cresskill N.J.: Hampton Press.

— (1998b) 'Information Economics Research: Points of Departure', *Information Economics and Policy*, vol. 10, pp. 325–30.

— (1998c) 'Language and Critical Mass', paper presented at the International Telecommunications 12th Biennial Conference, Stockholm, 21–24 June.

— (1999) 'Information: Pieces, Batches or Flows?', in S.C. Dow and P.E. Earl (eds), *Economic Organisation and Economic Knowledge. Essays in Honour of Brian Loasby*, Vol. 1, Cheltenham, UK: Edward Elgar.

Loasby, B.J. (1998) 'The Organization of Capabilities', *Journal of Economic Behavior and Organization*, vol. 35, pp. 139–60.

Macdonald, S. (1998) *Information for Innovation: Managing Change from an Information Perspective*, Oxford: Oxford University Press.

Madden, G. (1999) 'Asia-Pacific Information Flows and Trade', in S. Macdonald and J. Nightingale (eds), *Information and Organization*, Amsterdam: North-Holland.

Marschak, J. (1965) 'Economics of Language', in D.M. Lamberton (ed.), *The Economics of Communication and Information*, Cheltenham, UK: Edward Elgar.

Marschan, R., Welch, D. and Welch, L. (1997) 'Language: The Forgotten Factor in Multinational Management?', *European Management Journal* (October).

OECD (1971) *Information for a Changing Society: Some Policy Considerations*, Paris: OECD.

Pritchett, L. (1998) 'Divergence, Big Time', *Journal of Economic Perspectives*, vol. 11(3).

Reiter, S. (1996) 'On Endogenous Economic Regulation', *Economic Design*, vol. 2(2), pp. 211–43.

Rodrik, D. (1998) 'Why do More Open Economies have Bigger Governments?', *Journal of Political Economy*, vol. 106, pp. 997–1032.

Smythe, D. (1987) 'Radio Spectrum Policy and World Needs', *Prometheus*, vol. 5(2), pp. 263–83.

Snow, M.S. (1998) 'Economic, Statistical, and Linguistic Factors Affecting Success on the Test of English as a Foreign Language (TOEFL)', *Information Economics and Policy*, vol. 10(2), pp. 159–72.

Tinbergen, J. (1978) 'Alternative Forms of International Co-operation: Comparing their Efficiency', *International Social Science Journal*, vol. 30(2), pp. 223–37.

Wolfe, A.W. (1977) 'The Supranational Organization of Production: An Evolutionary Perspective', *Current Anthropology*, vol. 18, pp. 615–35.

9

Economic Integration and Regional Policy Cooperation

Jeffrey Petchey and Perry Shapiro

F42

F15

Introduction

Economic unions often begin by establishing common markets for trade in goods and services. In some cases, for example the European Union, common factor markets that allow the free flow of capital and labour are also established. Integration of factor markets implies that as a state chooses its policies it will change the distribution of mobile factors within the common market and hence have an effect on neighbouring states. In other words, integration implies increasing policy interdependence.

If states act competitively towards one another, ignoring the broader regional effects of their local decisions, the taxes and public policies chosen may be inefficient from the perspective of the region, though rational from the point of view of each state. Concerns over the difficulties created by competitive behaviour between nation-states in an integrated region are paramount in the Europe Union at present where there are moves to introduce tax policy cooperation between member states. In more mature federations, too, such as the United States, Canada and Australia, there are institutional mechanisms for coordinating sub-national government policies. The aim of cooperation is to choose tax and public spending policies in a way that takes account of regional interdependence. In principle, cooperative policies pursue the regional interest as a whole and have the potential to produce efficient outcomes.

Here we examine the efficiency properties of competitive versus cooperative behaviour in a region made up of independent nation-states sharing a common factor market. We do this by developing a model that captures the essence of common factor markets. The model supposes a common market of two member states. The population of each state is divided into two groups: immobile workers who receive the economic residual from production (which may include income from labour supplied), and a mobile group receiving only wage income. Each state chooses its tax and public policies competitively to maximize the net income of the immobile class who we suppose to be the politically dominant group. Mobile workers move freely between member states in response to these policies and seek to maximize their (equal) per capita utility.

We also allow the common factor market to be integrated with the world factor market. This is achieved by allowing the mobile group to migrate between the common market and the rest of the world in response to member states' tax and public policies. This means that the total supply of labour to the factor market varies in response to member state policies. The degree of this response is captured by a parameter, ε, which varies between zero and infinity. When ε is zero, the size of the labour market is fixed and invariant with regard to member state policies. When ε is between zero and infinity, there is some positive response of total labour supply to changes in state policies. The total size of the common labour market contracts and expands in response to member states' policies. Finally, when ε is infinite there is an infinite labour supply response to state policies.[1]

We then show how member states' tax and public policies influence the welfare of other member states through the free migration of workers within the common market, and also through the migration of workers between the market and the rest of the world. A competitive equilibrium between member states is characterized and it is shown that each state adopts policies to attract mobile migrants from outside the market and from other states within the union. They do this because the income of each state is an increasing function of the number of mobile workers within its borders.

General results that hold regardless of the degree of labour market integration are then presented for the competitive case. First, it is shown that provision of public policies is always efficient in the competitive equilibrium. This mirrors results in Scotchmer (1986) and Burbidge and Myers (1994), though neither of those results were obtained in a world with factor market integration. Second, it is shown that the allocation of mobile labour within the common labour market is generally inefficient. Thus, there is efficient provision of public policies but an inefficient allocation of labour between member states under competitive behaviour where states pursue their own interests and ignore the broader regional interest.

Next we examine the efficiency and equity effects of policy cooperation between member states. Two results follow. First, as in the competitive outcome, the supply of the public good is efficient when states cooperate.

Second, mobile labour is allocated efficiently. Therefore, cooperation is efficient in the sense that the mobile factor is allocated efficiently within the factor market. Cooperation allows states to choose policies that maximize the joint or regional interest, taking account of the policy interdependencies that exist between them (induced by the presence of the common factor market).

The chapter is organized as follows. In the next section we develop the model of a regional common factor market. We then characterize the competitive outcome, followed by an examination of the efficiency properties of policy cooperation. Conclusions are provided in the final section.

Model

Suppose there are two independent states (nations) $i = 1, 2$. In each there is a mobile population whose number is denoted n_i. Assume there is also an immobile group whose number in state i is denoted as L_i. The production function of state i is then:

$$y_i = f_i(n_i) \tag{1}$$

where $f_i' > 0$ and $f_i'' < 0$. We assume competitive labour markets in which mobile labour is paid its marginal product. Therefore, we have $f_i' = w_i$ where w_i is the mobile factor wage rate in state i. It is also supposed that mobile labour receives only wage income and that the immobile group receives the economic residual. This might be thought of literally as the economic rent accruing from ownership of some fixed factor, such as land, natural resources or fixed capital, or the return to any labour inputs provided by immobile citizens. Following Wildasin (1991), the immobile labour income can be aggregated with rents from ownership of fixed factors if this labour is inelastically supplied by the immobile workers, as we suppose here. The residual in state i, equivalent to immobile worker income, is:

$$R_i(n_i) = f_i(n_i) - w_i n_i. \tag{2}$$

Mobile residents have identical preferences regardless of which state they live in. This group consumes a private good, x_i and a state-provided pure local public good, q_i. The utility function of a representative mobile resident, continuous and twice differentiable, is $u(x_i, q_i)$. Immobile residents consume only the private good, and the preference function for a representative immobile citizen in state i is $U_i = U_i(X_i)$, also assumed to be continuous and twice differentiable.

All residents contribute to the cost of providing the public good, and the total contribution by immobile citizens of state i is:

$$T_i = q_i - t_i n_i \tag{3}$$

where t_i is the per capita lump sum tax paid by the mobile factor in state i to finance q_i and the marginal cost of q_i is one.

The aggregate budget constraint for immobile citizens in state i is:

$$X_i + q_i = f_i(n_i) - n_i(w_i - t_i) \tag{4}$$

where X_i is the immobile resident's total consumption of the private good. Equation (4) implies that $X_i = f_i(n_i) - n_i(w_i - t_i) - q_i$. Since immobile workers derive no utility from the public good, their interests can be represented by total residual income net of the expenditure on the public good, that is:

$$X_i(n_i, t_i, q_i) = R_i(n_i) + n_i t_i - q_i. \tag{5}$$

The budget constraint for a representative mobile citizen in state i is:

$$x_i + t_i = w_i(n_i). \tag{6}$$

As noted, mobile residents migrate freely between states to equate per capita utilities, and the free migration equilibrium condition is:

$$u(w_1 - t_1, q_1) = u(w_2 - t_2, q_2). \tag{7}$$

From equation (7), citizens migrate in response to changes in the tax and public policies of the two states. In equilibrium, per capita utilities are equated, but in general the levels of public policy provision and per capita taxes differ across states (as shown below). There is also a second migration equilibrium condition, namely:

$$n_1 + n_2 = N \cdot \left(\frac{u}{u^*}\right)^\varepsilon, \qquad \varepsilon \geq 0 \tag{8}$$

where u^* is the exogenous world utility level and u/u^* is the (equal) mobile utility in the common labour market, per unit of world utility. When $u/u^* > 1$, mobile factor utility in the common labour market exceeds the world level, and vice versa if $u/u^* < 1$. When $u/u^* = 1$, the common labour market utility equates to the world level. $\varepsilon \geq 0$ is a parameter that captures the responsiveness of $n_1 + n_2$ to changes in u relative to u^*. Since u is a function of state policies, the parameter also captures the response of $n_1 + n_2$ to changes in state policies within the common market, relative to the rest of the world.

There are three possibilities for the value of ε. First, if $\varepsilon = 0$, then there is no labour supply response to differences between the common market and world utility. Since from equation (7) common market utility is a function of state policies, this implies that there is no labour supply response to changes in state policies within the market, though there are still changes in the allocation of the given labour supply across states in response to state policies. If this is so, then equation (8) is $n_1 + n_2 = N$, where N is fixed. Second, if $\varepsilon > 0$, we have a more general case where the total supply of labour to the common labour market varies in response to state policies. The degree of supply response depends on the value of ε. Finally, if $\varepsilon = \infty$, then there is an infinite supply response to changes in state policies within the common market.

As noted earlier, previous models of common factor markets effectively assume that $\varepsilon = 0$ (for example Wildasin, 1991) and hence that there is a fixed pool of regional labour that moves freely between member states. Yet in most regions, Europe included, the link between the regional factor market and the world is an important one. In the European case immigration into the Union has become highly contentious and has held up implementation of the common labour market. The problem is that states such as France and Germany believe that the policies of other states, such as Italy, encourage the inward migration of too many migrants from outside the Union. Once in, these people are then free to move to other states, such as Germany and France. What this means is that through its independent public policies, one member state, Italy in this example, can influence the welfare of citizens living in other member states, because it changes the total pool of Union labour (through immigration) as well as the distribution of that labour between member states.

Competition

Many objectives could be pursued by states when choosing tax and public policies. One option is to suppose that they are efficient Pigouvian planners, an assumption often made in models of inter-state competition. We instead suppose that the fixed factor, the immobile landowners, control the public choice process and that the mobile factor is disenfranchised. The interests of the state are therefore synonymous with those of immobile citizens and q_i and t_i are chosen by state i to maximize equation (5). The interests of the mobile factor are ignored by the state, at least directly.

State policies are interdependent in two ways. First, when state i chooses its tax and public good policies to maximize equation (5), then through the internal migration condition, equation (7), these choices affect n_i, and hence n_j. Since state j's net income is a function of n_j, this means that state i's policies affect state j's income. Thus, we capture the direct effect that independent policies of the states have on one another through the common labour market. Second, because we also allow state policies to affect the total supply of labour to the market through the second equilibrium condition, equation (8), there is an additional source of interdependence. In particular, as state i chooses its tax and public good policies it also affects the total supply of labour to the common labour market through the right side of equation (8).

Interdependence raises the prospect that states will act strategically. In keeping with the literature, we adopt an equilibrium concept in which governments believe they can vary their policies without inducing any response from other governments. Each makes its policy choices to maximize the interests of immobile residents, taking as given the tax and public good policies of other states. In other words, states ignore the effect that their policy choices have on other states through the migration condition. However, states are assumed to take account of the migration response to their policies to the extent that this response affects their own welfare.

Thus, the problem of state i is to

$$\operatorname*{Max}_{t_i, q_i}\ X_i = f(n_i) - n_i(w_i - t_i) - q_i$$

$$\text{subject to}\quad u(w_1 - t_1, q_1) = u(w_2 - t_2, q_2)$$

$$n_1 + n_2 = N \cdot \left(\frac{u}{u^*}\right)^{\varepsilon}. \tag{9}$$

The necessary conditions for t_i and q_i in the competitive equilibrium (CE) are

$$t_i : (t_i - w_i n_i)\frac{\partial n_i}{\partial t_i} + n_i = 0, \qquad q_i : (t_i - w_i n_i)\frac{\partial n_i}{\partial q_i} - 1 = 0. \tag{10}$$

The following theorems and lemmas[2] use the necessary conditions to show how states choose their levels of public spending and taxes in the CE. The efficiency of these choices is also assessed.

Theorem 1: q_i and q_j are always provided efficiently in the CE.

The theorem shows that competition between states corrects for the potential inefficiency of the collective choice process by ensuring that the preferences of the disenfranchised group are accounted for in the provision of state public policy. The ability of citizens to 'shop' between states for different public good and tax packages gives states the incentive to take account of their interests indirectly through the migration condition, and to do so in a way that is efficient. This result is a formal demonstration of the competitive federalism notion of Breton (1984) that competition preserves the interests of the disenfranchised.

> *Theorem 2:* States levy positive though different taxes on the mobile factor in the CE.

This second theorem implies that the mobile factor per capita tax differs across states in the CE (except in the symmetric case). Thus, in the CE states choose an efficient supply of the public good and different tax rates on mobile labour.

We now examine whether the CE tax rates are optimal. The standard approach to answering this question in fiscal federalism models with factor mobility is to solve the Pareto-optimal problem (Myers, 1990). Here, the Pareto-optimal problem is to maximize the utility of mobile residents from one state, for example state 1, while holding the utility of the immobile landowners of both states and the utility of the mobile citizens of the other state, for example state 2, at some predetermined level, subject to a national feasibility constraint. The necessary conditions associated with this allocation are then compared with those derived from the CE to assess the efficiency of the latter. The Pareto optimal problem is:

$$\max_{\substack{(x_i, X_i \\ q_i, n_i, L_i)}} u(x_i, q_i)$$

subject to:

$$U(X_1, q_1) = \bar{U}_1, U(X_2, q_2) = \bar{U}_2, u(x_j, q_j) = \bar{u}_j, \frac{\partial n_i}{\partial t_i} =< 0$$

and

$$f_1(n_1, L_1) + f_2(n_2, L_2) - n_1 x_1 - n_2 x_2 - L_1 X_1 - L_2 X_2 - q_1 - q_2 = 0 \qquad (11)$$

> *Lemma 1:* Pareto optimality requires that the mobile group be allocated across states such that $w_1 - x_1 = w_2 - x_2$, which in turn implies that $t_1^* = t_2^*$.

We already know that $t_1^* \neq t_2^*$ in the CE. Therefore, the CE is inefficient, resulting in a sub-optimal allocation of the mobile factor across states. It should be noted that t_1 and t_2 are mobile factor tax externalities (since the public good is pure) and the efficiency condition of lemma 1 simply requires that these externalities be equated in equilibrium.

The public goods in this model are pure. Therefore, the tax externalities are perfect in the sense that they represent a perfect spillover from a migrant to the existing residents of a state. However, the externalities would be present even with less than perfect spillovers (for example impure local public goods). All that is needed for the tax externalities to distort the migration equilibrium is that there be some benefit to others provided by the tax contribution of any one mobile or immobile citizen.

While most public services provided by governments are unlikely to be pure local public goods, as assumed here, it does seem reasonable to expect that many of them have public good characteristics, that is, are impure public goods. For example, if a migrant to Germany makes a tax contribution that is used to fund additional hospitals, schools or roads, one would expect these additional facilities to benefit existing residents to some extent, depending on the degree of congestion associated with such expenditures. While these services are not necessarily pure public goods, they have public good characteristics. Thus, one would expect that in principle tax externalities are important sources of distortion if states tax mobile factors of production. If all state services are pure private goods, an extreme assumption, then the inefficiency characterized here disappears and state tax policies will be fully efficient. In this world, all taxes would be benefit taxes where the tax paid is exactly related to the benefit received, and the CE is efficient.

Note also that states that are rich, in terms of having more fixed factors, or more efficient production technologies, will have higher per capita incomes. In turn, such states will produce greater tax externalities in the competitive equilibrium, depending on the publicness of the services provided with their tax contributions. Such states might, for example, have better roads, schools and public health services, all of which can be enjoyed by migrating citizens from other states or outside the common market. In the European case, the richer states might be France and Germany. Our analysis suggests that these states will draw mobile citizens from other states, attracted by the relatively large tax externalities, as the European common labour market develops. This produces a competitive equilibrium in which the rich states have 'too many' mobile citizens, relative to the optimum defined by lemma 1, while the poorer states have 'too few'.

Apart from the symmetric case, another case where the CE is efficient is as follows:

Lemma 2: If $\varepsilon = \infty$ then $t_1^* = t_2^* = 0$ and the CE is efficient.

From the total labour supply condition, it is also the case that $u = u^*$ when $\varepsilon = \infty$. States must provide a tax and public policy package that yields the world per capita utility for the mobile factor. They lose discretionary power over the return to the mobile factor. Thus, if the mobile factor is perfectly mobile between the common factor market area and the rest of the world, the states will levy a zero mobile factor tax and provide the world utility level. By Theorem 1 they also provide the public good, which is enjoyed by the mobile factor, efficiently. However, the public good is funded entirely by the fixed factor with the mobile factor making no contribution.

Oates and Schwab (1988) have a model with a common factor market. In their model, capital rather than labour is perfectly mobile between the common factor market and the rest of the world. Thus, the Oates and Schwab model is analogous to our labour mobility model with $\varepsilon = \infty$. They obtain a result for capital that is consistent with Lemma 2: that states levy a zero capital tax. The implication for regions such as Europe is that if the emerging common labour market becomes fully integrated with the rest of the world, the tax on mobile labour will tend to zero. The public good, supplied efficiently by Theorem 1, will be funded entirely by the fixed factor, the immobile group.

Cooperation

Generally we expect ε to be less than infinite and the CE to be inefficient.[3] This implies that there is an efficiency role for policy cooperation between states. We now examine the efficiency properties of cooperation between states as representatives of the fixed factor. In doing so, we take the stability of a two-state coalition in which states coordinate their policies as given. Therefore, we do not consider the issue of coalitional stability (this is examined in Burbidge, DePater, Myers and Sengupta, 1997).

Gains to the states from cooperation are twofold. First, they can set tax and public good policies that take into account the migration-induced externality. In other words, they can maximize the joint or regional interest instead of their own individual interests. This creates a cooperative surplus to be divided between states. Second, states are able to exploit the mobile factor, and the scope for this depends on the degree of mobility possessed by the disenfranchised citizens.

It is supposed that states choose t_i and q_i cooperatively to maximize their net aggregate income. The necessary conditions are:

$$t_i : (t_i - w_i' n_i) \frac{\partial n_i}{\partial t_i} + (t_j - w_j' n_j) \frac{\partial n_j}{\partial t_i} + n_i = 0,$$

$$q_i : (t_i - w_i' n_i) \frac{\partial n_i}{\partial q_i} + (t_j - w_j' n_j) \frac{\partial n_j}{\partial q_i} - 1 = 0. \tag{12}$$

The following theorem establishes the efficiency properties of policy cooperation:

Theorem 3:   Supply of the public good and the allocation of the mobile factor are always efficient when states choose their policies cooperatively.

Thus, if states cooperate and choose their policies to make the aggregate net income of the fixed factor as large as possible, it is in their interests to provide the optimal quantity of public good in each state (as in the CE). However, the theorem also establishes that maximizing aggregate net income for the fixed factor requires that the tax rate levied on the mobile factor be identical across states (unlike the CE). Hence, the cooperative outcome in which states choose tax and spending policies cooperatively is efficient in the sense that public spending and the allocation of mobile workers is optimal. Policy cooperation, when states face policy inter-dependence because they share a common factor market, is therefore efficiency-enhancing, relative to the competitive outcome in which states pursue their own self-interest. Indeed, the cooperative outcome is an allocation on the utility possibilities frontier defined between the dominant classes (fixed factor) of each state.

Conclusion

A number of regions of the world, in particular Europe, are creating common regional factor markets in which capital and labour migrate freely across national boundaries. The implication of our analysis is that if member states continue to adopt competitive tax and spending policies in the presence of this mobility, the allocation of mobile factors may be inefficient. This arises due to regional policy interdependencies that are not taken into account by individual nation-states. States have an incentive to adopt 'beggar-thy-neighbour' policies to attract mobile factors, and, in doing so, act against the collective interest of the region as a whole.

The implication is that there may be efficiency gains from policy cooperation in regional common factor markets. Indeed, we have shown that if states cooperate to maximize their joint net income, such cooperation can yield an efficient spatial allocation of mobile resources within the region, and an efficient level of public spending. The innovation has been to show that this is so even when the common factor market is integrated with the world factor market.

Finally, it should be noted that we have not shown how cooperation affects the welfare of the mobile disenfranchised group. Therefore, we do not say whether cooperation is equitable, only that it is efficiency-enhancing.

Notes

1 Existing models of common labour markets, for example Wildasin (1991), assume ε equal to zero and hence that there is a fixed common labour market pool with no inward or outward migration. As far as we are aware, there has been no analysis of the more general case where mobile labour can migrate between the common labour market and the world, as in our model. Yet this is an important feature of common factor markets, including the European Union.

2 Proofs of these theorems and lemmas are available from the authors on request.

3 Myers (1990) argues that states might make optimal transfers voluntarily among themselves to secure an efficient distribution of mobile factors without any need for central intervention or cooperation. However, in models of the type constructed here, there is a conflict of interest between states. This means that states have no incentive to make optimal transfers (voluntarily) in the CE.

References

Breton, A. (1984) 'Towards a Theory of Competitive Federalism', in A. Breton, G. Galeotti, P. Salmon and R. Wintrobe (eds), Villa Colombella Papers on Federalism, Proceedings of the Seminar held at Villa Colombella, *European Journal of Political Economy*, Perugia, Italy, September 1984.

Burbidge, J.B. and Myers, G.M. (1994) 'Redistribution Within and Across the Regions of a Federation', *Canadian Journal of Economics*, vol. 27(3) (August), pp. 620–36.

Burbidge, J.B., DePater, J.A., Myers, G.M. and Sengupta, A. (1997) 'A Coalition-Formation Approach to Equilibrium Federations and Trading Blocs', *American Economic Review*, vol. 87(5) (December), pp. 940–56.

Myers, G. (1990) 'Optimality, Free Mobility and Regional Authority in a Federation', *Journal of Public Economics*, vol. 43.

Oates, W.E. and Schwab, R.M. (1988) 'Economic Competition Among Jurisdictions: Efficiency Enhancing or Distortion Inducing?', *Journal of Public Economics*, vol. 35, pp. 333–54.

Scotchmer, S. (1986) 'Local Public Goods in an Equilibrium: How Pecuniary Externalities Matter', *Regional Science and Urban Economics*, vol. 16, pp. 463–81.

Wildasin, D.E. (1991) 'Income Redistribution in a Common Labour Market', *American Economic Review*, vol. 81(4) (September).

10
Inside Australia's Contingent Protection Black Box

Donald Feaver and Kenneth Wilson

F13

F14

Introduction

For most countries, the globalization of the world economy has meant an increase in competitive pressures affecting the performance of domestic industries. Although the adjustment to new levels of competition has posed a challenge for some domestic industries and firms, the adjustment process is made more difficult if import competition is artificially competitive because of unfair trade practices.

The regulation of unfair international trade practices has prompted a debate revolving around the definition of what constitutes 'unfair trade'. A fine line exists between goods that are sold at highly competitive prices and those that are sold at anti-competitive prices. Consequently, efforts to clarify an economic concept of unfair or anti-competitive trade has diverged from the development of a political/legal definition of unfair trade under international trade agreements including the General Agreement on Tariffs and Trade 1994 (GATT).

The legal definition of unfair trade under the GATT is contained in the provisions regulating the trade practices of dumping and subsidization, anti-dumping/countervailing duty (AD/CVD, law and policy, Article VI and XVI). However, in recent years it has become apparent that some members of the World Trade Organization (WTO) are using AD/CVD law and policy as an instrument of protection rather than as a mechanism with which to regulate unfair trade. Several procedural features of the AD/CVD process provide ample opportunity for abuse and manipulation of the process. Figure 10.1 illustrates that a routine AD/CVD inquiry involves two investigations – first is the investigation into the *unfair trade practice*, and second is the *material injury determination*.[1] In focusing on the second step, Tharakan and Waelbroeck (1994, p. 171) conclude that 'those who are

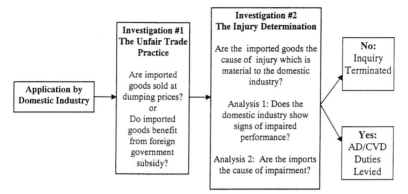

Figure 10.1 Anti-dumping investigations

interested in restraining the misuse of the anti-dumping provisions should concentrate their attention on the injury determination mechanism'.

Under the GATT Anti-Dumping and Subsidies Codes (hereafter the Codes), the material injury determination stipulates that only dumped or subsidized goods that *cause or threaten material injury* will be subject to AD/CVD action.[2] It is reasonably settled opinion that the multilateral rules direct regulatory authorities to conduct two distinct inquiries: (1) whether a domestic industry *is being injured* (the injury analysis); and (2) whether the unfair trade practice *is causing* the injury (the causation analysis) (Feaver and Wilson, 1998). Therefore, evidence of material injury is only the *first* necessary condition to obtaining a positive material injury determination (Kaplan, 1991).

The *second* condition, which is the focus of this chapter, is the most technically complicated and least administratively transparent aspect of the material injury determination. Bound up within it is the regulatory requirement that a *causal link* between dumping or subsidization and material injury must also be established. Although this requirement may appear simple on the surface, in practice 'unravelling an often confusing web of cause and effect is a precarious task' (Carmichael, 1986). This task is further complicated because the Codes provide very little clear guidance as to the precise method by which regulatory authorities are expected to arrive at satisfactory answers to the questions these requirements pose.

It is uncertain what method, if any, the Australian Anti-Dumping Authority (ADA) uses to establish whether a causal link exists. In its defence, whereas the multilateral rules provide insufficient guidance, the Australian law provides even less direction as to how the causation requirement is to be fulfilled. Consequently, the ADA has had to develop administrative and economic approaches to resolving the question within a legislative vacuum.

The aim of this chapter is simple, it is to examine the causation analysis in greater depth to gain a better understanding of the influences and factors the ADA considers in establishing causation. We present the first empirical model of contingent protection that, within an appropriate theoretical and regulatory framework, examines the decision-making processes of an AD/CVD regulatory authority in establishing the causation requirement under AD/CVD law and policy.

Regulatory imperatives

Most AD/CVD authorities around the world conduct the injury determination by endeavouring to answer the two economic questions: (1) whether a domestic industry *is being injured* (the injury analysis); and (2) whether the unfair trade practice *is causing* the injury (the causation analysis) (Kaplan, 1991).[3] A counter-intuitive feature of the injury determination is that, under the bifurcated analytical process, an *effects* analysis is conducted before an investigation into the precise cause, or causes, of a domestic industry's poor economic health. This occurs, as illustrated in Figure 10.2, for practical reasons because in the course of investigating the economic circumstances surrounding whether the domestic industry is suffering injury, valuable information helpful in determining causation is also acquired.

If it is found that a domestic industry is injured (thereby answering question 1 in the affirmative), the next step involves disentangling the complex interrelationship between *diminished domestic industrial perform-ance* and the extent to which the injury is being *caused by unfairly traded imports*. However, practical difficulties arise in establishing the causal link between the imports and injury where the domestic industry's poor performance can be linked to several contributing causes of injury.[4]

The methods of economic analysis used by regulatory authorities to, first, assess injury and, second, establish causation are not explicitly provided in the Codes. Nevertheless, the Codes do direct that a non-exhaustive list of economic factors be investigated and considered. Although these factors are listed as part of the injury analysis, a subsequent direction provides that the same factors should be considered in establishing causation. Consequently, a question of interpretation arises as to whether the same or different legal standards of assessment and hence economic analytical procedures must be used to satisfy the requirements of the separate economic questions.

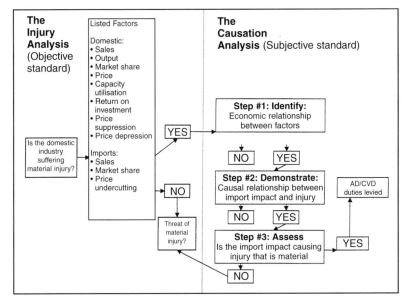

Figure 10.2 Inside the black box of contingent protection

It is suggested elsewhere that the Codes provide insufficient direction as to the treatment of the listed factors (Banks, 1990; Willet, 1996). However, an analysis of several key and fundamental distinctions between the injury and causation analysis provide the foundation for an interpretation that supports an analytical framework for the causation analysis.

First, the Code obligations include an important *substantive* difference between the injury and causation requirements by providing different analytical standards of assessment. On the one hand, the Codes provide that the injury test is satisfied if, using an *objective* standard of assessment, an observation that the economic condition of industry has deteriorated can be made.[5] By contrast, the causation test imposes a more rigorous subjective assessment standard. This requires that the causal link between the injury and the unfair trade practice be established by means of a *demonstration* that the dumped or subsidized imports are the cause of material injury.[6] In practice, the objective injury standard can be derived from static analysis. However, the causation demonstration implies that a dynamic analysis requiring more sophisticated economic techniques must be applied.

Further evidence that the Codes require a separate analysis of injury and causation arises from an important *procedural* distinction included in the Codes. The Codes direct that the objective observation of injury be conducted by examining a non-exhaustive list of economic factors indicative of the economic health of the domestic industry. The purpose of this investigation is to identify *directional trends in the movement* of key economic factors that provide evidence as to the overall health of the domestic industry. By contrast, the causation analysis focuses on the identification of *causal relationships between factors in light of their directional movements*. The purpose of this investigation is to provide the evidentiary basis for a *demonstration* of any 'cause and effect' relationship between the impact of the unfairly traded imports and the injury.

In briefly summarizing the Code requirements, and as shown in Figure 10.2, a causal link will be established if the impact of dumped and subsidized import shows:

1 evidence of an *economic relationship* between negative directional movements in listed factors (taking into account external factors);
2 sufficient to *demonstrate* injury as a result of import impact to the domestic industry; that
3 is *material* in magnitude.

However, the Codes omit to clarify three important elements that would assist national regulators. First, there is no guidance with respect to the method by which the demonstration requirement should be conducted. Second, although the Codes direct that *all* factors contributing to any injury other than dumped or subsidized imports must be considered, no method for separating between competing causes of injury is described. Finally, the Codes do not specify the measure of magnitude or degree of injury that is required to satisfy the 'material' requirement.

Therefore, in briefly summarizing the Code requirements, a basic analytical framework is proposed in a stepwise fashion as follows:

Step 1:   identify all economic factors showing evidence of an economic relationship between those factors and the injury being suffered by the domestic industry;

Step 2:   demonstrate a causal relationship between the impact of the dumped imports and the injury; and

Step 3:   assess whether the magnitude of the impact of imports alone is causing injury which is 'material'.

These steps provide a useful framework for considering the material injury determination. However, the absence of a clear description in the Codes of the mechanical processes required to conduct appropriate economic analysis has led to the situation where different national regulators have developed different analytical approaches of varying degrees of economic sophistication and legal fairness. Furthermore, to the extent that there are deficiencies inherent in the Code provisions, this is further exacerbated where national legislators have failed to enact transparently the more basic, but subtle, aspects of the Code requirements as part of national laws.

The causation analysis under Australian law

Even though the Codes can be interpreted as substantively and procedurally distinguishing between the injury and causation requirements, like US AD/CVD laws, the Australian law does not: (1) prescribe the objective injury and subjective causation assessment standards; or (2) direct that regulators conduct the causation analysis by *demonstrating a relationship* between and among movements in the economic factors. Herein lies the basis of the debate which has arisen in the USA as to whether the material injury determination contains a single or two separate analytical requirements (Knoll, 1989; Kaplan, 1991; Boltuck, 1991).

Since AD/CVD authorities must exercise their responsibilities pursuant to national laws, not the GATT rules, the ADA is under no legal obligation to distinguish between the injury and causation requirements. In both the US and Australian contexts, as long as regulators answer the question: *are dumped or subsidized imports causing material injury?*, the means by which it is accomplished cannot be subject to legal challenge (*ICI* v. *Fraser*, 1992, 106 ALR 257). Therefore, this eliminates any statutory obligation to conduct the injury and causation analyses using economically different analytical approaches in order to satisfy the different substantive assessment standards. Furthermore, the door is open to procedurally merge the two analytical steps into a single, unified economic analysis (Knoll, 1989; Boltuck, 1991).

Yet, even though the Customs Act does not provide different analytical standards for the injury and causation analyses, in practice the ADA does analyse injury and causation separately. This does not, however, mean that the ADA transparently follows the Code requirements in their entirety. A subtle, but critical departure by the ADA from the Code requirements is that rather than conducting a subjective *demonstration* of causation, it merely seeks to ascertain *observed* relationships between injury and cause. In using an objective standard of analysis (similar to that used for the injury assessment), the ADA uses a less-economically-sophisticated analytical method in conducting the causation analysis.

The danger in using an objective standard to judge the existence of a causal link is summed up by Kaplan's (1991) assessment of the use by some US International Trade Commission (USITC) Commissioners of an objective standard. In exactly the same respect, the fundamental flaw besetting the ADA's use of an objective test:

> is that the relationship between trends in causation factors and the condition of the domestic industry is never explained and is unreliable. This methodology fails to take into account the plethora of possible explanations for movements in a particular trend and the various alternative relationships between the trend and the condition of the domestic industry. Without a mechanism connecting the trend and the condition of the industry it is *impossible* to distinguish between causation and coincidence (p. 149).

To say that the ADA's use of an objective standard is opaque is an understatement. The inaccuracy, which flows from its reliance on the identification of apparent relationships, opens a great deal of latitude for data interpretation which is not transparent in either its empirical or deductive foundation.

More importantly, the mere identification of economic relationships using the listed or other factors is not the only step in the causation analysis (see Figure 10.2). The analysis is not complete unless the ADA demonstrates that a relationship exists between the import impact and the injury suffered by the domestic industry. Since the ADA does not conduct this demonstration, its analytical approach unravels at this point in the material injury determination.

Furthermore, since no demonstration between the import impact and injury is conducted, it follows that the ADA is in no position to accurately assess whether the extent of the injury caused by the imports qualifies as 'material'. Even disregarding the ADA's ambiguous and economically inadequate definition of the materiality standard as being *not insubstantial, inconsequential or immaterial* (see ADA *Report* No. 4), the ADA's failure to produce any evidence as to the magnitude of the import impact, it is *economically unable* to answer whether or not the imports have caused material injury to the domestic industry. This lack of precision in decision-making processes increases the opportunity, either intentionally or through inadequacy, to produce decisions which are biased or, in the case of the latter criticism, flawed.

Inside the black box of contingent protection

In Feaver and Wilson (1998) we describe the overall material injury determination as a decision-making process occurring within a *black box*. In order to unravel this process and gain better insight into how the ADA conducts the material injury determination, we distinguish between the different types of economic analyses which take place within the black box (see Figure 10.2). We explained how it is open to the Australian Customers Service (ACS) and ADA to decide that the domestic industry:

1   is not suffering any sign of injury, *material* or otherwise; or
2   is showing signs of injury, however, that injury is not *material*; or
3   is suffering *material injury*, but injury which is material has not been *caused* by the dumped or subsidized imports; or
4   is suffering *material injury that has been caused* by the dumped or subsidized imports.

Although corrective duties can only be levied under 4 where both material injury and causation are present, if the domestic industry does not show signs of present injury, or is materially injured for a reason not causally connected to dumped or subsidized imports, the ACS and ADA may still decide that:

5   a threat of material injury is foreseeable and imminent,[7] or
6   the establishment of a new industry is being materially hindered.

In either circumstance, duties can be levied even though the domestic industry has not been injured by dumped or subsidized imports.

   In focusing on the circumstances identified under 4, we assume that the ADA has completed the injury analysis and found in the affirmative that the domestic industry is suffering injury that is material. The challenge is to investigate how the ADA conducts a causation analysis and determines the existence of a causal link between injury and imports. In this regard, we seek to determine what evidence of 'cause' the ADA relies upon to make its finding that causation is present (and hence duties will be levied).

   Central to this question is the ADA's use of the non-exhaustive list of economic factors contained in the Codes and section 269TAE of the Customs Act. Although the ADA states that it proceeds by identifying 'observed' relationships between economic factors which may be indicative of causation, given the different economic characteristics of each factor, a strong argument can be made that each factor provides different economic information. In this regard, some factors are more indicative of injury to the domestic industry, and others indicative of import impact (and, hence, causation). Accordingly, it is useful to subdivide the listed factors into three categories which can be ranked as to their evidentiary weight in demonstrating a reliable evaluation of the impact of the imports and their economic relationship to the injury suffered by the domestic industry.

The first category includes factors consistent with subjective demonstration of causation. These factors are indicative of a direct relationship between domestic performance and import penetration and, for example, include relative changes in market shares and comparative sales increases or decreases. A second category of factors is consistent with a lower objective standard. This category includes, for example, price depression and its relationship to domestic market price changes characterized by the variable price suppression. The cause-and-effect relationship between these variables should be interpreted as providing evidence only of an indirect relationship between import impact and injury. The variables price suppression, and price depression, provide evidence of a strategic pricing response taken by the domestic industry in the face of all competitive pressures. Hence, these variables may be subject to manipulation by the applicants in order to contrive, or strategically manage, the appearance of harm leading to a finding of injury industry (Leidy, 1994; Staiger and Wolack, 1994).

A third category of factors includes a range of non-transparent variables. For example, profitability trends, capacity utilization and employment only provide indirect evidence of the possible effects of import penetration. In their own right, this group of variables provides evidence more of injury to the domestic industry as opposed to causation by dumped or subsidized imports. These are the least transparent factors in respect of the requirement of demonstrating a relationship between the impact of imports and domestic industrial injury.

In a theoretical sense, it follows that in order for the analytical processes used by the ADA to appear to be more economically sound, greater weight should be given by the ADA to the direct 'causation' variables. Much less weight should be given to those variables which indirectly provide evidence of causation. No weight should be given to the opaque injury variables. Furthermore, we have already identified that the ADA conducts a causation analysis by completing only the first step in the causation analysis described in Figure 10.2. Given that the ADA fails to identify those factors that are most economically relevant, by ascribing evidentiary weight to improper variables, the likelihood that it reaches erroneous conclusions is increased. Hence, this issue forms the basis of our empirical investigation into the ADA's causation decision.

Modelling causation

The Codes' substantive ambiguity and lack of procedural direction has stunted the development of empirical models of contingent protection. The broad objective of previous models of contingent protection has been to gain a more precise understanding of the administrative decision-making processes of AD/CVD authorities through the identification of political and economic factors influencing AD/CVD decision-making outcomes. In doing so, researchers have analysed modelling results with a view to seeking evidence of bias in the decision-making process. However, most previous studies modelling contingent protection fail to test decision-making outcomes within an appropriate regulatory/procedural context. In turn, this failure to distinguish between key regulatory requirements has the effect of distorting the performance and interpretation of modelling outcomes.[8]

In all of those studies that examine the material injury determination, none distinguish between the injury and causation analyses as separate steps of the material injury determination. Therefore, previous studies use the final, overall, material injury decision as the dependant variable without sufficiently differentiating between the procedural steps (or their separate economic analyses) which take place within the black box. As we identified above, since certain factors can be classified as having economic characteristics illustrative of either import impact or injury, previous studies have failed to specify models that test the importance of independent variables in an accurate regulatory context.

In attempting to model the causation decisions of the ADA we are aiming to answer several questions. Given the apparent inconsistency between the Codes and the Australian law, does the ADA appear to adopt an approach that is consistent with the Codes, given that the Codes require a subjective demonstration of causation. This leads us to test the following hypothesis.

> *Hypothesis 1* That the approach taken by the ADA appears, on the surface, to satisfy the GATT requirement of a subjective demonstration of causation.

However, we know that the ADA examines a broader range of factors consistent with the Australian law that shifts the analytical approach from a subjective to an objective assessment of a causal relationship. This leads us to test a second hypothesis.

> *Hypothesis 2* That the approach taken by the ADA appears to conform to a transparent objective standard of causal link.

Finally, because of the opaqueness of the ADA's decision-making processes, we expect that a model that includes a combination of subjective factors, transparent objective factors and opaque objective factors better explains causal link decisions. Hence we test a third hypothesis.

> *Hypothesis 3* That the causal link decisions of the ADA can be best explained by a model that includes non-transparent decision factors.

Accordingly, we present three models to test these hypotheses.

Data and modelling framework

Because the ADA does not use a clearly-defined analytical process to demonstrate if a causal link exists between dumping, subsidization and material injury to a domestic industry, a data-set comprised of variables corresponding to the principal factors mentioned by the ADA in its *Reports* has been constructed. These variables, in large part, correspond with the factors listed in subsection 269TAE of the Customs Act and the Codes. Because the Australian law does not explain what the factors are intended to indicate, both in isolation and relative to each other, we have treated them equally for the purpose of assessing their statistical influence as utilized by the ADA. In addition, as the material injury and causation assessments made by the ADA are identical irrespective of whether the unfair trade practice complained of is dumping or subsidization, it was not necessary to distinguish between injury resulting from the two different causes.

The majority of the data used in this analysis are contained in ADA *Reports* nos. 1–122, inclusive, published in the period January 1988 to January 1994, which provide a rich source of material for the researcher. The data-set covers a range of quantitative and qualitative variables identified in the relevant Australian law and the Codes; the variables are discussed below.

Where data on a specific variable was not provided in a single *Report*, in some cases it is possible to derive the data from information provided in other ADA or ACS Reports. An infrequent source of data proved to be Federal Court judgements, both reported and unreported. If these sources proved unhelpful, data was obtained from the Australian Bureau of Statistics (ABS) and Victoria University's Tradedata database, the least preferable sources of data. The ABS data on imports is unreliable because the ACS and ADA undertake to produce their own estimates of volume and price effects. Data submitted by parties to an inquiry cannot be considered reliable unless the ACS and ADA investigations verify it.

A second issue relates to the number of respondents or countries from which imports of a particular dumped or subsidized good arrive. In many of the ADA *Reports*, injury is analysed in light of effects of dumped or subsidized imports from several different national sources. Although a single material injury analysis of an industry's economic condition suffices irrespective of whether an application is brought against one or several sources, a separate causation analysis must be undertaken for each country against which an application is brought. Hence, a single observation represents a nation against which an application has been brought.[9] Data on all ADA causal-link assessments are included irrespective of whether they originated from dumping or subsidies cases. As causation assessments are not undertaken during the course of revocation inquiries,[10] these were rejected.

Because the direction requiring the consideration of the factors enumerated in the statute is permissive, the ADA considers only those factors that are appropriate under the circumstances. Consequently, the choice of variables was restricted to those for which a complete data-set could be obtained. Given these qualifications we have been able to construct a data-set comprising 184 separate causation analyses.

A subjective model of causation

The first model conforms to an interpretation of the Codes requiring that causation be established by means of a subjective demonstration. This entails an analysis of the relationship between the economic impact of the imports and the health of the domestic industry. A subjective assessment of this relationship requires a clear economic link between the cause of injury (the dumped imports) and its effects on domestic industry. Therefore we include only variables with a direct import impact. That is, this model includes only economic factors capable of demonstrating a direct relationship between imports and injury.

Direct import impact variables

ΔIMPT	Change in sales of the imported like-good over the inquiry period from 'dumping' countries, measured as the percentage change in sales turnover of the 'dumped' imported like-goods.
ΔDOMT	Change in sales of the domestically produced like-good over the inquiry period, measured as the percentage change in sales turnover of the domestic like-good.
IMPSH	Share of the total Australian market held by the 'dumped' imported like-good at the end of the inquiry period, measured as the proportion of sales turnover.
ΔIMPSH	Percentage change in the share of the total Australian market held by the 'dumped' imported like-good.
DOMSH	Share of the total Australian market held by the domestically-produced good at the end of the inquiry period, measured as the share of sales turnover.
ΔDOMSH	Percentage change in the share of the total Australian market held by the domestically-produced good.
PUC	Price undercutting; whether or not the selling price of the imported like-good was consistently below that of the domestically-produced good (1 = below, 0 = otherwise).
DM	The size of the dumping margin or subsidy expressed as the per cent difference between the export price and normal value.
CI	Whether dumped imports from several countries identified in a single application were aggregated for the purpose of the causation analysis in accordance with the cumulative injury rule (1 = cumulation, 0 = otherwise).
AD	Amount of imports expressed as a per cent identified as having originated from a country named in an application as having been dumped.

Dependent variable:

CALINK	Whether or not the ADA determined that a causal link between material injury and dumped or subsidized imports could be established (1 = yes, 0 = otherwise).

The subjective model (SM) may be represented as:

$$\text{CALINK}_{SM} = f(\overset{+}{\Delta IMPT}, \overset{-}{\Delta DOMT}, \overset{+}{IMPSH}, \overset{+}{\Delta IMPSH}, \overset{-}{DOMSH}, \overset{-}{\Delta DOMSH},$$

$$\overset{+}{PUC}, \overset{-}{DM}, \overset{+}{CI}, \overset{+}{AD}). \tag{1}$$

The expected pattern of the signs here requires brief explanation. The positive signing of ΔIMPT, IMPSH and ΔIMPSH are expected since increases in the sales and market share of the imported like-good are clearly indicative of import impact. Moreover, ΔDOMT and ΔDOMSH will enter with negative signs for similar reasons.[11]

Turning to the qualitative variables, all other things held equal, evidence of price undercutting (PUC) increases the likelihood of a finding of causation. A positive sign on DM is expected because the larger the dumping margin, the greater the negative impact on domestic industry is expected.[12] Similarly, the proportion of the imports imported at dumping prices (AD) and whether dumped imports from several sources are cumulated and treated by the ADA as a single homogenous source (CI) are both signed positively.

The ADA faces a binary choice between finding evidence of causation or not. If we denote a decision of causation by CALINK = 1 and a decision of no causal link by CALINK = 0, then we can model the probability of the ADA making a positive finding that a causal link between imports and injury does exist by a standard probit model:

$$Prob(CALINK = 1) = F(\mathbf{X'b})$$

$$Prob(CALINK = 0) = 1\text{-}F(\mathbf{X'b})$$

where F denotes the cumulative normal distribution function, X denotes the vector of variables introduced above, and b is a vector of parameters. The maximum likelihood estimates of b are known to be consistent and asymptotically efficient.

A transparent objective model of causation

Because the Australian law allows the ADA to consider a range of additional indirect impact variables consistent with an objective standard of judgement, we suggest the inclusion of the following additional variables. That is, the model now includes factors indirectly indicative of a causal relationship, as well as the direct injury impact variables. These indirect impact variables do not provide direct evidence of import impact and injury. Instead these indirect impact variables provide only circumstantial evidence of injury.

Indirect impact variables

PSUP   Price suppression; evidence that the domestic industry was unable to pass through to sales price any cost increases of making and selling the domestically produced good (1 = unable, 0 = otherwise).

PDEP   Price depression; whether the actual sales price of the domestically produced good fell during the inquiry period in real terms (1 = fall, 0 = otherwise).

ΔPIND   Whether the ratio of profit to domestic industry's sales revenue changes (1 = increase, 0 = otherwise).

ΔEMP   Whether there was a decline in the number of persons employed by the domestic industry (1 = decline, 0 = otherwise).

ΔCU   Whether there was a change in the utilization of plant/production capacity of the domestic industry (1 = decline, 0 = otherwise).

The transparent objective (TO) model may be represented as:

$$\text{CALINK}_{TO} = f(\overset{+}{\Delta\text{IMPT}}, \overset{-}{\Delta\text{DOMT}}, \overset{+}{\text{IMPSH}}, \overset{+}{\Delta\text{IMPSH}}, \overset{-}{\text{DOMSH}}, \overset{-}{\Delta\text{DOMSH}},$$

$$\overset{+}{\text{PUC}}, \overset{+}{\text{DM}}, \overset{+}{\text{CI}}, \overset{+}{\text{AD}}, \overset{+}{\text{PSUP}}, \overset{-}{\text{PDEP}}, \overset{+}{\Delta\text{PIND}}, \overset{+}{\Delta\text{EMP}}, \Delta\text{CU}) \quad (2)$$

All else held equal, price suppression (PSUP), price depression (PDEP), declines in employment (ΔEMP) and declines in capacity utilization (ΔCU) are all likely to increase the likelihood of a finding of causation, and, therefore, are signed positively. (ΔPIND, denoting increases in industry profits, is signed negatively on the grounds that an increase in industry profitability is less likely to lead to a finding of causation.)

An opaque objective model of causation

The imprecision and opaqueness of the Australian law allows the ADA to consider other factors beyond those identified above. That is, the ADA may also consider factors indicative of injury only, which do not provide any evidence of a causal relationship. For instance the ADA may take into account the ill-defined 'outside circumstances' as a factor contributing to injury. We therefore suggest the inclusion of the following additional non-injury impact variables.

Other injury related variables

ENCS   Whether the ADA identified and evaluated the effect of outside circumstances as factors apart from the imports that could be observed as a contributing cause of injury to the domestic industry and intimated relative influence (0 = no influence, 1 = minor, 2 = moderate, 3 = major).

ΔTOTMKT Percentage change in the total domestic market measured as aggregate sales of imported and domestically-produced like-goods.

TRF The level of tariff imposed upon the imported like-good.

PROFLOSS Whether, on the whole, the domestic industry experienced profitability or losses (1 = loss, 0 = otherwise).

ΔCTMS Cost to make and sell, measured as the change in the cost of the inputs and sales expenses (1 = increase, 0 = otherwise).

The Opaque Objective (OO) model may be represented as

$$\text{CALINK}_{OO} = f(\overset{+}{\Delta\text{IMPT}}, \overset{-}{\Delta\text{DOMT}}, \overset{+}{\text{IMPSH}}, \overset{+}{\Delta\text{IMPSH}}, \overset{-}{\text{DOMSH}}, \overset{-}{\Delta\text{DOMSH}},$$

$$\overset{+}{\text{PUC}}, \overset{+}{\text{DM}}, \overset{+}{\text{CI}}, \overset{+}{\text{AD}}, \overset{+}{\text{PSUP}}, \overset{+}{\text{PDEP}}, \overset{-}{\Delta\text{PIND}}, \overset{+}{\Delta\text{EMP}}, \overset{+}{\Delta\text{CU}},$$

$$\overset{-}{\text{ENCS}}, \overset{-}{\Delta\text{TOTMKT}}, \overset{+}{\text{TRF}}, \overset{-}{\text{PROFLOSS}}, \overset{+}{\Delta\text{CTMS}}) \qquad (3)$$

The variable ENCS requires further explanation. It is included to indicate where the ADA has made reference to outside economic events in its deliberations over causation, and is introduced to capture this opaque decision process; a weighted dummy variable has been constructed to capture this impact. It is clear from reading many *Reports* that where the ADA assigns importance to 'outside events', this diminishes the likelihood of a finding of causation between dumped imports and injury. ΔTOTMKT is expected to be negative since a declining domestic industry will be sensitive to any import competition. However, a declining domestic market in its own right is incapable of demonstrating causation. The higher the level of tariff imposed upon the imported like-good then the more likely is there to be a finding of causation. PROFLOSS, denoting cases where a domestic industry records accounting losses during the inquiry period is signed negatively, while CTMS is positively signed.

Results

In Table 10.1 we report the estimated probit coefficients, *t*-ratios and diagnostics for all three models. Column 1 contains results for the subjective model, column 2 provides results for the transparent objective model and column 3, the opaque objective model. A cursory examination

Table 10.1 Probit estimates for causal link determination ($n = 164$)

Regressor	Expected sign	1 (SM model)	2 (TO model)	3 (OO model)
CONSTANT		−4.188	−10.337	−8.632
		(−3.426)	(−4.668)	(−3.152)
Direct import impact variables				
ΔIMPT	(+)	0.133	0.826	0.148
		(1.642)	(0.873)	(1.175)
ΔDOMT	(−)	1.328	1.921	1.189
		(2.249)*	(2.733)**	(1.256)
IMPSH	(+)	3.482	6.140	6.825
		(2.361)**	(2.977)**	(3.089)**
ΔIMPSH	(+)	3.490	7.321	5.803
		(1.199)	(1.724)*	(1.227)
ΔOMSH	(?)	−0.169	1.925	1.119
		(−0.201)	(1.771)*	(0.774)
ΔDOMSH	(−)	−2.740	−3.445	−5.416
		(−1.626)	(−1.727)*	(−2.089)*
PUC	(+)	1.040	0.731	0.253
		(1.891)*	(1.044)	(0.313)
DM	(+)	2.160	2.064	0.730
		(3.071)**	(2.502)**	(0.756)
CI	(+)	0.567	1.424	1.560
		(2.116)*	(3.639)**	(3.597)**
AD	(+)	1.735	2.345	2.390
		(2.275)*	(2.532)**	(2.303)*
Indirect import impact variables				
PSUP	(+)		4.212	4.856
			(3.270)**	(3.331)**
PDEP	(+)		−0.342	−0.508
			(−1.030)	(−0.995)
ΔPIND	(−)		−1.009	−1.605
			(−2.293)*	(−1.663)*
ΔEMP	(+)		1.590	1.231
			(3.406)**	(2.218)*
ΔCU	(+)		0.355	0.834
			(1.107)	(1.878)*
Other injury variables				
ENCS	(−)			−0.759
				(−2.857)**
ΔTOTMKT	(−)			−0.509
				(−0.426)
TRF	(+)			2.262
				(0.928)

Table 10.1 (continued.)

PROFLOSS	(–)			–0.468
				(–0.773)
ΔCTMS	(+)			0.995
				(0.250)
Log Likelihood		–77.686	–59.481	–53.171
LR-test		–112.45	105.94	118.56
Maddala R-square		0.3456	0.4759	0.5147
Cragg–Uhler R-square		0.4630	0.637	0.689
McFadden R-square		0.3091	0.471	0.527
% Correct predictions		79.86	83.53	87.80

Notes: Significance at the 5 per cent level is indicated by * and at the 1 per cent level by ** using a one-tail test of significance, except for DOMSH which is tested with a two-tail test.

of the results indicates that the subjective model performs well with a prediction success of almost 80 per cent. Of the explanatory variables, five are significantly different from zero at acceptable decision levels and enter with expected signs; whether the share of the total Australian market held by the dumped imported like-good at the end of the inquiry period (IMPSH), price undercutting (PUC), dumping margin (DM), cumulative injury (CI), and amount dumped (AD). Of the remaining five variables, only the percentage change in sales of the domestically produced like-good (ΔDOMT) enters significantly with the wrong sign. The remaining four variables enter with the correct sign but are not significantly different from zero.

The results from testing the transparent objective model are contained in Column 2. We see that the predictive success improves to almost 84 per cent and the diagnostics also indicate an improvement over the subjective model. These diagnostics support the superiority of the transparent objective model over the subjective model. All the same variables that are significant in the subjective model continue to be significant in the transparent opaque model. Although ΔDOMSH, the change in the share of the total Australian market held by the domestically-produced like-good, is now significant at the 5 per cent level, and with the expected sign. ΔDOMT continues to be statistically significant but with a counter-intuitive negative sign.

Importantly, three of the additional indirect import impact variables are statistically significant at acceptable decision levels and enter with correct signs. Of these, PSUP, evidence that the domestic industry was unable to pass through to sales price any cost increases of making and selling the domestically-produced like-good is significant at the 1 per cent level. Similarly, change in employment (ΔEMP) is also significant at the 1 per cent level.

Column 3 includes the results obtained from a test of the opaque objective model. Prediction success again improves to almost 88 per cent and all three R^2 statistics improve. Important changes can be observed in the performance of explanatory variables. We observe that a fourth indirect import impact variable ΔCU, the change in capacity utilization, is now statistically significant at acceptable decision levels along with PSUP, ΔPIND and ΔEMP. PSUP is statistically the most important indirect import impact variable in this model. As before, of the direct import impact variables, IMPSH, ΔDOMSH, CI and AD are all significantly different from zero at acceptable decision levels. Interestingly, DM is no longer significant, just failing the 5 per cent test, whilst ΔDOMT, which previously entered with a counter-intuitive and significant negative sign is no longer significantly different from zero at acceptable decision levels.

Turning to the specific hypothesis identified above, the pattern of regression results across all three models confirms our prior beliefs. First, model 1 was constructed using only direct import impact variables capable of testing for a direct cause and effect relationship. Given that model 1 emulates the subjective demonstration standard contained in the Codes, it provides a useful framework for testing whether causal link decisions appear to conform broadly with the multilateral standard. Therefore, the results of model 1 give the appearance that the ADA's causation analysis is not inconsistent with Australia's multilateral obligations.

However, as we know, the ADA examines a broader range of factors and uses an objective standard of assessing changes in the 'observed' relationship among the variables. Hence, this led us to identify a second hypothesis. The good performance of the indirect import impact variables combined with the improved overall performance of the model confirms our prior belief that the causal link decisions of the ADA appear to conform to a broader transparent objective standard.

Finally, because of the opaqueness of the ADA's decision-making process and its lack of a clear methodology of assessing causation, we further hypothesize that the ADA considers an even broader range of non-transparent decision-factors. The improved performance of the model, which now includes 'other' injury variables, combined with the statistical significance of ENCS (a very non-transparent proxy for the propensity of the ADA to consider the importance of outside circumstances), supports our belief that the causation decisions of the ADA are best explained by a model that encompasses non-transparent explanatory variables.

Conclusion

The processes national AD/CVD regulatory authorities must follow in disentangling the interrelationship between *diminished domestic industrial performance* and the extent it is *caused by unfairly traded imports* is unclear. The want of a clear theoretical and administrative framework has contributed to a situation whereby, according to Pangratis and Vermulst (1994) the:

> inadequate guidance provided by the Code(s) combined with the lack of consensus on the economic analyses concerning basic injury-related concepts has resulted in a multitude of national rules and practices concerning the injury-side of the anti-dumping (and countervailing) instrument(s). (p. 26)

The lack of consensus is attributed to the ambiguity and lack of prescription of the Codes. More importantly, this problem is exacerbated by the failure of Code signatories to legislate subtle, but critical, requirements into national AD/CVD rules.

The regression results confirm our belief that the ADA uses methods of determining causation that leaves it open to the accusation of bias. This is highlighted by the improved performance of the modelling framework as we move from a very transparent subjective model of economic cause and effect to increasingly non-transparent models incorporating a range of indirect and opaque explanatory variables. In particular, the statistical significance of PSUP and ENCS are cause for concern. Whereas PSUP is influential in improving the ability of the regression model to explain positive findings in favour of causation, ENCS is important in better explaining those situations where the ADA uses the opaque excuse of 'other circumstances' to find against causation.

The policy implications of this outcome are clear. Any review of AD/ CVD law and policy must tackle the difficult problem of seeking a method of establishing causation which is consistent with the rules designed to govern the regulatory process, economic theory and fairness in the decision-making process. At present, the causation analysis does not exhibit any of these qualities and, therefore, remains the weakest aspect of the material injury determination and the entire AD/CVD decision-making process.

A revision of the rules designed to inject greater transparency into the decision-making process would alleviate some concerns surrounding the protectionist characteristics of the process. In addition, a more transparent material injury determination should be restricted to an analysis of the competitive relationship between the dumped imports and alleged injury caused to the domestic industry. This focus would reduce the opportunity for AD/CVD regulators to resort to a consideration of extraneous factors that open the door to abusing the process to achieve biased and protectionist outcomes.

Notes

1   As the focus of this chapter is not the dumping margin/subsidization investigation, it does not examine the methods by which either is calculated. For a description of the EC calculation process see Waer (1993) and Vermulst and Waer (1991); refer to Customs Act section 269TAC for Australian procedures. The existence, or magnitude, of a dumping margin or subsidy may be influenced by the choice of assessment method regulatory authorities are directed to use under the GATT Codes and national law. The assessment method is, in large part, determined by the circumstances of each good's importation.

2   The material injury determination is the subject of Article 3 of the Agreement on Implementation of Article VI of the General Agreement on Tariffs and Trade 1994 (the Anti-Dumping Code); and Article 15 of the Agreement on Subsidies and Countervailing Measures (the Subsidies Code). Apart from their differing application to different trade practices, the material injury provisions of the two Articles are nearly identical in all substantive respects.

3   Under US law, other than reference to the requirement that dumped imports must be found to 'cause or threaten to cause material injury' no distinction between material injury and causation is made. Several US authors have proposed that, consistent with the law, the relationship between injury and causation can, in theory as well as practice, be established (using counter-factual models) within a single analytical step (Knoll; 1989, Murray and Rousslang, 1989; Boltuck, 1991; Francois, 1992). Therefore, the argument is put forward that the two-step approach is unnecessary and contributes to inaccurate decision-making. Although this holds true of the US and Australian law, the Codes do, however, distinguish between injury and causation requirements.

4   Among contributors to poor performance are fluctuations in the business cycle, domestic macro-economic factors such as interest rates and labour costs, domestic and international low-cost competition, poor internal efficiencies, qualitative factors contributing to consumers substitution, to name just a few.

5   Article 3.1 of the Anti-Dumping Code states that 'a determination of injury ... shall be based on positive evidence and involve an *objective* examination ...'

6   Article 3.5 of the Anti-Dumping Code states that it 'must be demonstrated that the dumped imports are, through the effects of dumping ... causing injury within the meaning of this Agreement.

7 For further information regarding the threat of material injury determination see Feaver (1997).
8 In Feaver and Wilson (1998), we describe how other researchers have developed several different approaches towards modelling contingent protection (for example Finger, Hall and Nelson, 1982; Tharakan and Waelbroeck, 1994; Baldwin and Steagall, 1994). Although the broad objective of most of these studies has been to gain a better insight into the influences affecting the administrative decision-making processes of AD/CVD authorities, different modelling approaches have been developed to test whether regulatory outcomes can be ascribed to a range of political and economic considerations. However, it is our belief that most previous studies modelling contingent protection fail to test decision-making outcomes within appropriate regulatory/procedural context. In turn, this failure to distinguish between key regulatory requirements has the effect of distorting the performance and interpretation of modelling outcomes.
9 Where a domestic industry identifies dumped or subsidized imported goods from more than one country, applications are brought against each country from which those goods originate. For example, in *Report* nos. 34, 38 and 40, applications for duties were made against 16 countries. As the aggregate effect of all imports affected the domestic industry as a single entity, a single injury assessment was able to capture the cumulative effect of those imports (in addition to other factors influencing the industry's performance).
10 The ADA following an earlier positive finding against a foreign exporter conducts a revocation inquiry. The foreign exporter may apply at a later date to have the duty against its product revoked.
11 In most cases, IMPSH and DOMSH do not add to equal 100% of the market, and are therefore not perfectly multicollinear, because IMPSH reflects only the market share of imports originating from countries named in the dumping complaint. As non-dumped imports from other sources are not included in IMPSH, together the sum of IMPSH, DOMSH and non-dumped imports equals 100% of the market.
12 This argument is somewhat misleading in that the dumping margin measures the price below the home market price at which the import is sold. If the normal value is high relative to world or export market prices, a much lower export price will be required in order for that product to generate sales in a more price-competitive market. Therefore, the size of the dumping margin should not be construed as being an indication of price undercutting in the export market.

References

Antidumping Authority (various years) *Reports*, Canberra: Australian Government Publishing Service.
Baldwin, R. and Steagall, J.W. (1994) 'An Analysis of ITC Decisions in Antidumping, Countervailing Duty and Safeguard Cases' *Weltwirtschaftliches Archives*, vol. 130, pp. 290–307.
Banks, G. (1990) 'Australia's Anti-Dumping Experience', The World Bank Working Paper series no. WPS 551, December.
Boltuck, R. (1991) 'Assessing the Effects on the Domestic Industry of Price Dumping', in P.K.M. Tharakan (ed.), *Policy Implications of Antidumping Measures*, Amsterdam: North-Holland.

Carmicheal, W.B. (1986) 'Review of the Customs Tariff (Anti-Dumping) Act: Submission by Chairman', Industries Assistance Commission, Canberra, February.

Feaver, D. (1997) 'Forces Affecting the Administration of Anti-Dumping and Countervailing Policy in Australia: Statutory Failure or Regulatory Capture?' *Australian Journal of Public Administration*, vol. 56, pp. 67–77.

— and Wilson, K. (1998) 'Unlocking Australia's Contingent Protection Black Box, *Economic Record*, vol. 74, pp. 62–73.

Finger, J. Hall, H. and Nelson, D. (1982) 'The Political Economy of Administered Protection', *American Economic Review*, vol. 72, pp. 452–66.

Francois, J. (1992) 'Countervailing the Effects of Subsidies: An Economic Analysis' *Journal of World Trade*, vol. 36, pp. 5–13.

Kaplan, S. (1991) 'Injury and Causation in USITC Anti-Dumping Determinations: Five Recent Approaches' in P.K.M. Tharakan (ed.), *Policy Implications of Antidumping Measures*, Amsterdam: North-Holland.

Knoll, M. (1989) 'An Economic Approach to the Determination of Injury under United States Antidumping and Countervailing Law', *International Law and Politics*, vol. 22, pp. 37–116.

Leidy, M.P. (1994) 'Trade Policy and Indirect Rent-Seeking: A Synthesis of Recent Work', *Economics and Politics*, vol. 6(2), pp. 97–118.

Murray, T. and Rousslang, D. (1989) 'A Method for Estimating Injury Caused by Unfair Trade Practices', *International Review of Law and Economics*, vol. 9, pp. 149–64.

Pangratis, A. and Vermulst, E. (1994) 'Injury in Anti-Dumping Proceedings: The Need to Look Beyond the Uruguay Round Results', *Journal of World Trade*, vol. 28(5) pp. 61–96.

Staiger, R.W. and Wolack, F.A. (1994) 'Measuring Industry Specific protection: Antidumping in the United States', *NBER Working Paper Series No. W4696*, (Cambridge, Mass.: National Bureau of Economic Research.

Tharakan, P.K.M. and Waelbroeck, J. (1994) 'Antidumping and Countervailing Duty Decisions in the EC and in the US', *European Economic Review*, vol. 38, pp. 171–93.

Vermulst, E. and Waer, P. (1991) 'The Calculation of Injury Margins in EC Anti-Dumping Proceedings', *Journal of World Trade*, vol. 25, no. 6, pp. 5–42.

Waer, P. (1993) 'Constructed Normal Values in EC Dumping Margin Calculations', *Journal of World Trade*, vol. 27, no. 4, pp. 47–80.

Willet, L. (1996) *Inquiry into Australia's Antidumping System (The Willet Report)*, Canberra: Australian Government Publishing Service.

Part IV

International Comparisons of Economic Performance

11

Ō19 E23
Ō47
F43

Export-Led Growth in Asia: Long-Run Relationships and Structural Change

*Peter M. Summers**

(US, Japan, S. Korea, Malaysia, Taiwan)

Introduction

This chapter presents new evidence in support of the export-led growth hypothesis in a small group of Asian countries and the United States. The evidence comes from an *ad hoc* model similar to ones used in many empirical investigations of export-led growth, which is really just a plausible specification of a possible cointegrating relationship between output, exports, imports and the terms of trade.

I find, in all the countries studied, that a cointegrating relationship exists between (the levels of) exports, imports, the terms of trade, industrial production and OECD output. There is also, however, considerable evidence of structural instability in these cointegrating relationships. In particular, it appears that in all the countries studied there was a significant structural break in the relationship between exports and industrial output. For Japan and the USA, this break seems to coincide with the dramatic rise in the US current account deficit in 1982–84. In the other countries, the break occurred somewhat later, around the time of the Plaza Accord.

* This material was prepared for a conference on 'Creating an International Competitive Economy', held by the Institute for Research into International Competitiveness (IRIC) at Curtin University in Western Australia. I am grateful to the conference participants, the editors, and to Ólan Henry for helpful discussions. I also wish to thank Bruce Hansen and James MacKinnon for making their computer code available via the Internet (at http://www2.bc.edu/~hansenb/14 June and http://qed.econ.queensu.ca/pub/faculty/mackinnon/ 14 June respectively). Some of their code was used in the estimation reported here. Any remaining errors are solely my responsibility.

Export-led growth and cointegration

Previous evidence

In this section I investigate the question of whether a cointegrating relationship exists between monthly industrial production and monthly real exports in five countries: Japan, Korea, Malaysia, Taiwan and the United States. As noted above, many previous studies have investigated the export-led growth hypothesis in the context of cointegration and error-correction modelling. In many cases this seems to be a consequence of the time-series interpretation of export-led growth as a unidirectional Granger causal ordering. It is well known that valid inference regarding Granger causality must take explicit account of the stationarity and cointegration properties of the data series under investigation.

Time-series investigations of the export-led growth hypothesis typically begin with an equation such as the following:

$$y_t = \alpha + \gamma_1 x_t + \gamma_2 z_t + \varepsilon_t \qquad (1)$$

where y_t is a measure of output; x_t represents exports, and z is a vector of other variables that may be thought to influence the export–growth relationship. Examples of such variables that can be found in the literature are the terms of trade, world output, imports, and measures of physical and/or human capital. Equation (1), or a variant thereof, has been used extensively in empirical tests of the export-led growth hypothesis in Asia. Ahmad and Harnhirun (1995) estimated the model using GDP as their measure of output, with only exports appearing on the right-hand side. Using annual data for the ASEAN countries (Indonesia, Malaysia, the Philippines, Singapore and Thailand), they found evidence of a cointegrating relationship only in Singapore. Their Granger causality tests revealed bi-directional causality between exports and GDP.

In their study of export-led growth in Malaysia, Ghatak, Milner and Utkulu (1997) also used variants of equation (1), with y_t measured as both GDP and non-export GDP.[1] Using total exports as the only explanatory variable, they found evidence of a cointegrating relationship in which a 1 per cent increase in the *level* of exports led to a 1.1 per cent increase in the *level* of GDP. They also found a uni-directional Granger causal ordering from export *growth* to income *growth*, for both measures of GDP. Ghatak *et al.* estimated equation (1) using measures of disaggregated exports (that is, manufactured exports, fuel and non-fuel primary commodities), along with the share of gross domestic investment in GDP, and the primary and secondary school enrolment ratio included as components of z. Their results from this extended model suggested that exports of manufactures have the largest output elasticity (in the cointegrating relationship) of the three categories, followed by fuel exports. Primary commodity exports actually had a negative estimated elasticity (see their table 7, p. 221).

Islam (1998) tested for the export-led growth hypothesis in a sample of 15 Asian countries. Again using a bivariate version of equation (1) with y measured by GDP and x by the share of exports in GDP, he found a cointegrating relationship in only five of the 15 countries: Bangladesh, India, Nepal, Sri Lanka and Fiji. Islam further extended model (1) by including the GDP shares of imports, non-defense government expenditures, and total investment. Islam's Granger causality tests (accounting for cointegration where appropriate) showed bi-directional causality in seven countries, with the export share causally prior to GDP growth in six countries.

Bodman (1998) estimated equation (1) using quarterly data for Australia and Canada. His specification included labour productivity as a measure of output, with manufacturing exports, the terms of trade, and OECD industrial production on the right-hand side. He found a single cointegrating vector among the four variables for each country. In addition, he found that 'exports are a direct cause of economic (productivity) growth' in both countries, although the effects were small in magnitude.

Some additional evidence

The cointegrating relationship analysed in this chapter can be written as follows:

$$y_t = \alpha + \gamma_1 x_t + \gamma_2 m_t + \gamma_3 q_t + \gamma_4 w_t + \varepsilon_t \qquad (2)$$

where y_t is an index of industrial production; x_t and m_t are real exports and imports, respectively, in national currency; q_t is the terms of trade, measured as 100 times the ratio of the export unit value index to the import unit value index; w_t is an index of OECD industrial production; and ε_t is an error term. All variables are measured in logarithms. I obtained monthly data for Japan, Korea, Taiwan, Malaysia and the United States from the *International Financial Statistics* database via Datastream.

Throughout the analysis presented here, I estimated equation (2) using single-equation methods. I had two main reasons for using this method as opposed to multivariate methods such as Johansen's (1988) maximum likelihood estimator. First, a major motivation is the analysis of possible structural breaks in the long-run relationship (if any) between exports and growth. There are currently several procedures for testing for the presence and timing of structural breaks in univariate cointegrating systems, examples are Hansen (1992a, b) or Gregory and Hansen (1996a, b). Multivariate versions of these tests are not yet as well-advanced. The second major motivation in this project is to assess the evidence for any long-run relationship between exports and growth; that is, to detect *at least one* cointegrating vector between the five variables. I did not attempt a thorough structural interpretation of any long-run relationships I detected. Preliminary analysis using Johansen's maximum eigenvalue and trace statistics generally indicated the presence of a single cointegrating vector. If more than one cointegrating vector exists, single-equation methods will still give consistent estimates, and the residuals ε_t will be uncorrelated with any other linear combination of the cointegrating variables (see Hamilton, 1994, pp. 590–1).

Are exports and output cointegrated?

Following standard practice, I tested for the degree of integration of the data series prior to testing for cointegration. I performed both the augmented Dickey–Fuller (ADF) test of the unit-root null hypothesis, and the Kwiatkowski *et al.* (1992, KPSS) test of the null of stationarity. The results of these tests clearly indicated that nearly all the series are I(1) in levels but I(0) in first differences.[2] In the only ambiguous case (Korean exports), the ADF test rejected the unit root null while the KPSS tests rejected the stationarity null. Hence, the data seem to be relatively uninformative about the presence of a unit root in this case. Given the absence of compelling evidence either way, I proceeded on the assumption that all the monthly data series have exactly one unit root.

Table 11.1 gives the OLS estimates of equation (2), along with ADF and KPSS tests for the stationarity of the residuals, ε_t. Note that in this case, the null hypothesis of the ADF test is no cointegration, while the null of the KPSS test is cointegration. The two residual tests provided conflicting evidence regarding a cointegrating relationship. The KPSS test indicated that for all countries, the OLS residuals are mean-stationary, although there is some dependence of this result on the number of lags used in computing the long-run variance estimate used in the test.[3] The ADF tests generally rejected cointegration, although the z-test was slightly more supportive than the τ-test. There is strong evidence of cointegration among the five variables for Korea, and somewhat weaker evidence for the United States. The data are not particularly informative regarding cointegration for the other countries. Note that the export elasticity of output is significantly positive for all countries except the USA.

The next step was to estimate an error-correction model (ECM) based on equation (2). This model includes only variables that are I(0), and can be written as:

Table 11.1   Estimates of cointegrating regression

	Japan	Korea	Taiwan	Malaysia	USA
			Constant		
coefficient	−5.96	−9.55	−9.69	−5.37	−0.34
std. error	0.22	0.37	0.27	0.25	0.12
t ratio	−27.38	−25.81	−36.46	−21.23	−2.87
msl[a]	0.00	0.00	0.00	0.00	0.00
			Exports		
coefficient	0.23	0.20	0.47	0.46	0.01
std. error	0.02	0.03	0.03	0.04	0.01
t ratio	11.13	7.05	15.13	11.24	1.07
msl[a]	0.00	0.00	0.00	0.00	0.28
			Terms of trade		
coefficient	0.11	−0.03	0.16	0.08	0.00
std. error	0.02	0.07	0.07	0.04	0.02
t ratio	4.77	−0.39	2.38	1.85	−0.06
msl[a]	0.00	0.69	0.02	0.07	0.95
			Imports		
coefficient	0.04	0.34	−0.01	0.12	0.16
std. error	0.02	0.04	0.04	0.03	0.02
t ratio	1.72	9.57	−0.35	4.29	10.31
msl[a]	0.09	0.00	0.73	0.00	0.00
			OECD industrial production		
coefficient	1.31	1.31	1.30	1.00	0.67
std. error	0.02	0.17	0.12	0.10	0.04
t ratio	65.65	7.58	11.00	9.97	16.70
msl[a]	0.00	0.00	0.00	0.00	0.00
			Stationarity of residuals		
ADF τ	−2.08	−5.48	−1.63	−3.49	−3.39
msl[b]	0.85	0.00	0.95	0.19	0.23
ADF z	−14.67	−33.71	−9.07	−26.06	−22.98
msl[b]	0.59	0.05	0.86	0.15	0.01
KPSS $\eta(\mu)$	0.44	0.44	0.43	0.31	0.45
k[c]	3	6	4	1	2
Sample	1/62–1/98	1/64–1/97	1/76–2/97	1/71–4/97	1/69–1/98
(# obs.)	(433)	(397)	(264)	(316)	(349)

Notes: [a] Marginal significance level (*p*-value); [b] computed using MacKinnon's program 'urcdist', available at http://qed.econ.queensu.ca/pub/faculty/mackinnon/; [c] 10% and 5% critical values for the $\eta(\mu)$ test are 0.347 and 0.463, respectively. Test statistics are reported for the indicated value of *k*, representing the number of lags used in computing the long-run variance estimate (see Kwiatkowski *et al.*, 1992). The null of stationarity is accepted for all values of *k* greater than the indicated value, up to a maximum of 12.

$$\Delta y_t = \alpha + \beta_1 \Delta y_{t-1} + \beta_2 \Delta x_{t-1} + \beta_3 \Delta m_{t-1} + \beta_4 \Delta q_{t-1} + \beta_5 \Delta w_{t-1} + \delta \varepsilon_{t-1} + u_t$$
(3)

with Δ the lag operator. Note that the ECM representation of equation (3) remains valid even if there is no cointegration; in this case $\delta = 0$. In general, one would test for the appropriate number of lags of the variables to be included on the right-hand side; this was done using the BIC model selection criterion. For all countries but the USA, a single lag was chosen; the appropriate lag length for the USA was 2. Because the focus of the remainder of this chapter is on possible structural breaks, I do not report coefficient estimates of the ECM.

While estimating the ECM for each country, I also performed Hansen's (1992a) L_c test for parameter stability. These tests can be thought of as generalizations of the Chow test for a single structural break at a known point in time; the test allows for possible instability in each individual parameter, plus instability in the overall equation. The results of these tests are presented in Table 11.2.[4] The table clearly shows evidence of substantial parameter instability; in all countries except Taiwan, overall stability of the ECM relationship is rejected. Notice in particular that stability of the residual variance is rejected at the 5 per cent level in Korea,

Table 11.2   Tests for parameter stability in ECM[a]

	Japan	Korea	Taiwan	Malaysia	USA
Constant	2.22	0.79	0.16	0.10	0.09
y_{t-1}	2.78	0.35	0.03	0.18	0.13
y_{t-2}					0.09
x_{t-1}	0.90	0.35	0.33	0.22	0.11
x_{t-2}					0.09
m_{t-1}	1.32	0.35	0.27	0.27	0.03
m_{t-2}					0.07
q_{t-1}	0.08	0.65	0.08	0.33	0.04
q_{t-2}					0.06
w_{t-1}	1.89	0.45	0.10	0.10	0.21
w_{t-2}					0.17
ε_{t-1}	0.10	0.33	0.25	0.35	0.50
Variance	0.37	0.49	0.07	0.59	1.35
Overall stability	5.6	2.67	1.25	2.18	3.25

Notes: [a] Table entries are Hansen's (1992a) L_c statistics which test the null of parameter stability over the sample period. 10% and 5% critical values for the individual parameter tests are 0.353 and 0.470, respectively. Corresponding critical values for the overall stability test are 1.89 and 2.11 for all countries but the USA; critical values for the USA are 2.89 and 3.15.

Malaysia and the United States, and at the 10 per cent level (critical value 0.353) in Japan. Hansen (1992a) presented Monte Carlo evidence that instability in the variance term can cause a substantial loss of power in the stability tests for the other parameters. Hence the true extent of parameter instability may be *understated* by the results in Table 11.2.

Also of concern here is the evidence of instability in the coefficient on lagged exports. Stability of this parameter is rejected at the 5 per cent level for Japan, and at nearly the 10 per cent level for Korea and Taiwan. Also note that δ, the coefficient on the error-correction term, appears unstable in the United States. The results in Table 11.2 therefore suggest a closer examination of the nature of the export–growth relationship over time. This analysis is the subject of the next section.

Structural change and export-led growth

Structural change

While Hansen's L_c test gives an indication of possible parameter instability, it cannot detect when any structural breaks may have occurred. In order to investigate the issue of the timing of structural changes, I performed the recursive cointegration tests of Gregory and Hansen (1996a, b). These tests are conceptually and computationally straightforward, and in order to explain their operation it is convenient to rewrite equation (2) as follows:

$$y_t = \alpha + \beta t + \gamma Z_t + \varepsilon_t \tag{4}$$

where $Z_t = (x_t, m_t, q_t, w_t)$ and $\gamma = (\gamma_1, \gamma_2, \gamma_3, \gamma_4)'$. Note that a linear trend has also been added. Now define the dummy variable $D_{\tau t}$, which takes the value 1 if $t \geq \tau$, and zero otherwise, and let $\delta = (\delta_1, \delta_2, \delta_3, \delta_4)$. The most general form of the Gregory–Hansen test involves estimating:

$$y_t = \alpha + \theta D_{\tau t} + \beta t + \phi D_{\tau t} t + \gamma Z_t + \delta'(D_{\tau t} Z_t) + \varepsilon_t \tag{5}$$

for each date τ in a certain range.[5] Other versions of the test allow for structural breaks in only a subset of the parameters, such as the constant. At each step, perform a unit root test on the residuals ε_t, and save the test statistic (the ADF-τ statistic, for example). The null hypothesis of no cointegration is rejected if the minimum of the sequence of ADF-τ statistics falls below the critical values tabulated by Gregory and Hansen. The date at which the minimium occurs is the estimated date of the structural break.[6] In performing the structural-break tests, I tested for the stationarity of the residuals using the ADF-τ test, and the Z_t and Z_α tests of

Phillips (1987). The Phillips tests allow for fairly general serial correlation in the estimated residuals from equation (5). The results of these tests are shown in Table 11.3.

The effect of the serial correlation corrections of the Phillips tests is readily apparent in Table 11.3. None of the ADF-τ tests reject the no-cointegration null, whereas all of the Phillips tests do.[7] The Phillips tests provide considerable evidence of cointegration in all five countries, and, further, the estimated break dates from the various tests are within a few months of each other, with the exceptions of Japan and the United States. For each country, both of the Phillips tests give the same break date. This suggests that all three tests are sending the same signal, but the ADF test is not rejecting because the residuals are not independently and identically distributed.

Export-led growth

In order to investigate the possibility that the structural change in these countries involves the changing relationship between exports and output, I computed the recursive estimates of the export elasticity $(\gamma_1 + \delta_1)$ from the Gregory–Hansen tests based on equation (5). This gives the total effect of (the log level of) exports on (the log level of) industrial production at each date for which the Gregory–Hansen tests are computed. Plots of these recursive estimates and the associated 2-standard-error bands are presented in Figures 11.1 to 11.5. The estimated break dates from Table 11.3 are also shown on the figures.[8]

The most striking feature of the figures is their similarity. In all five countries, the long-run elasticity of output with respect to exports is

Table 11.3 Gregory–Hansen recursive cointegration tests[a]

	Japan	Korea	Taiwan	Malaysia	USA
Estimation range	5/67–8/92	1/69–10/92	4/79–9/94	11/74–5/93	4/73–9/93
Min ADF	–5.17	–5.5	–4.71	–6.09	–5.33
Break date	7/88	3/76	8/89	11/83	11/77
Min Z_t	–7.28	–10.97	–9.34	–14.61	–7.06
Break date	7/77	3/76	1/90	2/84	11/74
Min Z_α	–90.01	–176.94	–124.66	–234.29	–80.36
Break date	7/77	3/76	1/90	2/84	11/74

Note: [a] 10% and 5% critical values for the min ADF and min Z_t tests are –6.58 and –6.84, respectively. Corresponding critical values for the Z_α test are –82.30 and –88.47 (see Gregory and Hansen, 1996b, table 1).

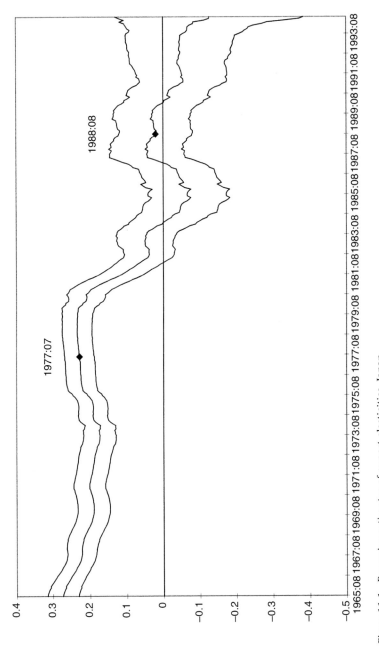

Figure 11.1 Recursive estimates of export elasticities, Japan

200

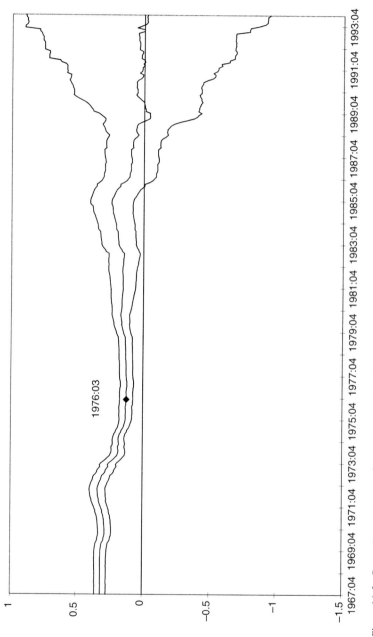

1967:04 1969:04 1971:04 1973:04 1975:04 1977:04 1979:04 1981:04 1983:04 1985:04 1987:04 1989:04 1991:04 1993:04

1976:03

Figure 11.2 Recursive estimates of export elasticities, Korea

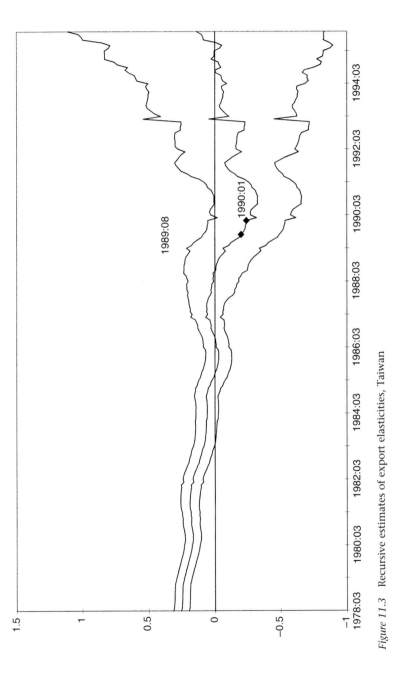

1989:08

1990:01

Figure 11.3 Recursive estimates of export elasticities, Taiwan

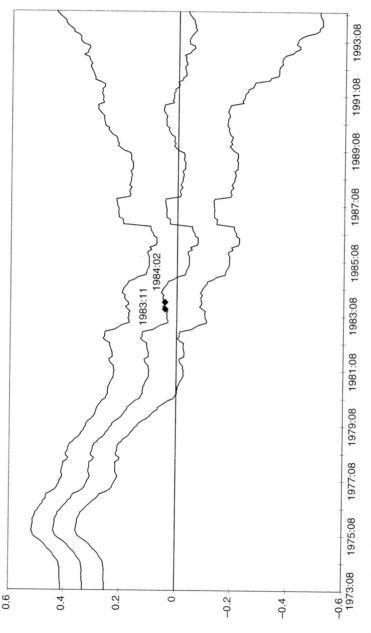

Figure 11.4 Recursive estimates of export elasticities, Malaysia

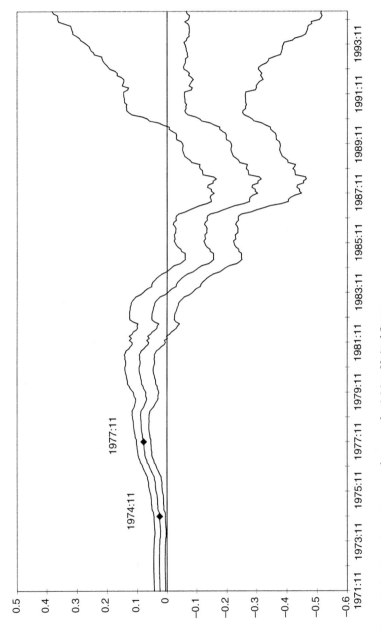

Figure 11.5 Recursive estimates of export elasticities, United States

significant and positive in the early part of the sample. Furthermore, the elasticities are all in the neighbourhood of 0.2, with the possible exception of the USA. All of the estimates then become statistically insignificant sometime in the early to mid-1980s, with the US export elasticity actually becoming significantly negative. None of the Gregory–Hansen estimated break dates correspond particularly well to the changes in the recursive export elasticity estimates. Finally, note that the changes in the USA and in Japan seem to predate the changes in the other countries.

One interpretation of the changes in Figures 11.1 to 11.5 is the following. The rapid and substantial increase in the US current account deficit in 1982–84 was financed mainly by an inflow of Japanese capital. This period also corresponded to the early phase of a prolonged US expansion which ended in the recession of late 1990. During this time there was downward pressure on US exports due to the strong dollar; strong output growth was thus associated with lower exports. In other words, the negative US export elasticity during most of the 1980s reflects a 'reverse causality' phenomenon (see Figure 11.5). In Japan, during this time, it may well be that investment and equity flows served as the dominant engine of growth. Increased offshore production of export goods and foreign direct investment may have contributed to the drop in the estimates in Figure 11.1.

The drop in export elasticities in the other countries seems to be fairly closely associated with the Plaza Accord of 1985, although the Malaysian case appears somewhat anomalous.

Conclusion

This chapter has presented evidence of a long-run relationship (that is, cointegration) between industrial production, trade, the terms of trade and OECD output for Japan, Korea, Taiwan, Malaysia and the United States. There is considerable evidence *against* these long-run relationships being stable. Furthermore, in many cases the evidence for cointegration only becomes apparent once the possibility of structural breaks is explicitly accounted for.

The nature of the long-run relationship between the level of exports and the level of output appears to have changed dramatically in all of these countries over the sample period considered here. One implication of this finding concerns the 'conventional wisdom' that the countries hardest hit by the Asian economic crisis will ultimately recover by exporting their way out of recession. The evidence presented here suggests that such an argument is not as straightforward as it might at first seem. One important issue that remains unresolved is the effect of export *composition* on both the level and growth rate of output over this same period. This issue is the subject of ongoing work.

Notes

1 The latter measure is designed to address the problem of simultaneity caused by exports being a component of GDP; see Michaely (1977).
2 The results of these tests are available from the author on request. Note that all results refer to the logarithms of the variables.
3 KPSS (1992) describe the use of the long-run variance estimate in the test, and also note that inference depends on this estimate in some cases.
4 The 5 per cent asymptotic critical value for the individual parameter tests is 0.47; for the joint stability test, the critical value varies with the number of parameters, as shown in the table.
5 Some trimming of the sample is necessary to prevent the test statistic from diverging to infinity near the endpoints. I follow Gregory and Hansen (1996b) and omit the first and last 15% of the sample for each country in estimating equation (5).
6 These tests are designed to detect a *single* structural break at an unknown date. The possibility of more than one break is not considered here.
7 Actually, the null hypothesis of the Gregory–Hansen test is that there is neither cointegration *nor* a structural break. The tests will have power in the case of non-cointegrated series with structural breaks.
8 The standard errors in the figures are from the uncorrected OLS covariance matrix, and are therefore probably wider than would be obtained from efficient estimation techniques such as Phillips and Hansen's (1990) fully-modified procedure. Thus, these figures should be taken as indicative only.

References

Ahmad, J. and Harnhirun, S. (1995) 'Unit Roots and Cointegration in Estimating Causality between Exports and Economic Growth: Empirical Evidence from the ASEAN Countries', *Economics Letters*, vol. 49, pp. 329–34.
Bodman, P.M. (1998) 'A Contribution on the Empirics of Trade, Migration and Economic Growth for Australia and Canada', *International Economic Journal*, vol. 12, pp. 41–62.
Ghatak, S., Milner, C. and Utkulu, U. (1997) 'Exports, Export Composition and Growth: Cointegration and Causality Evidence for Malaysia', *Applied Economics*, vol. 29, pp. 213–23.
Gregory, A.W. and Hansen, B.E. (1996a) 'Residual-Based Tests for Cointegration in Models with Regime Shifts', *Journal of Econometrics*, vol. 70, pp. 99–126.
— and — (1996b) 'Tests for Cointegration in Models with Regime and Trend Shifts', *Oxford Bulletin of Economics and Statistics*, pp. 555–60.
Hamilton, J.D. (1994) *Time Series Analysis*, Princeton, N.J.: Princeton University Press.
Hansen, B.E. (1992a) 'Testing for Parameter Instability in Linear Models', *Journal of Policy Modeling*, vol. 14(4), pp. 517–33.
— (1992b) 'Tests for Parameter Instability in Regressions with I(1) Processes', *Journal of Business and Economic Statistics*, vol. 10(3), pp. 321–35.

Islam, M.N. (1998) 'Export Expansion and Economic Growth: Testing for Cointegration and Causality', *Applied Economics*, vol. 30, pp. 415–25.

Johansen, S. (1988) 'Statistical Analysis of Cointegration Vectors', *Journal of Economic Dynamics and Control*, vol. 12, pp. 231–54.

Kwiatkowski, D., Phillips, P.C.B., Schmidt, P. and Shin, Y. (1992) 'Testing the Null Hypothesis of Stationarity against the Alternative of a Unit Root: How Sure are we that Economic Time Series have a Unit Root?' *Journal of Econometrics*, vol. 54, pp. 159–78.

Michaely, M. (1977) 'Exports and Growth: An Empirical Investigation', *Journal of Development Economics*, vol. 4, pp. 49–53.

Phillips, P.C.B. (1987) 'Time Series Regression with a Unit Root', *Econometrica*, vol. 55, pp. 277–301.

— and Hansen, B.E. (1990) 'Statistical Inference in Instrumental Variables Regression with I(1) Processes', *Review of Economic Studies*, vol. 57, pp. 99–125.

12
The International Diffusion of Technology: Technological Catch-up and Economic Growth

Mark Rogers

033

034

Introduction

Do countries that are better at absorbing technology from overseas experience faster economic growth? This question is associated with the idea of 'technological catch-up', which states that countries facing a technology gap with the world's best practice have the opportunity to grow faster. The existence of a technology gap is a necessary but not sufficient condition for the process of technological catch-up. A country must have sufficient 'absorptive capability' – defined as the capability to learn, absorb and implement relevant overseas technology to the benefit of the domestic economy. The concepts of the 'technology gap' and 'absorptive capability' are therefore central to understanding the process of technology diffusion and economic growth. Both concepts are difficult to define and measure, but they are the key to understanding the link between diffusion and economic growth.

The concept of benefiting from the technology in other countries goes back at least as far as Francis Bacon (1561–1626) who advocated the formation of an institute that would send fellows abroad to bring back useful inventions (Cardwell, 1994, p. 81). More recently, Abramovitz (1986) and Baumol (1986) began an empirical literature that assesses the extent and nature of technological catch-up for a large cross-section of countries. This literature considers similar issues to work on international spillovers of knowledge (see Coe and Helpman, 1995; Keller, 1996), technology transfer (Reddy and Zhao, 1990) and product cycles (Bernard and Ravenhill, 1995). The essence of each of these approaches is that countries can benefit from technology in other countries. The word 'technology' refers not only to scientific-based improvements in processes or products, but also to knowledge concerning management, marketing, advertising, accounting, investment planning and other areas. In other words, 'technology' is used as shorthand for any knowledge that could improve economic performance.

The structure of the chapter is as follows. In the next section some simple models of catch-up are discussed, which clearly indicate the role of the technology gap and absorptive capability. We then define absorptive capability and discuss a set of new variables that aim to proxy important elements of that capability. The empirical investigation of the association of these variables with economic growth is the central aim of this chapter. An empirical analysis is then presented which includes a variety of ways of testing the importance of each new variable, followed by a conclusion.

Some simple mathematics for technological catch-up[1]

This section assumes that we can express the technology levels and absorptive capabilities of countries with scalars. Given this, a point of departure is to assume that the growth rate of knowledge (A) for a follower country is defined by:

$$\frac{dA}{dt}/A = \phi(\cdot)\left[\frac{T-A}{A}\right] \tag{1}$$

where T represents the world level of best-practice technology and $\phi(\cdot)$ is a function representing absorptive capability. This equation originates in work by Nelson and Phelps (1966) and has been used by Hansson and Henrekson (1994) in the context of technological catch-up. Assuming that T grows at an exogenous constant rate g, the system of differential equations (that is, equation (1) and $dT/dt = gT$) can be solved to show that, in the long run, the growth of A must equal g. Intuitively, unless the growth rate of A equals the growth rate of T, the right-hand side of (1) must be changing, which in turn means the growth rate of A must be changing. Figure 12.1 illustrates this result graphically. The figure shows that a follower country which starts with a technology ratio (A/T) below the long-run equilibrium level ($\phi/(\phi+g)$) will experience rapid growth (relative to g). Conversely, countries which start with a technology ratio above $\phi/(\phi+g)$ will experience growth rates lower than g.

The functional form of equation (1) is essentially arbitrary. In general, any functional form that satisfies the condition that knowledge growth is zero when the technology gap is zero could be considered. An alternative functional form is:

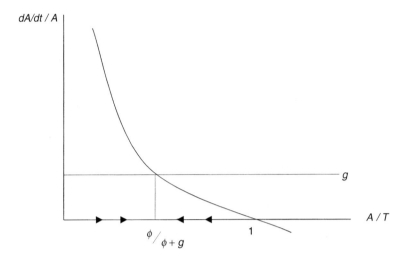

Figure 12.1 A monotonic technological-gap model

$$\frac{dA}{dt}/A = \phi(\cdot) \ln\left[\frac{T}{A}\right] \tag{2}$$

which is common in empirical growth work.[2] Both functional forms of
equations (1) and (2), however, have the unfortunate property that as the
technology gap tends to infinity (that is, $A/T \to 0$ in Figure 12.1), the
growth rate of technology tends to infinity. This implies that extremely
poor countries should be growing at high rates (note that this is the case as
long as $\phi(\cdot) > 0$). In contrast, the empirical work on catch-up has shown
that many poor countries do not grow at very fast rates. There are various
ways in which we can alter the theory to take such a fact into account.
One method would be to assume that the $\phi(\cdot)$ function is a step function
with very poor countries having a value of 0. This makes sense if the
economic, political and social institutions of a country are so adverse to
learning and implementing technology that they prevent technological
catch-up. Alternatively, we could redefine the technology gap (T/A) as the
appropriate technology gap and assume that this falls if countries fall too
far behind.[3] In essence, both of these methods try and capture the fact
that very poor countries may fail to benefit from overseas technology.

This brief section on the mathematics of technological catch-up
provides some guidance for empirical work. Specifically, it has highlighted
the importance of absorptive capability and the technology gap. But we

must also be realistic about its limitations. Firstly, the equations deal only with the rate of absorption of technology from overseas: there is no allowance for the generation of internal technology. Secondly, the equations describe a world of only two economies, a leader and a follower. In reality, a poor country may also be able to learn knowledge from economies at an intermediate level of technology. There is also the fact that this section only considers the growth of technology which is not necessarily equivalent to the rate of economic growth (which is the normal dependent variable in regression work). This means that the empirical specification will need to be richer than the theory discussed here.

Absorptive capability

What determines absorptive capability?

As the previous section indicates, absorptive capability plays an important role in technological catch-up. It can be considered as having three major elements: accessibility to overseas technology, learning ability, and the incentives or barriers to implementing new technologies. Abramovitz (1986) also considers three elements to his similar term 'social capability', namely: the facilities for the diffusion of knowledge, the conditions facilitating or hindering structural change, and the macroeconomic and monetary conditions encouraging investment.[4] The 'accessibility' term used here is similar to Abramovitz's term 'diffusion facilities'. Equally, Abramovitz's last two elements can be considered as influencing the incentives to implement new technologies.

Accessibility to overseas technology depends on such factors as the extent of interpersonal links with other countries (whether this is related to business, educational, academic or personal reasons), the level of trade in goods and services, and foreign investment. The ability to learn technology depends on a wide range of factors. At the most basic level, literacy is a fundamental element of learning capability. In addition, foreign language skills are important,[5] and more specialized 'language' skills, such as used in engineering, are also required in order to communicate technical information. These type of skills might be referred to as human capital, but there are obviously specific skills that are vital in certain contexts. With this in mind, the principal aim of the empirical work presented below is to proxy the accessibility and learning components of absorptive capability.

The last aspect of absorptive capability is the incentive to implement new technologies. The existence and size of these incentives depends on a range of economic, social and political factors, predominant among which are the existence of property rights, the rule of law and the degree of corruption. Government policies with regard to taxation, competition and finance, especially the consistency of their implementation, are also important. Equally, incentives are likely to be very low when political or civil disruption creates high levels of uncertainty. The macroeconomic and monetary factors emphasized by Abramovitz (1986), especially the banking and credit system, are also clearly vital, and lastly, basic factors concerning health and life expectancy may also have an impact on the capacity and incentive to invest in economic change. These are some of the factors that are often thought to affect growth and economic development; they are relevant not only to implementing ideas from abroad but also for implementing any new idea. Absorptive capability is therefore heavily influenced by all the common factors thought to be associated with economic growth, and in addition many of the factors determining absorptive capability will also determine the ability of a country to create and implement its own new ideas. This means that in empirical work it will be difficult to separate the effects of certain variables, for example to what extent education acts on growth through absorptive capability and the technology gap, as opposed to domestic invention and innovation.

New variables that proxy accessibility and learning

Given the above discussion, previous empirical work on growth can be interpreted as investigating the role of absorptive capability, with authors considering trade openness, foreign direct investment and human capital as proxies for the level of absorptive capability. In this chapter we expand the range of variables that can be used to proxy absorptive capability by considering study abroad, telecommunications and publications data. The method used is to look at the economic growth rate of 61 countries over the period 1965 to 1985 and consider whether these variables have significant partial correlations with the growth rate. To avoid the criticism of endogeneity, the values of the absorptive capability proxies come from the 1960s. Table 12.1 lists the absorptive capability proxies used.

Although the proxies in Table 12.1 may appear to be solely related to either the accessibility or learning components of absorptive capability, such appearances may be deceptive. For example, while the number of students studying abroad may at first sight appear to proxy accessibility to international knowledge, it may be that only countries with strong learning capabilities (such as foreign language skills) send students abroad. Similarly, if the students who were studying abroad return home,

Table 12.1 Absorptive capability proxies

Description	Source	Year(s)
Study abroad in higher education-based		
Students studying overseas p.t.	UNESCO	1962–65
Students studying in USA p.t.	UNESCO	1963
Students overseas studying natural sciences p.t.	UNESCO	1966
Students overseas studying social sciences p.t.	UNESCO	1966
Students overseas studying engineering p.t.	UNESCO	1966
Telecommunications-based		
International outgoing telegrams p.t.	ITU	1965
Main telephone lines per 100 population	ITU	1965
Telex subscribers p.t.	ITU	1965
Publications-based		
Periodicals published p.t.	UNESCO	1960, 65
Applied science books published p.t.	UNESCO	1960–64
Pure science books published p.t.	UNESCO	1960–64
Volumes in national library p.c.	UNESCO	1964
Volumes in university library p.c.	UNESCO	1964
Volumes in specialist library p.c.	UNESCO	1964
Newspaper circulation p.t.	UNESCO	1962–65
Patent-based		
Patent applications per thousand workers	WIPO	1962–65
Trade-based		
Exports of equipment/GDP	IEDB	1965–69
Exports of basic manufactures/GDP	IEDB	1965–69
Imports of equipment/GDP	IEDB	1965–69
Trade openness (X + M/GDP)*100	PWT	1962–64

Notes: p.t. = per thousand; p.c. = per capita; UNESCO – *Statistical Yearbook* various years; ITU – International Telecommunications Union database; IEDB – STARS/International Economic Data Bank at ANU; WIPO – World Industrial Property Organization; PWT – *Penn World Table*.

they will then represent domestic learning capability (for example they are particularly suited to being able to understand foreign knowledge). Lastly, foreign-educated people may become innovators and inventors, thereby raising the rate of domestic knowledge generation. Despite these observations, it is likely that a key aspect of sending students abroad is the technology or knowledge that students bring home. Such knowledge could come from their formal educational knowledge, or from observation of and interaction with the host country. A concern with using students in higher education overseas data is that students may fail to return home after their study period (a 'brain drain' effect). In particular, differences in the return rate of students across countries, and over time, would make finding a positive correlation (if one exists) between students studying abroad and subsequent economic growth less likely. Unfortunately, data on the return rate of students are not available and it is not possible to control for this potential bias.

The telecommunication variables listed in Table 12.1 are indicators of the level of infrastructure present in a country that is principally concerned with the transfer of information. The main telephone lines per population is an indicator of domestic infrastructure, and Easterly and Levine (1995) use data for telephones per worker in regression work and find a significant positive partial correlation with growth rates.[6] The telegrams and telex-based variables are included as proxies for the extent of international communication. Considering the publication-based variables in Table 12.1, the newspaper circulation and the periodical variables are primarily proxies for the degree of literacy and knowledge dissemination within an economy.[7] The publications of applied science and pure science books are proxies for the level of specialist knowledge within a country and the level of demand for such knowledge. We might hypothesize that the greater the level of specialist knowledge, and the higher the demand for such knowledge, the greater the publication of such books, including new books, second editions or translations. The library-based measures are proxies for a number of related factors. Firstly, countries with large numbers of volumes per capita may devote substantial effort to human capital formation. Secondly, the variables may also reflect literacy rates. Thirdly, the numbers of volumes in libraries may reflect the effort and importance devoted to the dissemination of knowledge within the country. The patent applications per thousand workers ratio is primarily an indicator of the creation of domestic technology (although both resident and non-resident applications are included). Domestic technological capability is likely to be a prerequisite for the ability to understand and implement overseas technology.

The trade openness variable has been used in previous studies as a proxy for international knowledge diffusion,[8] and the recent work by Sachs and Warner (1997) which we use in the empirical analysis below has developed new trade openness variables. A summary of the previous work and the many different variables used is contained in Edwards (1998). Another method is to disaggregate trade flows. The imports of equipment to GDP ratio has been found to be positively correlated with economic growth, and De Long and Summers (1993) use this ratio averaged over the growth period considered as a measure of real investment in equipment. Here, we use the ratio of imports of equipment to GDP at the *beginning* of the growth period to avoid endogeneity issues. The exports of basic manufactures and equipment to GDP ratio includes only those exports to developed countries. Hobday (1995), in a case study of Korea, Taiwan, Hong Kong and Singapore, has stressed the importance of the technology supplied by firms in export markets (that is, the importing firms in developed countries assist with design and production technology). Pack and Page (1994) also use the ratio of such exports to GDP as an explanatory variable in a cross-country growth regression. They find it has a positive coefficient, and also that it is a better explanator than trade openness. Alwyn Young, in a comment at the end of their paper, casts doubt on their results, pointing out the unreliable nature of the data (Pack and Page use World Bank data) and the fact that the export share is taken from the growth period, thus raising doubts about endogeneity (indeed, Young provides some regressions that show no link between pre-growth period values and subsequent growth). Since the variable used here is from UN trade data, and is also taken from the start of the growth period, our results contribute to this debate.

One variable that is lacking from the absorptive capability proxies listed above is foreign direct investment (FDI). The impact of this variable is explored in detail in the following chapter of this volume by Balasu-bramanyam, Salisu and Sapsford. Given that the role of FDI has been explored, together with the problems of obtaining reliable data, we do not include an FDI variable. Although this is an omission, we do not consider that this will bias the results on other variables.

Empirical analysis

Empirical specification

The central aim of this study is to empirically investigate the importance of a set of new absorptive capability proxies in determining economic growth. The basic method used is the so-called empirical cross-country regression approach, using the growth rate of GDP per worker (or per capita) as the dependent variable and then entering a set of other explanatory variables. A first point to make about this literature is that much of it is not based directly on a formal theory of economic growth; instead, various models and insights are used as motivation for the inclusion of explanatory variables. Partly as a result of this, the number of explanatory variables that have been investigated is large (Sala-i-Martin, 1997, counts 62). This obviously causes a problem of which variables are 'core' explanatory variables (that is, the omission of which might seriously bias the results). Table 12.2 shows the core variables used by five recent studies. Common to these studies are the inclusion of the log of initial income (often interpreted as either a test of classical convergence or technological catch-up) and some measure of human capital. Although there appears to be substantial variation in included explanatory variables, it should be borne in mind that some of the variables (for example institutional quality and market distortions) may be highly correlated. In our study we use the most recent Sachs and Warner (1997) paper as a benchmark (although we also present some results using Barro and Sala-i-Martin (1995) as a benchmark specification in Appendix 1). Both of these regressions include the log of the technology gap which has a positive and significant coefficient, which can be interpreted as evidence to support the general technological catch-up hypothesis.

Initial regression results

Our initial investigation into the importance of absorptive capability proxies involves adding each of the variables individually to the baseline regressions models discussed above. Adding each proxy individually avoids multi-collinearity problems since many of the proxies are highly correlated. Due to data limitations on many of the new absorptive capability proxies, our sample size is restricted to 61 countries, which is less than Sachs and Warner's (SW) 83 countries. Since not all of the SW explanatory variables are significant for our 61-country sample, we drop statistically insignificant explanators (at the 10% level); Appendix 1 presents the full baseline models used. The dependent variable is the trend growth rate of GDP per worker over the period 1965 to 1985 (expressed in per cent). Table 12.3 shows the coefficients and t-statistics from adding the log of the absorptive capability proxies to the baseline SW model.

The results in Table 12.3 show that six coefficients are significant, with all but one of these positive. The coefficients on students studying abroad in social sciences and engineering per thousand are significant and positive, as is the coefficient on the number of telex subscribers per thousand. Two trade-based coefficients are also positive and significant, despite the fact that the SW model also includes a variable for the fraction of years over the period 1965 to 1990 for which trade was adjudged to be open.[10] Note that the coefficient on the exports of equipment to GDP ratio is positive and

Table 12.2 Core variables used in five recent empirical growth studies

Explanatory variables	Levine and Renelt (1992)	Levine and Zervos (1993)	Barro and Sala-i-Martin (1995)	Sala-i-Martin (1997)[9]	Sachs and Warner (1997)
Log of initial GDP p.c.	x	x	x	x	x
Human capital measures	x	x	x	x	x
Population growth	x				x
Capital investment	x		x		
Political instability		x	x		
Government spending			x		x
Terms of trade			x		
Market distortions			x		
Trade openness					x
Institutional quality					x
Natural resources					x
Geography					x

Notes: Human capital measures include various measures based on schooling and life expectancy.

Table 12.3   Adding the log of absorptive capability variables to the Sachs and Warner baseline regression. (Dependent variable: trend growth in GDP per worker, 1965–85)

Description	Coefficient	(t-stat)
Study abroad-based		
Students studying in USA p.t.	0.396	(0.218)
Students studying o'seas p.t.	0.174	(0.956)
Students o'seas studying natural sciences p.t.	3.972	(1.237)
Students o'seas studying social sciences p.t.	*2.806*	*(2.665)*
Students o'seas studying engineering p.t.	*4.177*	*(2.637)*
Telecommunications-based		
Main telephone lines per 100 population	0.132	(0.352)
International outgoing telegrams p.t.	0.098	(0.366)
Telex subscribers p.t.	*0.378*	*(2.431)*
Publications-based		
Periodicals published p.t.	−0.055	(−0.288)
Pure science books published p.t.	−0.053	(−0.305)
Applied science books published p.t.	*−0.429*	*(−2.782)*
Volumes in national library p.c.	0.681	(0.737)
Volumes in university library p.c.	0.907	(0.888)
Volumes in specialist library p.c.	1.062	(1.197)
Newspaper circulation p.t.	−0.271	(−0.830)
Patent-based		
Patent applications p.t. workers	*0.378*	*(1.733)*
Trade-based		
Trade openness $(X + M)$ (GDP)*100	*0.554*	*(1.980)*
Imports of equipment/GDP	−0.316	(−1.285)
Exports of basic manufactures/GDP	−0.055	(−0.506)
Exports of equipment/GDP	*0.176*	*(1.813)*

Notes: Results show coefficient (*t*-statistic) from adding each variable to SW baseline regression (Appendix 1). Italicized coefficients are significant at the 10% level; maximum number of observations is 61; all *t*-statistics are White's corrected. All variables have been added to the regression in log form (where zero values occur, the log of one plus the value is taken). Entering the variables in levels does change some of the results. In summary, the coefficient on the students abroad variable is positive and significant. The coefficient on telex subscribers, patents and exports of equipment are no longer significant. In addition, the coefficient on pure science books published is significant and negative.

significant (this supports the results of Pack and Page, 1994). Lastly, the coefficient on the patent applications per thousand workers is positive and significant.[11]

Interaction effects

The theory discussed earlier suggests that the effect of absorptive capability should be related to the size of the technology gap (that is, an interaction effect, which appears in equation (2) as $\phi(\cdot)\ln(T/A)$). In other words, if two countries have the same absorptive capability but face different technology gaps, the country facing the largest technology gap should experience a stronger impact on economic growth *ceteris paribus*. To test this idea fully would require an accurate index of absorptive capability which, as we have discussed, is made up of a large number of factors. However, a partial test involves interacting the set of absorptive capability proxies listed above with the technology gap, and entering each interaction term as an explanatory variable in a separate regression. If the coefficient on the interaction term is positive and significant it lends some support to the idea of technological catch-up.[12]

Table 12.4 shows the results of adding separate interaction terms to the baseline SW model,[13] and the results show a similar pattern to Table 12.3 above. The coefficients on the interaction terms with study abroad in social science or engineering are positive and significant, as are the coefficients on the interaction terms that include telex subscribers and exports of machinery. In contrast, the coefficients on the interaction terms of the applied-science books and trade openness are now insignificant. The coefficient on the interaction term with patents per worker is also just insignificant (10.8%). Table 12.4 shows the coefficient on the interactive term that includes the number of telephone lines per 100 population is positive and significant.[14]

Threshold effects

A further aspect highlighted by our earlier discussion of theory was the potential problem with using a monotonic technology-gap model. Such a model implies that as the technology gap becomes large, the very poorest countries receive large growth effects. One method of avoiding this issue is to include a quadratic technology-gap term in an empirical specification. The Barro and Sala-i-Martin (BSiM) (1995) baseline model includes such a term and this substantially improved the fit of the regression (see Appendix 1). The SW model does not include a quadratic technology-gap term, although it does include the square of the log of life expectancy. In regressions run on the sample of countries here, the inclusion of this term is vital to ensuring a significant coefficient on the log of life-expectancy term. Since the log of life expectancy and the log of the technology gap are highly correlated (–0.85) in our sample, the inclusion of this term is similar to including a quadratic technology-gap

Table 12.4 Adding interaction terms to the Sachs and Warner baseline regression. (Dependent variable: trend growth in GDP per worker, 1965–85)

Description	Coefficient	(*t*-stat)
Study abroad-based		
Students studying in USA p.t.	–0.036	(–0.024)
Students studying o'seas p.t.	0.078	(0.631)
Students o'seas studying natural sciences p.t.	2.283	(0.973)
Students o'seas studying social sciences p.t.	*1.947*	*(2.661)*
Students o'seas studying engineering p.t.	*3.377*	*(2.658)*
Telecommunications-based		
Main telephone lines per 100 population	*0.478*	*(2.139)*
International outgoing telegrams p.t.	0.008	(0.065)
Telex subscribers p.t.	*0.162*	*(1.776)*
Publications-based		
Periodicals published p.t.	0.031	(0.312)
Pure science books published p.t.	0.054	(0.402)
Applied science books published p.t.	–0.144	(–1.347)
Volumes in national library p.c.	1.981	(1.074)
Volumes in university library p.c.	1.353	(1.159)
Volumes in specialist library p.c.	1.743	(0.998)
Newspaper circulation p.t.	0.029	(0.199)
Patent-based		
Patent applications/GDP	0.144	(1.636)
Trade-based		
Trade openness $(X + M)/(GDP)^*100$	0.250	(1.433)
Imports of equipment/GDP	–0.208	(–1.145)
Exports of basic manufactures/GDP	–0.041	(–0.943)
Exports of equipment/GDP	*0.084*	*(2.335)*

Note: All variables entered as interaction terms with the log (technology gap). Results show coefficient (*t*-statistic) from adding each variable to SW baseline regression (Appendix 1). Italicized coefficients are significant at the 10% level; maximum number of observations is 61; all *t*-statistics are White's corrected. All variables have been added to the regression in log form (where zero values occur, the log of one plus the value is taken). Entering the variables in levels does change some of the results. In summary, the coefficient on the students abroad variable is positive and significant. The coefficient on telex subscribers, patents and exports of equipment are no longer significant. In addition, the coefficient on pure science books published is significant and negative.

term.[15] Thus, both baseline models include variables that control for, to some extent, the fact that technological catch-up is not available to the poorest countries (there are, of course, alternative explanations for such 'poverty-trap' arguments).

In this section we investigate another method of introducing a non-linearity into the estimating equation. Specifically, we are interested in testing whether absorptive capability has a threshold level below which countries are not able to benefit from overseas technology. In terms of equation (2), this means we hypothesis that the $\phi(\cdot)$ function is a step function: zero for low values of absorptive capability, then jumping to a positive value at some threshold level.

One method of investigating the possibility of a threshold level of absorptive capability is to create a dummy which is zero for low values of the variable under consideration. This dummy can then be interacted with the variable itself to produce a proxy step function for $\phi(\cdot)$. This method effectively sets low values of a variable to zero. Although this is a crude method, it does capture the idea that a low level of absorptive capability may not enhance growth. To investigate this idea we create a series of dummies for a variable: the first is zero for the lowest value and one for all other values; the second is zero for the two lowest values and one for all others; and so on. These dummies are then interacted with the variable itself and the interaction term is entered in a regression. For each absorptive capability proxy we create 29 dummies, run a separate regression for each interaction term and record the estimated coefficient and t-statistic.

The results for four variables are shown in Figures 12.2 to 12.5. Each figure plots the t-statistic on the interaction term as increasing numbers of low values are effectively set to zero. Figure 12.2 shows the t-statistic on the interaction term for the log of students studying abroad. The coefficient on this variables was positive but insignificant in Table 12.3 (t-statistic of 0.96). This value is the first value shown on the far left of the figure. The figure shows that when the lowest value is set to zero, in this case Brazil, the t-statistic on the coefficient rises to about 1.6. Setting other low values to zero tends to raise the t-statistic further – although not monotonically. The figure suggests that a possible threshold level for the numbers of students sent abroad is around 0.04 per thousand (as indicated on the horizontal axis).

Figure 12.3 shows a similar plot but this time for the log of one plus the number of students studying in the USA per thousand. No increase in the t-statistic is seen across the graph with the coefficient on the interaction term always remaining insignificant. In this case there appears to be no threshold effect. One possible reason, which would require investigation, is that students studying in the USA return home less frequently than the average.

Figures 12.4 and 12.5 show similar graphs for trade openness and the number of applied-science books published per thousand population.

221

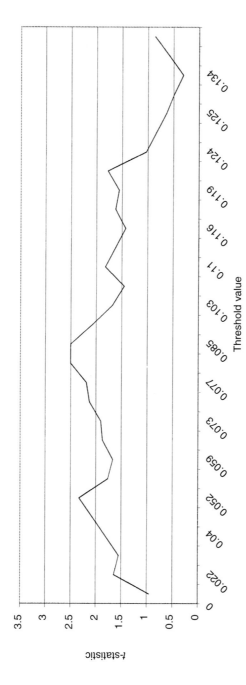

Figure 12.2 Threshold analysis for students studying overseas p.t.

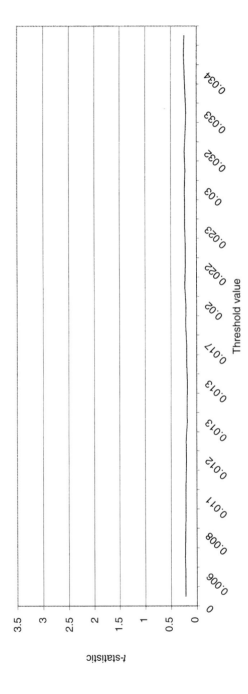

Figure 12.3 Threshold analysis for students studying overseas in the USA p.t.

223

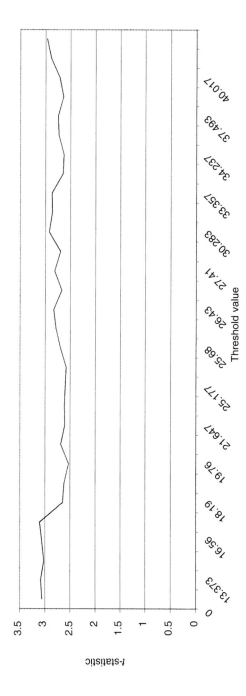

Figure 12.4 Threshold analysis for trade openness

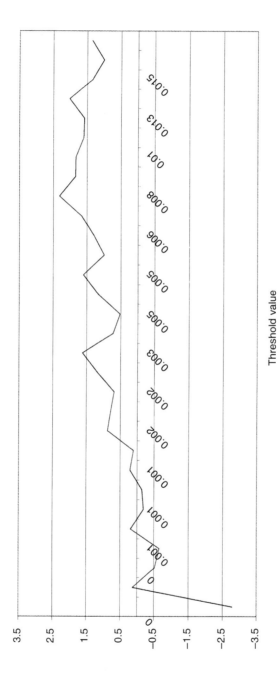

Figure 12.5 Threshold analysis for applied books published per thousand

Figure 12.4 is based on the trade openness entered in level, not log, form which is why the initial *t*-statistic is different from that in Table 12.3. The *t*-statistic shows that trade-openness has a significant positive correlation with subsequent economic growth through the range of trade-openness values. In contrast, the number of books published in applied science variable – which was the only variable to have a negative and significant coefficient in Table 12.3 – shows a change in sign and a gradual increase in significance when the lowest values are progressively set to zero. Once the ratio reaches 0.01 books per thousand population, the coefficient is close to significant at the 10 per cent level (this equates to the lowest 20 countries' values being set to zero).

In this section we have only investigated four variables, but the results suggest that for some variables the concept of a threshold value does have relevance. This lends some support for the theory discussed earlier and the general hypothesis on technological catch-up and the importance of absorptive capability. Further investigation is needed for the other variables, including the commonly-used human-capital proxies. However, caution should also be expressed about these results; the limited sample size and the complex nature of economic growth imply that other explanations for the results here may exist.

Conclusions

In this chapter we have investigated the importance of technological catch-up in explaining economic growth in a sample of 61 countries over the period 1965 to 1985. All the regressions reported here include a technology-gap term which is always positive and significant. This is a familiar result in the cross-country regression literature. We have argued that the technology gap is only part of the technological catch-up story, and that absorptive capability, defined as the ability to access, learn and implement new technology from overseas, is also vital. The technology gap a country faces and its absorptive capability interact to give rise to the growth effect due to catch-up. We investigated the importance of absorptive capability by considering a set of new proxies based on students studying overseas, telecommunications, publications, patent and trade data.

The new proxies for absorptive capability were tested in various ways. First, each was added individually to a growth regression. The results show that out of the 20 proxies, 7 are statistically significant and of these 6 are positive. The important variables appear to be students studying engineering or social sciences abroad, the number of telex subscribers, the number of patent applications and trade openness. It is important to note that the data from these variables are taken from before the growth period considered, to minimize the endogeneity problems. If more data were available and instrumental variables used the results may have been stronger.

Second, the proxies were entered as interactive terms with the log of the technology gap. This specification is suggested by the models of technology catch-up outlined earlier in the chapter. The results from these regressions (again each interactive term was entered individually in a growth regression) indicate that the results above still hold: students abroad, telex subscribers, trade openness and patents all appear to proxy absorptive capability. Third, we investigated whether there are non-linearities in absorptive capability; specifically, whether very low values of absorptive capability appear to be of no use in fostering economic growth. Here we have found mixed results, and some variables such as trade openness appear to have no threshold effects. The implication is that countries can benefit from a marginal increase in trade openness whatever its current level. Other variables, such as publications of applied-science books, suggest that low levels of publications per capita may have no growth effect. It is difficult to take these results as any more than indicative of such a relationship. It is highly likely that the various absorptive proxies used are positively correlated with a range of other variables and indeed, this is one reason for choosing them. This means that it is unreasonable to make strong statements concerning the threshold levels for specific variables, and is also a reason why we have refrained from assessing the economic impact (that is, interpreting the coefficients in economic terms) of the results.

Taking the overall set of results, they indicate that, as the theory suggests, absorptive capability has an influence in determining economic growth. The set of proxies we have considered suggests a number of variables may be important elements of absorptive capability. However, the difficulty of proxying such a broad concept as absorptive capability still stands out as a key problem.

Appendix 1   Baseline regressions

Table A1.1   Baseline regression with dependent variable = trend growth in GDP per worker, 1965–85

Explanatory variable	Modified Sachs and Warner (1997)	Modified Barro and Sala-I-Martin (1995)
Log (GDP per worker in US/GDP per worker in country)	1.034 (2.71)	4.161 (6.30)

Share of years open, 1965–90	11.914	
	(2.49)	
Share of years open * GDP per worker, 1965	–1.178	
	(–2.05)	
Central government budget balance, 1970–90	0.107	
	(2.20)	
Dummy for tropical country	–1.306	
	(–2.52)	
Share of natural-resource exports in GDP, 1970	–4.451	
	(–2.08)	
Log of life expectancy	107.127	4.048
	(1.94)	(2.67)
Square of log of life expectancy	–13.237	
	(–1.91)	
Square of log (GAP)		–0.628
		(–3.78)
Average years of secondary schooling, 1965		0.567
		(1.74)
Government to GDP ratio		–11.659
		(–3.38)
Log (1 + black-market premium)		–2.462
		(–4.91)
Change in terms of trade		23.875
		(3.76)
Observations	61	64
R-square	0.61	0.612

Note: Figures in brackets are *t*-statistics.
Sources: Barro and Sala-i-Martin variables from Barro and Lee (1994) data-set. Sachs and Warner (SW) data from NBER database. Specifications-based on SW (1997, p. 187) and BSiM (1995, p. 425, (1)). Insignificant coefficients (10% level) omitted. Quadratic technology-gap term added to BSiM.

Appendix 2   Summary statistics

Table A2.1   Summary statistics of log of absorptive capability variables added to Sachs and Warner baseline regression

Log of variable	No of observations	Mean	Std devn	Min.	Max.
Students studying in USA p.t.	61	0.075	0.118	0.000	0.616
Students studying o'seas p.t.	61	–1.698	1.107	–4.053	1.884
Students o'seas in nat. sciences p.t.	61	0.040	0.059	0.000	0.352
Students o'seas in soc. sciences p.t.	61	0.071	0.157	0.000	1.181
Students o'seas in engineering p.t.	61	0.054	0.090	0.000	0.434
Main telephone lines per 100 pop.	50	1.368	1.146	0.000	3.664
Int'l outgoing telegrams p.t.	44	3.997	1.383	1.385	7.083

Telex subscribers p.t.	40	−3.056	2.065	−7.574	0.223
Newspaper circulation p.t.	60	4.068	1.529	−0.051	6.217
Periodicals published p.t.	61	−3.770	1.607	−7.581	−0.490
Pure-science books published p.t.	47	−5.291	1.752	−8.961	−2.247
Applied-sc.books published p.t.	52	−4.561	1.678	−7.754	−2.034
Volumes in national library p.c.	54	0.096	0.132	0.000	0.754
Volumes in university library p.c.	48	0.170	0.196	0.000	0.785
Volumes in specialist library p.c.	42	0.148	0.242	0.001	0.923
Trade openness	61	3.705	0.596	2.398	5.607
Imports of equipment/GDP	59	−3.260	0.621	−5.340	−2.169
Exports of basic manufactures/GDP	58	−5.143	2.098	−11.773	−0.916
Exports of equipment/GDP	55	−7.547	3.186	−14.175	−2.914
Patent applications p.t. workers	54	−1.136	1.829	−5.578	1.796

Note: Where a variable has a minimum Log value of 0 this means the Log (1 + value) transformation was used (so that original values of 0 in the data can be transformed). This is a method used by Barro and others in transforming the black-market premium – which is zero for many countries – into log form.

Table A2.2   Summary statistics for SW baseline variables

Explanatory variable	No. of observations	Mean	Std devn	Min.	Max.
Trend growth in GDP per worker, 1965–85	61	2.272	1.761	−1.414	6.069
Log (GDP per worker in US/GDP p.w.)	61	1.509	0.911	0.116	3.721
Share of years open, 1965–90	61	0.500	0.448	0.000	1.000
Share of years open * GDP p.w., 1965	61	4.380	4.023	0.000	9.744
Central government budget balance, 1970–90	61	1.256	3.374	−5.244	9.599
Dummy for tropical country	61	0.462	0.483	0.000	1.000
Share of natural-resource X in GDP, 1970	61	0.113	0.092	0.010	0.540
Log of life expectancy	61	4.047	0.200	3.648	4.299
Square of Log of life expectancy	61	16.417	1.602	13.308	18.478

Table A2.3   Summary statistics for Barro and Sala-i-Martin baseline variables

Explanatory variable	No. of observations	Mean	Std devn	Min.	Max.
Trend growth in GDP per worker, 1965–85	64	2.272	1.761	−1.414	6.069
Log (GDP per worker in US/GDP p.w.)	64	1.509	0.911	0.116	3.721
Square of above	64	3.198	3.254	0.013	13.844
Log of life expectancy	64	4.040	0.201	3.648	4.299
Av. years of secondary schooling	64	0.703	0.627	0.013	2.573
Government spending/GDP	64	0.085	0.054	0.000	0.252
Log (1 + black-market prem.)	64	0.194	0.323	0.000	1.747
Growth in terms of trade	64	−0.005	0.025	−0.044	0.083

Table A2.4   Country list

Country	Growth (%)	SW	Country	Growth (%)	SW
Algeria	3.86		Kenya	2.14	1
Argentina	1.16	1	Korea	6.07	1
Australia	1.19	1	Malawi	1.44	1
Austria	2.67	1	Malaysia	4.46	1
Belgium	2.18	1	Mexico	2.14	1
Benin	0.26	1	Netherlands	1.52	1
Bolivia	1.97	1	New Zealand	0.51	1
Brazil	3.52	1	Norway	2.39	1
Cameroon	4.75	1	Pakistan	1.54	1
Canada	1.42	1	Panama	2.53	.
Chile	−0.59	1	Paraguay	3.38	1
Colombia	2.4	1	Peru	−0.02	1
Costa Rica	0.71	1	Philippines	2.06	1
Denmark	1.09	1	Portugal	3	1
Dominican Rep.	2.58	1	Senegal	0.62	1
Ecuador	3.98	1	Singapore	6.03	1
Finland	2.72	1	Spain	2.53	1
France	2.26	1	Sri Lanka	2.44	1
German, Fed. Rep.	2.39	1	Sweden	1.01	1
Ghana	0.11	1	Switzerland	0.95	1
Greece	3.7	1	Syria	5.24	1
Guatemala	1.88	1	Tanzania	1.58	1
Honduras	1.56	1	Thailand	3.63	1
Hong Kong	4.9	1	Togo	1.75	.
India	2.26	1	Tunisia	3.73	1
Indonesia	5.7	1	Turkey	3.04	1
Ireland	3.3	1	Uganda	−0.12	1
Israel	2.87	1	United Kingdom	1.46	1
Italy	3.16	1	Uruguay	1.08	1
Jamaica	−1.11	1	Venezuela	−1.41	1
Japan	4.22	1	Zambia	−1.11	1
Jordan	6.01	1	Zimbabwe	2.07	1

Notes: '1' in the SW column indicates that the country is included in the Sachs and Warner regression. Growth is 'Trend growth in GDP per worker 1965–85'.

Notes

1   A more comprehensive discussion of this section along with proofs is contained in Rogers (1997).

2   Equation (2) can be thought of as either a separate functional form or an approximation to equation (1), since

$$\left[\frac{T-A}{A}\right] \approx \ln\left[\frac{T-A}{A} + 1\right] = \ln\left[\frac{T}{A}\right].$$

Such an approximation is good if A is close to T.

3   Baumol (1986, p. 1080) made this point in the following way, '[a] less developed country that produces no cars cannot benefit from the invention and adoption of a better car-producing robot in Japan.' Baumol, Blackman and Wolff (1989, p. 70) assert 'those countries that are so far behind the leaders that it will be impractical for them to profit substantially from the leaders' knowledge will generally not be able to participate from the convergence process at all.' Helliwell and Chung (1991, pp. 289–90) also consider qualifications to the ability of countries to catch up, including inappropriate technology. David (1993, p. 240) makes a similar point by using the idea of tacit knowledge (the knowledge or know-how that is difficult (costly) or impossible to codify for transmission), '[t]he greater the technological distance between firms in terms of the degree of overlap or disjointness in the domain of production experiences, the more serious is the problem posed by tacit knowledge.'

4   See Abramovitz and David (1996) for a slightly updated treatment of technological catch-up and social capability.

5   An unpublished paper by Hall and Jones (1996) includes such a foreign language variable (the fraction of a country's population that speaks an international language). The authors find this variable yields a positive and significant coefficient in a regression on output per worker.

6   Easterly and Levine (1995) use the log of telephones per worker as an explanatory variable where the value taken is an average over the growth period. Hence, the variable can be criticized as being endogenous.

7   Romer (1990) uses the log of newsprint consumption, and the number of radios per thousand population, as instruments for the initial level of income per capita. He does not, however, enter these as separate explanatory variables, or discuss them as proxies for knowledge diffusion.

8   For example, Helliwell (1992, pp. 8–9) states, '[f]or a given country size, larger trade flows might be a good proxy for the freer flows of ideas, on the presumption that whatever pattern of access and opportunities gave rise to the trade flows would also apply to knowledge transfers. This is over-simplified reasoning, but it may provide a sensible starting point.' Of course, trade openness may have other beneficial effects on growth that are unrelated to knowledge diffusion. Tybout (1992) contains a review of the effects of trade on productivity.

9   We should also note that Sala-i-Martin (1997) conducted a form of robustness test on 59 other variables finding 22 of them were significant explanators (including geographic dummies, political, religious, market distortions, investment, natural resources and trade openness variables) – although not all 22 variables were entered in the regression together.

10   The SW variable does not exactly match with the growth period used here, but given the difficulty of adjusting the SW measure to the 1965 to 1985 period used here, and the likelihood that such a variable would be highly correlated with the measure for 1965 to match with 1990, we use the SW variable as is.

11   An issue in empirical growth analysis is the potential for influential observations to drive the results on certain coefficients. To investigate this, all the regressions reported in Table 12.3 were re-estimated excluding countries with high values for each of the absorptive capability proxies (a high value is defined as above the 95th percentile of the distribution). The

results of these regressions show that all of the positive coefficients, apart from the coefficient on trade openness, remain significant.

12 The use of interaction effects to investigate such issues is not new. In fact, both the Sachs and Warner (SW) and Barro and Sala-i-Martin (BSiM) models use interaction terms to capture, in part, the role of technological catch-up. SW used their openness measure interacted with log of initial GDP per worker, while BSiM used a human capital measure interacted with initial GDP.

13 We omit SW's interaction term (openness * log $\text{GDP}_{\text{initial}}$) to prevent multi-collinearity problems.

14 As before, we also investigate the role of potential influential observations by running regressions omitting the observations with the largest values of the respective absorptive capability variable (again the cut off point being the 95th percentile). We find that all of the coefficients that were significant in the full sample are still significant. In addition, the coefficients on four other interaction terms are significant. Three of these have positive coefficients, namely, the interactive terms that include students studying in the USA, students studying natural sciences abroad, and books in specialized libraries.

15 Sachs and Warner (1997, p. 187), however, state that they do not find evidence of a non-linear technology-gap variable.

References

Abramovitz, M. (1986) 'Catching Up, Forging Ahead, and Falling Behind', *Journal of Economic History*, vol. xlvi, (2), pp. 385–406.

Abramovitz, M. and David, P. (1996) 'Convergence and Deferred Catch-up: Productivity Leadership and the Waning of American Exceptionalism', in R. Landau, T. Taylor and G. Wright (eds), *The Mosaic of Economic Growth*, San Francisco: Stanford University Press.

Barro, R. and Sala-i-Martin, X. (1995) *Economic Growth*, New York: McGraw-Hill.

Barro, R. and Lee, J.W. (1994) 'Losers and Winners in Economic Growth', in M. Bruno and B. Plesovic (eds), *Proceedings of the World Bank Annual Conference on Development Economics 1993*, Washington, DC: World Bank.

Baumol, W. (1986) 'Productivity Growth, Convergence, and Welfare: What the Long Run Data Show', *American Economic Review*, vol. 76(5)1, pp. 1072–85.

—, Blackman, S. Wolff, E. (1989) *Productivity and American Leadership: The Long View*, Cambridge, Mass.: MIT Press.

Bernard, M. and Ravenhill, J. (1995) 'Beyond Product Cycles and Flying Geese', *World Politics*, 47, pp. 171–209.

Cardwell, D. (1994) *The Fontana History of Technology*, London: Fontana Press.

Coe, D. and Helpman, E. (1995) 'International R&D Spillovers', *European Economic Review* vol. 39, pp. 859–87.

David, P.A. (1993) 'Path-Dependence and Predictability in Dynamic Systems with Local Network Externalities: A Paradigm for Historical Economics', in D. Foray and C. Freeman (eds), *Technology and the Wealth of Nations*, Paris: OECD.

De Long, J. and Summers, L. (1993) 'How Strongly do Developing Economies Benefit from Equipment Investment?', *Journal of Monetary Economics*, vol. 32, pp. 395–415.

Easterly, W. and Levine, R. (1995) 'Africa's Growth Tragedy: A Retrospective, 1960–89'. World Bank, Policy Research Paper no. 1503.

Edwards, S. (1998) 'Openness, Productivity and Growth: What do we Really Know?', *Economic Journal*, vol. 108(447), pp. 383–98.

Hall, R. and Jones, C. (1996) 'The Productivity of Nations', memos, Stanford University.

Hansson, P. and Henrekson, M. (1994) 'What Makes a Country Socially Capable of Catching Up?', *Weltwirtschaftliches Archiv*, vol. 130 (4), pp. 760–83.

Helliwell, J. (1992) 'Trade and Technical Progress', NBER Working Paper no. 4226.

Helliwell, J. and Chung, A. (1991) 'Globalization, Convergence, and the Prospects for Economic Growth', in J. Cornwall (ed.), *The Capitalists Economies: Prospects for the 1990s*, New York: Edward Elgar.

Hobday, M. (1995) *Innovation in East Asia*, Aldershot, UK: Edward Elgar.

Keller, W. (1996), 'Are International R&D Spillovers Trade-Related? Analyzing Spillovers Among Randomly Matched Trade Partners', University of Wisconsin, Madison, SSRI, 9607.

Levine, R. and Renelt, D. (1992) 'A Sensitivity Analysis of Cross-Country Growth Regressions', *American Economic Review*, vol. 82 (4), pp. 942–63.

— and Zervos, S. (1993) 'What we have Learned about Policy and Growth from Cross-country Regressions', *American Economic Review*, vol. 83 (2), pp. 426–30.

Nelson, R. and Phelps, E. (1966) 'Investment in Humans, Technological Diffusion, and Economic Growth', *American Economic Review*, vol. 56, pp. 69–75.

Pack, H. and Page, J. (1994) 'Accumulation, Exports, and Growth in the High-Performing Asian Economies', *Carnegie-Rochester Conference Series on Public Policy*, vol. 40, pp. 199–236.

Reddy, N. and Zhao, L. (1990) 'International Technology Transfer', *Research Policy*, vol. 19, pp. 285–307.

Rogers, M. (1997) 'The Diffusion of Knowledge and Economic Growth', PhD thesis, Economics Program, RSSS. Canberra: Australian National University.

Romer, P. (1990) 'Human Capital and Growth: Theory and Evidence', *Carnegie-Rochester Conference Series on Public Policy*, vol. 32, pp. 251–86.

Sachs, J. and Warner, A. (1997) 'Fundamental Sources of Long Run Growth', *American Economic Review*, vol. 87(2), pp. 184–8.

Sala-i-Martin, X. (1997) 'I Just Ran Two Million Regressions', *American Economic Review, Papers and Proceedings*, vol. 87(2), pp. 178–83.

Tybout, J. (1992) 'Linking Trade and Productivity: New Research Directions', *World Bank Economic Review*, vol. 6(2), pp. 189–211.

13

Foreign Direct Investment and Economic Growth in LDCs: Some Further Evidence[*]

V.N. Balasubramanyam, Mohammed Salisu and David Sapsford

F21 047
019 F43

Introduction

The phenomenon of foreign direct investment (FDI) has generated a large and still growing literature. Particular interest in the last decade (no doubt encouraged by the development of the so-called 'new' theory of economic growth) has been directed to the role played by FDI in determining the pace of economic growth in less-developed countries (LDCs), and it this topic that forms the subject matter of this chapter. Our motivation in writing this chapter is twofold. First, while the relationship between FDI and growth has been intensely debated in the literature, the precise nature of the relationship and the preconditions required for FDI to promote growth and the mechanisms through which it does so remain largely unexplored. Second, recent developments in growth theory provide a convenient framework within which to analyse the relationship between FDI and growth. Indeed, many of the growth-promoting factors, such as human capital and externalities, have long been recognized to be the main ingredients of FDI.

This chapter aims to identify the preconditions necessary for the effective utilization of FDI and the mechanisms through which it can promote growth, and the exploration of these aspects is grounded in the framework of new growth theory. The chapter is organized as follows: the

[*] This chapter is a revised and extended version of the paper presented at the conference Creating an Internationally Competitive Economy that was held at Curtin University of Technology, Perth, Western Australia between 27 and 28 August 1998. We are grateful to both the seminar participants and the editors of this volume for their helpful comments.

next two sections provide an overview of the major issues involved and set out the four major hypotheses to be considered. We than provide some empirical evidence relating to the four hypotheses, followed by an exploration of some specific issues relating to the influences of human capital, domestic competition and physical infrastructure upon the growth-enhancing effects of FDI. Finally we provide a summary and offer some concluding remarks.

The nature and character of FDI

Although there is no consensus, the following appear to be the major actors identified in the literature on FDI.[1]

1 FDI is a composite bundle of capital, know-how and technology.
2 Its main contribution to growth is through technology transfer and technology and skill diffusion in the countries importing FDI.
3 The effectiveness of FDI in promoting growth is, amongst other things, a function of the type of trade regime in place in the host country. FDI in the presence of a protectionist regime is likely to reduce growth, where as a liberal trade regime is likely to promote growth.[2]
4 Most empirical studies suggest that foreign-owned firms in comparable industry groups exhibit superior productive efficiency relative to that of locally-owned firms on most criteria of efficiency. But whether or not the social rate of return to FDI is on a par with the private rate of return is a matter of dispute.

There is, however, little empirical analysis relating to the impact of FDI on growth in general. While much of the recent literature has addressed the impact of exports on growth, relatively little attention has been paid to the relationship between FDI and growth.

FDI and economic growth

In a recent paper (Balasubramanyam, Salisu and Sapsford, 1996) we addressed the issue of the impact of FDI on economic growth under differing trade-policy regimes, specifically setting out to test the hypothesis proposed by Bhagwati (1978) that, given other factors, the efficiency of FDI in promoting growth is likely to be higher in countries pursuing an export promotion (EP) strategy than in countries pursuing an import substitution (IS) strategy. An EP strategy is defined as one which is neutral in terms of policy-oriented incentives provided for export and import substitution industries. The results of the statistical exercise provided support for Bhagwati's hypothesis, but the precise reasons for the observed efficacy of FDI in EP countries are yet to be established.

In this chapter, we argue that some of the tenets of new growth theory (see for example Pack, 1994) provide an appropriate framework for identifying the factors underlying the observed efficacy of FDI in promoting growth in countries pursuing liberal foreign trade and investment regimes. In this context we will identify a number of testable hypotheses.

The essence of new growth theory is that contrary to neoclassical wisdom, growth can be endogenous. In the neoclassical Solow (1957)-type models, embodying constant returns to scale (CRS), production functions and standard utility maximization behaviour, increased capital accumulation will result in diminishing returns to capital. This, of course, discourages both savings and investment. Given such diminishing returns, growth can occur only in the presence of labour force growth or technical change. Both these sources are exogenous, with the former altering the slope of the production function and the latter shifting it outwards. Furthermore, the extant models provide no explanation for either technical change or the growth attributed to the 'A' term in the familiar Cobb–Douglas type of production function.

Endogenous growth results from mechanisms which prevent the unbounded decline in the marginal physical product of capital. This could come about through increasing returns to scale, imperfect competition, human capital accumulation or spillover effects. While there are a variety of models, most emphasize human capital and knowledge spillover effects or externalities inherent in R&D. One idea is that while private rates of return to investment in R&D could decline over time, the social rate of return could remain high. A divergence between social and private rates of return to investment is a common feature of these models, it is this high social rate of return via externalities which provides a floor to the decline in the marginal product of capital in the aggregate. Another idea is that returns to the accumulation of human capital do not meet with diminishing returns in the same fashion as returns to the accumulation of physical capital. Such investment increases not only private returns but also social returns.

The hypotheses

New growth theory emphasizes precisely those factors which are supposed to characterize FDI. To the extent that FDI is believed to transfer technology, promote learning by doing, train labour, and in general result in spillovers of human skills and technology it should promote growth. For all this to occur, however, several conditions should hold and we therefore propose the following four hypotheses:

Hypothesis 1   FDI can promote growth in the presence of a liberal trade regime; and the fruits of FDI should be transferable abroad by the investors. In other words FDI, economic growth and exports are intertwined.

Hypothesis 2   FDI does not, in itself, transfer sufficient volumes of human capital. But, rather, it augments existing human capital. More precisely, we argue that a threshold level of endowments of human capital is a necessary condition for the promotion of growth through FDI.

Hypothesis 3   Effective utilization of human capital in conjunction with FDI requires an adequate domestic market for the goods produced. In other words, mere importation of FDI through the offer of policy-induced incentives and investments in the production of human capital through investments in education may generate export enclaves. FDI has to be coordinated with investments in human capital. This can occur in the presence of a domestic market.

Hypothesis 4   Technology and skill spillovers from FDI do not materialize from the mere presence of FDI, they have to be engineered with effective policies. These include effective competition from locally-owned firms through both investments in R&D and domestic production. In other words, dualistic structures make for promotion of growth through FDI.

We believe that the foregoing hypotheses provide the basis of an explanation of the growth-enhancing effects of FDI in general, and in particular for the observed efficacy of FDI in promoting growth in countries operating within the context of a liberalized as opposed to an inwardly-oriented trade policy regime.

Some empirical evidence

In this section we describe some results that were obtained in attempting to test the above four hypotheses.[3] It is convenient to begin with a brief overview of the estimation framework to be used.

The model we use to test this hypothesis is derived, in conventional manner, from a production function in which FDI is introduced as an input in addition to labour and domestic capital. As stated earlier, FDI is the prime source of human capital and new technology to developing countries and this variable is included in the production function in order to capture the externalities, *learning by watching* and spillover effects associated with FDI. We also introduce exports as an additional factor input into the production function, following the large number of empirical studies which investigate the export-led growth hypothesis (see for example Feder, 1983; Balassa, 1985; Salvatore and Hatcher, 1991; Greenaway and Sapsford, 1994). In the usual notation the production function can be written as follows:

$$Y = g(L, K, F, X, t) \tag{1}$$

where: Y is the gross domestic product (GDP) in real terms; L is labour input; K the domestic capital stock; F the stock of foreign capital; X is exports; and t is a time trend, capturing technical progress.

Assuming equation (1) to be linear in logs, taking logs and differencing we obtain the following expression describing the determinants of the growth rate of GDP:

$$y = \alpha + \beta l + \gamma k + \psi f + \varphi x \tag{2}$$

where lower case letters denote the rate of growth of individual variables and the parameters β, γ, ψ and φ are output elasticities of labour, domestic capital, foreign capital and exports respectively. Alternatively, these parameters may be interpreted as the partial derivatives of the growth rate of GDP with respect to the growth rate of the respective right-hand side variables in equation (1).

In view of the well-known and formidable problems associated with attempts to measure the capital stock – especially in the context of less-developed countries – we follow the precedent set in numerous previous studies by approximating the rate of growth of the capital stock by the share of investment in GDP. Accordingly, replacing the rates of change in domestic and foreign capital inputs by the share of domestic investment and foreign direct investment in GDP yields the following growth equation:

$$y = \alpha + \beta l + \gamma(I/Y) + \psi(FDI/Y) + \varphi x \tag{3}$$

In the econometric analysis which follows, the parameter ψ, the elasticity of output with respect to foreign capital is of particular interest. The model is estimated against annual average data relating to a cross-section of 46 countries over the period 1970 to 1985.[4]

Hypothesis 1

This hypothesis is concerned with the influence of the trade policy regime upon the strength of the growth-promoting influence of FDI. This issue was explored in some depth in our earlier paper (Balasubramanyam, Salisu and Sapsford, 1996) in the context of Bhagwati's (1978) classification of trade policy regimes as either EP or IS. In that study (see the results summarized in Table 13.1) we found evidence indicating that the coefficient of the FDI to GDP ratio in the growth equation (3) is not only positive but also significantly greater for the export-oriented countries than for those countries which pursued an import-substituting trade policy. Because of the spillover effects and externalities associated with human capital, and the higher rate of technical innovation associated with foreign direct (as opposed to domestic) investment, we also argued in that paper that it seems reasonable to expect that, at least for the export-oriented group of countries, foreign investment is a more powerful driving force in the growth process than is domestic investment. This supplementary hypothesis (according to which the elasticity of output with respect to foreign capital is predicted as exceeding that with respect to domestic capital) was also found to be consistent with the data. Looked at from an alternative perspective, our evidence relating to this supplementary hypothesis suggests that foreign investment is more important than domestic investment in terms of its individual contribution to the (calculated value of the) growth rate, as the dependent variable in equation (3).

The classification of alternative trade policy regimes is neither a straightforward nor a non-controversial exercise. Although the primary purpose of our earlier study was to focus upon Bhagwati's classificatory system of EP versus IS regimes, we also report in Table 13.1 the results which emerged when our sample was subdivided according to the World Bank's well-known alternative classification (World Bank, 1987; Greenaway and Nam, 1988) of countries according to the apparent outwardness of their trade policy regime. As can be seen from the results reported as equations (1.7) to (1.10), essentially the same conclusions follow when the analysis is replicated using this alternative classification.[5]

Hypothesis 2

Central to our second hypothesis is the concept of human capital, the measurement of which, as distinct from the size of the workforce, is by no means a straightforward matter. In our analysis we follow Crafts and Thomas (1986), amongst others, by proxying inputs of human capital by a real wage variable. A common approach to this issue is to proxy human

Table 13.1 Cross-section regression analysis of determinants of growth rate of real GDP, 1970–85 (annual averages)

Eqn No.	Sample	Estimated coefficients of:										Estimation method
		Cons	FDI/Y	I/Y	l	x	R^2	LM_1	LM_2	LM_3	LM_s	
1.1	All countries (n = 46)	-0.20 (0.16)	1.84** (3.86)	-0.004 (0.09)	1.07** (2.73)	0.22** (4.74)	0.57	1.27	1.01	0.99	n.a.	OLS
1.2	EP countries (n = 18)	-0.63 (0.39)	1.83** (3.71)	0.01 (0.19)	0.95 (1.67)	0.30** (4.45)	0.79	0.40	1.11	0.94	n.a.	OLS
1.3	IS countries (n = 28)	0.72 (0.34)	1.77 (1.39)	-0.03 (0.45)	1.07* (1.85)	0.16* (2.35)	0.37	2.40	0.37	0.86	n.a.	OLS
1.4	All countries (n = 46)	-0.18 (0.14)	1.65** (2.68)	-0.002 (0.05)	1.07** (2.73)	0.22** (4.76)	0.57	0.01	0.88	1.11	4.53	GIVE
1.5	EP countries (n = 18)	-0.52 (0.32)	1.68** (3.20)	0.01 (0.21)	0.93 (1.62)	0.30** (4.49)	0.79	0.76	1.01	1.62	4.28	GIVE
1.6	IS countries (n = 28)	-2.14 (0.40)	-10.16 (0.90)	0.22 (0.79)	1.21 (0.94)	0.30 (1.52)	0.01	1.31	3.71	1.10	0.86	GIVE
1.7	EP countries† (n = 10)	-3.25 (1.66)	1.54* (3.43)	0.06 (0.86)	2.09* (3.83)	0.22 (2.31)	0.90	1.29	0.27	0.62	n.a.	OLS
1.8	IS countries† (n = 24)	1.57 (0.83)	-0.14 (0.08)	-0.05 (0.71)	0.90 (1.61)	0.21 (2.02)	0.33	3.88	5.86	0.06	n.a.	OLS
1.9	EP countries† (n = 10)	-3.27 (1.66)	1.43* (2.93)	0.06 (0.91)	2.11* (3.83)	0.22 (2.28)	0.90	0.00	0.32	0.66	4.13	GIVE
1.10	IS countries† (n = 24)	0.81 (0.21)	-13.71 (0.96)	0.18 (0.67)	0.32 (0.25)	0.35 (1.37)	0.01	1.42	3.38	0.36	0.12	GIVE

Notes: Figures in parenthesis are absolute 't' values. A single asterisk denotes an estimated coefficient which is significantly different from zero at the 5 per cent level, while a double asterisk denotes significance at the 1 per cent level. LM_1 denotes Ramsey's RESET test of functional form, LM_2 denotes the Jarque–Bera test for residual normality, LM_3 denotes the Lagrange multiplier test for heteroscedasticity, while LM_s denotes Sargan's general misspecification test for instrumental variable estimation. On the relevant null-hypothesis these test statistics are distributed as χ^2 with 1, 2, 1 and 2 degrees of freedom respectively.

† Based on World Bank classification; GIVE = generalized instrumental variable estimator; OLS = ordinary least squares.

Source: Summary of results from Balasubramanyam, Salisu and Sapsford (1996).

capital inputs by (capitalized) difference between the industry wage rate and some unskilled wage rate as the measure of average per capita human capital in a sector. In the interests of simplicity we adopt a one-period horizon and utilize the manufacturing real wage as our proxy. As we are working with cross-sectional country (as distinct from industry) data we can interpret this measure as capturing the human-capital premium relative to the country in the sample which possesses the lowest real wage and, by implication, the smallest endowment of human capital.[6]

Equation (2.1) in Table 13.2 summarizes the results that were obtained when model (3), augmented by the real wage growth variable (*WR*), specified as a proxy for the growth in human capital inputs, was estimated against our sample of 46 developing countries. As can be seen, the real wage growth variable has the hypothesized positive value and is significantly different from zero at the 1 per cent level on a one-tailed test. In a separate study we have produced evidence to show that after controlling for differences in input growth, the South-east Asian and Pacific Rim countries in our sample have experienced more rapid growth in real output than their Latin and Central American counterparts. Since such differences were found to manifest themselves in a significant difference in the intercept term (seen as a measure of autonomous growth) in growth model (3) as between these groups of countries, equation (2.1) is reestimated with intercept dummies corresponding to these two sub-groups of countries (denoted, respectively, by *ASIA* and *LATIN*) included. As may be seen from equation (2.2) in Table 13.2, the Southeast Asian and Pacific Rim dummy is positive (although not significant) whereas the Central and Latin American dummy is negatively signed and significantly different from zero at the 5 per cent level.

Our second hypothesis is, in essence, concerned with the interactions which occur between human capital and FDI in the context of the growth process and, as such, may be easily investigated by adding an interaction term between these two variables to model (3). The results that were obtained when such an interaction term (denoted by *FDIWR*) was specified for all countries in our sample are reported as equation (2.3) in Table 13.2. Although the estimated coefficient of the FDI-human capital interaction term in this equation is found to be positive, in accordance with the hypothesis, it fails to achieve statistical significance. However, our second hypothesis holds that a certain threshold level of human capital endowments is necessary before the interaction effects begin to make their presence felt. In order to allow for this threshold mechanism, the countries in our sample were ranked according to their inputs of human capital (as proxied by the real wage) and a set of modified interaction terms

Estimated coefficients of:

Eqn No.	Cons	FDI/Y	I/Y	l	x	wr	ASIA	LATIN	FDIwr	FDIfwr	GDPP	MFG VA	L_{70} (Infra)	HK_{70} (FDIlnf)	R^2	LM_1	LM_2	LM_3
2.1	-0.52 (0.45)	1.31** (2.72)	0.001 (0.04)	0.95** (2.62)	0.18** (4.03)	0.20** (2.83)									0.64	0.28	0.50	1.38
2.2	-0.58 (0.56)	1.27** (2.94)	0.02 (0.49)	1.03** (3.14)	0.17** (4.19)	0.16* (2.48)	0.75 (1.16)	-1.15* (2.18)							0.73	2.66	0.23	0.99
2.3	-0.52 (0.48)	0.95 (0.58)	0.02 (0.52)	1.02** (2.99)	0.17** (4.14)	0.15* (2.21)	0.72 (1.07)	-1.14* (2.14)	0.04 (0.20)						0.73	4.63	0.23	0.87
2.4	-0.11 (0.09)	0.30 (0.27)	0.01 (0.16)	0.84** (2.22)	0.17** (3.75)	0.18* (2.59)				0.05 (1.02)					0.65	2.77	0.48	1.03
2.5	1.66 (1.41)	0.11 (0.12)	-0.03 (0.79)	0.80* (2.43)	0.14** (3.48)	0.21** (3.42)				0.09* (2.20)	-.0006** (3.61)				0.74	2.31	1.40	0.17
2.6	1.39 (1.19)	-0.12 (0.12)	-0.04 (1.21)	0.77** (2.38)	0.10* (2.20)	0.22** (3.57)				0.11* (2.60)	-0.001** (3.82)	0.08 (1.61)			0.76	2.48	5.51	0.51
2.7[†]	0.98 (0.68)	0.58 (0.44)	-0.032 (0.82)	1.05* (2.64)	0.173** (3.36)	0.013 (0.644)				0.013 (1.58)	-0.001* (2.47)	0.08 (0.5)			0.65	2.24	0.88	0.09
2.8[†]	1.54 (1.05)	0.96 (0.95)	-0.041 (1.04)	0.92* (2.33)	0.165** (3.13)	-0.10 (0.39)				0.17* (1.81)	-0.001* (2.27)	0.03 (1.03)			0.65	0.51	2.12	0.64
2.9[‡]	-1.08 (0.64)	2.77** (4.91)	-0.03 (0.89)	1.17** (3.12)	0.20** (3.96)	-0.08 (0.43)					-0.0003 (1.62)	-0.04 (0.68)	0.37* (1.95)	0.82 (1.16)	0.66	1.72	1.81	0.00
2.10[++]	0.97 (0.71)	-0.075 (0.06)	-0.03 (0.88)	0.92** (2.62)	0.10* (1.99)	0.18** (2.54)				0.10* (1.85)	-0.001** (3.32)	0.07 (1.45)	0.011 (0.89)	0.009 (0.49)	0.77	1.51	2.85	1.24

Notes: As for Table 13.1. All variables are as defined in Table 13.1 except *wr*, which is the growth rate of the real wage rate, *ASIA* which is an intercept dummy for Asian countries, while *LATIN* is an intercept dummy for Latin American countries. *FDIfwr* is an interaction term between *FDI/Y*, *l* and *wr* utilizing a threshold level for *wr* (second quartile). *GDPP* is real GDP per capita and *MFGVA* is the share of manufacturing in total value added. *m* is the growth rate of the share in GDP of imports of machinery and equipment from industrial countries.

[†] In equations (2.7) and (2.8) the variable *wr* is replaced in each relevant term by the *secondary school enrolment rate* (as obtained from the World Bank's *World Data 1995* cd-rom) and by the Barro–Lee measure of the stock of educational attainment respectively. [‡] In equation (2.9), the variable *wr* is replaced by Gemmell's measure of the average rate of growth of human capital over the period 1970 to 1985. In this equation the term L_{70} denotes the initial (i.e. 1970) labour force, while the term HK_{70} denotes the initial stock of human capital, calculated according to the method set out in Gemmell (1996). [++] In equation (2.10), columns 14 and 15 relate, respectively, to the infrastructure variable (*Infra*) and an interaction term (*FDIlnf*) between this variable and FDI.

constructed. The first of these takes the value zero for all countries in the lowest quartile of the distribution according to human capital inputs, and the product of FDI growth and real wage growth for all other countries. The second such variable takes as its dividing line the second quartile, while the third takes the third quartile. The results thus obtained failed to reveal a significant interaction coefficient. One possible explanation for this is simply that the interaction occurs between FDI and growth in both dimensions of labour input; namely, quantity (as measured by labour input, in person hours) and quality (as measured by human capital inputs). Accordingly, the analysis was repeated with the interaction term specified as the interaction between growth in FDI and growth in *total* labour input, with the latter represented by the growth rate of labour input (in persons) plus the growth rate of human capital inputs as represented by real wage growth. For all quartiles the estimated coefficient of this interaction variable (denoted by *FDLFWRD*) was found to be positive. Judged in terms of significance, the most appropriate threshold seems to be a little below the second quartile. A sequential search procedure suggested the threshold as occurring at the twentieth observation in our sample of countries ranked according to the real wage level which gives rise to a '*t*' value of 1.05. Although a long way from significance it is felt, especially given the crudity of our human capital measure, that this interactive effect is worthy of further investigation. The performance of this interaction term might be improved if data relating to labour hours could be brought into the picture, although the absence of available data for the countries in our sample prevents us from doing so at this time.

Hypothesis 3

Our third hypothesis concerns the role of the domestic market for the goods produced as a result of FDI. The basic argument is that the existence of an adequate domestic market is an essential prerequisite if the potential growth-enhancing effects are to be fully realized. Perhaps the simplest proxy that may be adopted to capture the effect of the domestic market in this context is real GDP per capita (denoted by *GDPP*). Equation (2.5) reports the results which emerge when equation (2.4) is reestimated after the inclusion of such a variable. As can be seen from equation (2.5), the estimated coefficient of the real GDP per capita is negative and statistically significant at the 1 per cent level. However, the argument underlying hypothesis 3 suggests that the real GDP per capita variable will possess a positive sign. One plausible interpretation of the observed negative coefficient is that this variable is picking up (the dominance of) convergence effects of the sort widely observed elsewhere in the endogenous growth literature (see, for example, Levine and Renelt, 1992; Barro and Sala-i-Martin, 1992).

The results reported in equation (2.5) are interesting in that they show that once one controls for the effects of the domestic market/convergence (as proxied by GDP per capita), the interaction between the FDI variable and total labour input growth (the growth in persons plus the growth in human capital inputs) that was the subject of hypothesis 2 becomes statistically significant when evaluated in relation to the second quartile as the threshold. We did investigate the possible existence of a spillover effect between real GDP per capita and FDI but could find no evidence to indicate a significant coefficient. In essence what these results would seem to suggest is that the domestic market does have a role to play in the growth process and that once this is controlled for, a significant positive interaction between FDI and labour input above a threshold level of human capital emerges.

Hypothesis 4

In order to test this particular hypothesis we would ideally like to use data relating to real domestic expenditures on R&D. Unfortunately such data are not currently available to us. The second dimension to this hypothesis concerns the strength of competition from locally-owned firms. In order to test this dimension one would ideally employ data relating to concentration ratios seen as a measure of the domestic competitive climate. Once again, however, data constraints prevent us from so doing. However, it is possible to capture, in a rather crude way, the role of local competition by using some measure of domestic output share (Chenery and Syrquin, 1975). Accordingly, the share of manufacturing value added in total value added (*MFGVA*) was included as an additional explanatory variable in model (3).

In addition we explored various interaction terms between FDI growth and this variable of the sort discussed above in connection with hypothesis 2. While no convincing evidence of significant interaction effects between FDI and the value-added share emerged from this exercise, it is important to notice (see equation (2.6)) that once we control for the influence of local competition (as proxied by the value-added share of manufacturing) the interaction between FDI and labour plus human capital input considered under hypothesis 2 emerges as positive *and* statistically significant. In addition, it may be noted that both the Southeast Asia and Pacific Rim dummy and the Latin and Central American dummy become insignificant once the domestic market and local competition variables are included, a result that might be taken to suggest that the apparent differences in autonomous growth performance for countries in these two sub-groups may be due to differences in their domestic markets, the strength of local competition and FDI-labour (including human capital) interaction.

Some further results

In this section we explore further a number of issues relating to the measurement of human capital, the importance of structure of the domestic market and the possible role of investments in the physical infrastructure.[7]

Alternative measures of human capital

As already noted, the measurement of human capital inputs is by no means a straightforward matter. For reasons already discussed, our chosen measure in the preceding empirical analysis was the real wage seen, in essence, as an *output*-based measure. In many previous studies investigators have chosen to employ what amount to *input*-based measures of human capital. The two most commonly used proxies for human capital of this sort are, first, the secondary-school enrolment rate (see for example Levine and Renelt, 1992), and, second, some measure of the stock of educational attainment (for example Barro and Lee, 1993). In order to explore the robustness, or otherwise, of our findings to alternative proxies of the human capital stock the preceding empirical analysis was repeated using both the secondary-school enrolment rate and the Barro–Lee measure of the stock of educational achievements. As can be seen from the results summarized in equations (2.7) and (2.8) of Table 13.2, which replicate (2.6) but employ, respectively, the secondary-school enrolment rate and the Barro and Lee stock measure in place of the previous real wage measure of human capital, the overall character of our results is little altered by the use of these alternative measures of human capital.[8]

In a recent study of the impact of human capital on growth performance, Gemmell (1996), recognizing that the stock of human capital is determined not only by the rates of growth of the labour force and school enrolments but also by their initial values, argues that the widespread use of the school enrolment rate as a measure of human capital in growth equations may be flawed because in the typically specified equation this variable, in effect, encapsulates both human capital *stock* and *accumulation* effects. His analysis demonstrates that, in essence, when school enrolment rates are used in growth equations the estimated coefficients on labour-growth terms will capture not only the effects of physical increases in labour inputs, but also some part of the effects of human capital stocks or investment, with the consequence that failure to find significant effects associated with school enrolment variables does not necessarily imply the absence of human capital effects. In order to overcome this problem, Gemmell proposes an extended formulation which includes two separate (sets of) explanatory variables; the first being designed to capture the effects on growth of *initial* stocks of human capital, and the second to capture the effects of a change in the pace of human capital *accumulation*. The results which were obtained when our model was reestimated after the inclusion of the additional explanatory variables suggested by Gemmell's analysis (namely the labour force and stock of human capital in the initial year of our sample period and the average rate of growth of human capital over our study period[9]) are reported in equation (2.9) in Table 13.2. As may be seen from these results, neither the initial stock of human capital (HK_{70}) nor its average growth rate over the period 1970 to 1985 exerted significant effects upon growth. However, the results do suggest that, in contrast, the initial size of the labour force exerted a positive and significant effect upon growth performance in our sample of countries. In an important sense this finding might perhaps be taken to suggest that previous studies that have relied principally on measures of school enrolment to proxy human capital might in fact have been picking up no more than the significant effect of the initial labour force upon growth performance over the study period. This is a possibility that warrants further investigation.

Domestic market size: depth vs breadth

When testing hypothesis 3 we found evidence, using GDP per capita as our size measure, to suggest that convergence effects appeared to dominate possible size effects. In one sense it might be argued that while a variable such as GDP per capita provides a measure of market *depth* (in that, other things equal, one would expect the range of goods and services consumed in the domestic economy to be positively related to its average level of GDP per capita), it fails to capture the pure size (or breadth) of the domestic economy. One straightforward proxy for the *breadth* dimension is provided by the size of the population. However in some previous preliminary work we were unable to find any evidence to suggest that population exerts a significant effect upon growth in the context of the current model for further discussion see Balasubramanyam, Salisu and Sapsford, 1997).

Overseas competition in the domestic market

In our discussion of hypothesis 4, attention was focused on the strength of competition from locally-owned firms. However, equally relevant is the strength of competition from foreign-produced imports. In order to test for the influence of such foreign competition our model may be extended by the inclusion of the share of imports to total domestic demand as an additional explanatory variable. (See Balasubramanyam, Salisu and Sapsford (1997) for some preliminary econometric evidence using this measure, the results of which appear to suggest that foreign competition may have a significant role to play).

Physical infrastructure

One further determinant of economic growth in general, and the growth-enhancing effects of FDI in particular, implicit in much of the new growth theory literature is the existence of an 'adequate' physical infrastructure. Unfortunately, the precise meaning of adequacy in this context is all too often left to the imagination of the reader, as indeed is the particular dimension of the physical infrastructure that is seen as relevant. As far as economic growth in LDCs is concerned, there can surely be little doubt that an inadequate infrastructure of roads (and perhaps also telecommunications) can act as an impediment to growth performance. Although not without its limitations, one useful proxy for the adequacy of the basic physical communications infrastructure is provided by the World Bank's index of the percentage of total road length that is paved, as published on its *World Development Indicators* (1997) cd-rom. In order to allow for the possible effects of physical infrastructure, our model was augmented by this index. And in order to test for possible complementarities in the growth process between FDI and the adequacy of the physical communications infrastructure, an interaction term between these two variables was included as a further explanatory variable.

The results obtained when equation (2.6) was extended to include the population, import share and infrastructure variables described above are summarized in equation (2.10).[10] As can be seen from these results, although both the infrastructure coefficient and the coefficient of the interaction term with respect to FDI possess the expected positive sign, neither achieves significance. Further work is clearly needed in order to ascertain whether this result reflects the inadequacy of our infrastructure proxy or the genuine absence of infrastructural effects.

Concluding remarks

Our objective in this work has been to develop and test some new hypotheses relating to the growth-enhancing effects of FDI. Tentative results presented here suggest that an important role is played by both the size of the domestic market and the competitive climate relative to both local producers and foreign competitors. In addition, we have explored various alternative approaches to measuring the role of human capital in the context of LDC growth and produced some evidence which would seem to suggest that the approach adopted in a number of previous investigations may have yielded misleading results. Perhaps the strongest result to emerge from our study concerns the apparently significant role played by FDI–labour (*including* human capital) interactions in the growth process.

Notes

1   For further discussion, see Balasubramanyam and Salisu (1991).
2   There are a number of theoretical arguments to support item 3. For a (partial) review see Balasubramanyam, Salisu and Sapsford (1996).
3   The results reported in this section in relation to hypothesis 1 were obtained in Balasubramanyam, Salisu and Sapsford (1996), while those relating to hypotheses 2 to 4 were initially reported in Balasubramanyam, Salisu and Sapsford (1999).
4   *Data sources*   Real GDP growth data were derived from Summers and Heston (1988) while data relating to domestic investment and import shares and real exports were derived from the International Monetary Fund's *International Financial Statistics* (various editions). Labour force data were obtained from the *World Development Report* (various issues) and FDI data from various editions of *Transnational Corporations in World Development* (United Nations: New York).
5   Although not reported in the present chapter, we did repeat the analysis using the so-called *residual* approach to the measurement of trade policy orientation. This approach, which was developed by Balassa (1985), involves the construction as an index of trade policy of the deviation of the actual volume of exports from the volume of exports predicted by what he saw as a simple structural model of trade. Assuming exports to be a linear function of *only* per capita income, population and the availability of mineral resources, Balassa interpreted positive residuals as reflecting *export promotion* policies and negative residuals as indicating *inward orientation*. Repetition of the analysis with countries classified according to Balassa's method (results available on request) was found to yield essentially the same conclusions regarding the influence of the trade policy regime upon the growth-enhancing power of FDI as emerged from both Bhagwati's classification and that of the World Bank.
6   Since the model is estimated in logarithmic first-difference form, the results will be invariant whether the real wage or its deviation from the lowest value observed in the sample is employed in the estimation. For ease of interpretation the former specification is adopted.
7   Central to any modern analysis of the determinants of the pace of economic growth is the issue of technical progress. In the preceding analysis we employed what amounts to a conventional Cobb–Douglas production function. It therefore follows on the basis of the usual assumption that technical progress occurs in equation (1) at some constant exponential rate,

that the intercept in our estimated growth equation (3) above may be interpreted as the (exogenously given) rate of neutral technical progress. In order to provide a more complete explanation of the determinants of growth it is therefore necessary to endogenize the rate at which technical progress occurs in the country or countries being investigated. In a recent study Coe, Helpman and Hoffmaister (1997) have produced some strong evidence to suggest that in a sample of developing countries the rate of growth of total factor productivity is positively and significantly related to the change in the share in GDP of machinery and equipment imports from industrial countries. The basic argument here is that developing countries that do little or no research and development themselves have an opportunity to benefit from R&D that is undertaken in the industrial countries through their trade with such countries. By importing a larger share of intermediate and capital goods it is argued that a developing country can boost its domestic factor productivity. In essence, the argument here is that by importing from the industrialized countries machinery and equipment embodying foreign knowledge, the countries of the developing world can acquire useful information that would otherwise be costly to obtain. See Balasubramanyam, Salisu and Sapsford (1999) for a test of this hypothesis.

8   One noteworthy feature, however, is the fact that neither of these two alternative human capital variables achieves significance. Notice also that the share of manufacturing value added in total value added becomes insignificant when each of these two alternative human capital variables is utilized.

9   Measures of the latter two of these variables were constructed from the available (including school enrolment rate) data by following the procedures described in Gemmell (1996, pp. 25–6).

10   For reasons of brevity the estimated coefficients relating to the population and import-share variables are not reported in equation (2.10) in Table 12.2. In neither case was the estimated parameter found to be significantly different from zero; the relevant estimates (with 't' ratios in parentheses) being 0.0007 (0.26) and –0.027 (0.77) respectively.

References

Balassa, B. (1985) 'Exports, Policy Choices, and Economic Growth in Developing Countries after the 1973 Oil Shock', *Journal of Development Economics*, vol. 18, pp. 23–35.

Balasubramanyam, V.N. and Salisu, M. (1991) 'EP, IS and Direct Foreign Investment in LDCs', in A. Koekkoek, and L.B.M. Mennes, (eds), *International Trade and Global Development*, London: Routledge.

— and Sapsford, D. (1996) 'Foreign Direct Investment and Growth in EP and IS Countries's, *Economic Journal*, vol. 106(434), pp. 92–105.

—, — and — D. (1997) 'Foreign Direct Investment and Growth: New Hypotheses and Evidence', Paper presented at the Royal Economic Society Conference, 26 March.

—, — and — (1999) 'Foreign Direct Investment as an Engine of Growth', *Journal of International Trade and Economic Development*, vol. 8(1), pp. 27–40.

Bhagwati, J.N. (1978) *Anatomy and Consequences of Exchange Control Regimes*, Vol. 1, Studies in International Economic Relations, No. 10, New York: National Bureau of Economic Research.

Barro, R.J. and Lee, J.W. (1993) 'International Comparisons of Educational Attainment', *Journal of Monetary Economics*, vol. 32(3), pp. 363–94.

— and Sala-i-Martin, X. (1992) 'Convergence', *Journal of Political Economy*, vol. 100(2), pp. 223–51.

Chenery, H. and Syrquin, M. (1975) *Patterns of Development*, Oxford: Oxford University Press.

Coe, D.T., Helpman, E. and Hoffmaister, A.W. (1997), 'North–South R&D Spillovers', *Economic Journal*, vol. 107, No. 440, pp. 134–49.

Crafts, N. and Thomas, M. (1986) 'Comparative Advantage in UK Manufacturing Trade, 1910–1935', *Economic Journal*, vol. 96(383), pp. 629–45.

Feder, G. (1983) 'On Exports and Economic Growth', *Journal of Development Economics*, vol. 12, pp. 59–73.

Gemmell, N. (1996) 'Evaluating the Impacts of Human Capital Stocks and Accumulation on Economic Growth: Some New Evidence', *Oxford Bulletin of Economics and Statistics*, vol. 58(1), pp. 9–28.

Greenaway, D. and Nam, C. H. (1988) 'Industrialization and Macroeconomic Performance in Developing Countries under Alternative Trade Strategies', *Kyklos*, vol. 41(3), pp. 419–35.

— and Sapsford, D. (1994) 'What Does Liberalisation Do for Exports and Growth', *Weltwirtschaftliches Archiv*, vol. 130(1), pp. 152–73.

Levine, R and Renelt, D. (1992) 'A Sensitivity Analysis of Cross-Country Growth Regressions', *American Economic Review*, vol. 82(4), pp. 942–63.

Pack, H. (1994) 'Endogenous Growth Theory: Intellectual Appeal and Empirical Shortcomings', *Journal of Economic Perspectives*, vol. 8(1), pp. 55–72.

Salvatore, D. and Hatcher, T. (1991) 'Inward Oriented and Outward Oriented Trade Strategies', *Journal of Development Studies*, vol. 27, pp. 7–25.

Solow, R.M. (1957) 'Technical Change and the Aggregate Production Function', *Review of Economics and Statistics*, vol. 39, pp. 312–20.

Summers, R. and Heston, A (1988) 'A New Set of International Comparisons of Real Product and Price Levels: Estimates for 130 Countries, 1950–85', *Review of Income and Wealth*, vol. 34, pp. 1–25.

World Bank (1987) *World Development Report*, New York: Oxford University Press.

14

Transaction Efficiency in New Zealand and Australia, 1961–96

Tim Hazledine[*]

Introduction

In 1984 the New Zealand government began a sequence of, to date, more than one hundred major economic reforms which converted what had been the most regulated of OECD economies into perhaps now the most open and least regulated.[1] This remarkable programme of forced change – which perhaps is better suited to the word 'revolution' than 'reforms' – was motivated, or at least justified, by dissatisfaction with the performance of the New Zealand economy before 1984, which was blamed on rigidities and inefficiencies to be corrected by the imposition of 'free market' principles.

By now, fifteen years on, there is a fairly general sense of disappointment in New Zealand with the results of the reforms; in particular with productivity and growth performance. Whereas over the much-maligned 1978–85 'Muldoon period'[2] annual real GDP and labour productivity growth averaged 3.0 per cent and 1.9 per cent respectively compared to Australia's 3.2 per cent and 1.7 per cent, from 1985 to 1996 the New Zealand numbers were 1.5 per cent and 0.7 per cent whereas the Australian economy, which had not been subjected to a major reform process, showed GDP growth averaging 3.1 per cent and productivity increases averaging 1.1 per cent. Whilst poor results in the first years of the reforms might be blamed on adjustment costs and/ or the legacy (especially public sector debt) of the Muldoon excesses, by now – with many of the reforms in place for a decade or more – the

[*] Thanks to my discussant, Phil Lewis, and other participants at the conference Creating an Internationally Competitive Economy for their helpful comments and suggestions.

continued weak performance of the New Zealand economy seems to require a more fundamental, long-run explanation.

This chapter will put forward an hypothesis about where the explanation is to be found, and show data consistent with this. The hypothesis is that the *transaction costs* of operating the New Zealand economy have increased as a result of the reforms, counterbalancing improvements in allocative efficiency resulting from market liberalization. We do not here test this hypothesis in full, because we do not focus on allocative efficiencies (for which, see Hazledine and Murphy, 1996), but we do present evidence on transaction costs, using the Australian economy as our 'control'. The inputs devoted to transaction-type activities in New Zealand do indeed appear to have increased quite sharply.

The procedure is as follows. First we identify the analytical core of the New Zealand reform process; then we suggest how this should be reflected in the data – specifically in the data on the composition of the workforce. We then test this prediction with census data for New Zealand and Australia from 1961 through 1996.

What were the reforms all about?

There is an impressive theoretical cogency to the post-1984 reform programme. Bollard *et al.* (1996, p. 7) write:

> Economic reform can be opportunistic, pragmatic and carried out piecemeal without a strong theoretical underpinning. The opposite situation occurred in New Zealand. The reforms were notable for being based on an integrated theoretical framework. Central to this framework were the 'new microeconomic' theories of contestability, principal–agency and public choice.

Easton (1997) has summarized the economic content of the application of these theories in two terms; commercialization and liberalization. To liberalize is to open up activities to actual or potential competition; to commercialize is to focus economic agents on narrow, usually profit-oriented goals. Thus, one term refers to how people behave, and the other to the environment they behave in, and so they will often be linked. For example, liberalizing domestic markets by reducing tariffs may force local firms to behave more commercially, in the sense of sharpening their concern with profitability.

However, commercialization can proceed without liberalization. For example, the 1989 *Reserve Bank Act* narrowed the responsibility for monetary policy to the Governor (previously the Board of the Reserve Bank had shouldered ultimate responsibility), and narrowed the objectives or goals to just maintaining price stability, quite narrowly defined, with the Governor's contract containing financial incentives to achieve that goal. This is certainly commercialization, in comparison with the previous fuzzy-objective, civil-service procedures, but there was no liberalization – indeed by concentrating power in one person, the conduct of monetary policy was made less 'contestable' than it had been before (unless the threat of being sacked if the performance target was not met can be thought of as introducing input market competition, just as the threat of stockmarket takeover is supposed to constrain the performance of the managers of even monopolistic firms).

Commercialization with or without explicit liberalization is a pervasive feature of the reforms – micro and macro; private and public sector – and can be expected to spread beyond the immediately affected activities and sectors to permeate economic life in general. It represents a major, perhaps revolutionary regime shift which should show up in the data. How? What would be the manifestation in the economic statistics of massive commercialization? The usual data disaggregations are not likely to be informative here. We do not expect systematic changes in capital/labour ratios; nor even in the sectoral composition of output. Commercialization is probably something that applies *within* firms and industries, affecting the way that business is done, rather than changes in relative input or output prices that would induce inter-industry or factor proportion shifts.

The hypothesis advanced here is that commercialization and liberalization have resulted in an increase in transaction costs. Greater use of markets to allocate resources requires more resources devoted to market-making and market-using activities, and a more commercial attitude to achieving specific output goals requires increased measuring and monitoring efforts.

Of course these resources have to be taken away from other uses – that is from directly productive 'transformation' activities. This is the great quality versus quantity trade-off of more-market reforms: you want (and expect) them to yield improvements in resource allocation but those improvements themselves have a resource cost, meaning fewer resources to be allocated to actual, now more efficient production of goods and services. This chapter assesses the terms of the trade-off by estimating the labour inputs devoted to transaction and transformation work, over time and in both Australia and New Zealand.

Conceptual issues in measuring transaction costs

In nearly all textbooks and most journal articles, economists follow Adam Smith in assuming zero coordination costs: supply and demand are brought together with no visible effort; firms are 'atoms' of optimizing behaviour, with no internal structure. Yet in reality real resources are devoted to the coordination of economic activity – both within and between firms and other institutions. How could we measure these resources? First we must clearly conceptualize just what we wish to measure, and this turns out to be non-trivial.

The methodology to be used is, with modifications, that of Wallis and North (1986), who begin by noting that specialization and the division of labour *necessarily* introduce the need for coordination. Specialization means that each productive unit produces a surplus (to their personal requirements) of a small range of goods and services, which must be exchanged for the surpluses of other producers to achieve a balanced consumption portfolio. The division of labour (which does not necessarily involve specialization in the sense of exploiting comparative advantages) requires supervision and control.

Possible methods of coordination and control include main force (theft), chance (lotteries) and custom. Modern civil society, however, relies on two technologies for effecting the allocation of resources: price-mediated voluntary exchange in markets, and submission to established authority relationships within organizations such as firms. That is, when the price and the transfer of good or service are linked directly, we are in a 'market' situation; when the exchange occurs 'upstream' of the priced transaction – as when a worker on, say, a monthly contract performs tasks within that month as assigned by a manager – we are in the world of 'administration' or 'hierarchy', as found within firms.

The distinction maintained by Wallis and North is between 'transformation' and 'transaction' activities. Transformation is the act of adding inherent value; it may involve the physical transformation of material objects, such as combining wood and nails into the frame of a house, or spatial/temporal transformation as when the wood and nails are delivered from the factory or shop to the building site, or intellectual transformation as when an architect produces a plan for the house.

What, then, are transaction activities? These involve the transfer and protection of property rights. In the case of a house, they arise in particular when the house is sold, and include the expenses born by the buyer which are not passed on to the seller, and those incurred by the seller which would not have been necessary had the house not been sold.

Wallis and North include in the buyer's transaction expenses the legal fees, financing costs and costs of searching for houses and gathering market information. The seller has to pay real estate agents' expenses and/ or commissions, and also bears the damage and inconvenience of having prospective buyers and curious neighbours tramp through the house on Open Days, and so on.

For the case of sales workers in general (of whom real estate agents are a particular example), it will perhaps help the reader if we run through the reasoning needed to distinguish transformation and transaction activities. When you, a potential customer, enter a shop, what are the sales people doing? If they are stocking the shelves and guiding you to the goods you seek, that is 'transforming' – moving things and people from where they are not useful to where they are.[3] If they are taking your payment and making sure you don't steal the stock; those are transaction activities, which would not be needed if you produced the goods for yourself.

When property rights are not being transferred, they must be safely 'stored', an activity which involves the legal system, police and guards, insurance, and the expenditure by the houseowner on locks and alarms and perhaps the emotional stress of lying awake at night being frightened by strange noises (the last of which will again not be possible to tease out of the available aggregated statistics). The guarding-the-stock activity can be described as preventing involuntary (on the part of one party) exchange. We call this a transaction activity because, without it, the system based on voluntary exchange transactions could not function efficiently.

The above discussion refers to market exchange situations between voluntary buyers and sellers. The other great class of economic transactions occurs within firms and other organizations, when goods or services are passed along a value-adding chain with no money changing hands (though input services are eventually paid for) and to an extent involuntarily (by order of a supervisor). All managers, administrators and supervisors are judged by Wallis and North to be properly counted as transaction workers, who would not be needed if the division of labour did not introduce the jobs of coordination and monitoring. There must be some overestimation here since managers also do 'creative' work such as visualizing new combinations of value-yielding resources: on the other hand, many primarily transformation workers, especially more highly-skilled technicians and professionals, have some involvement in management activities, be this as informal or part-time supervisors of other workers or in interactions (such as meetings) with managers. It should perhaps be noted here that 'decision making' is not *per se* a transaction activity. Workers making decisions for themselves are basically pitting their own strength and knowledge against the laws of nature – 'if I cut these bits of woods in these places and nail them together in this pattern I will make a house'; it is someone telling *someone else* what to do to build a house – rather than do it themselves – who is involved in a transaction, as a supervisor or manager.

Clerks, data processors and other bookkeepers are record-keepers for transactions. Secretaries are complementary inputs to managers. Servicing workers (repairs and so on) are counted as belonging to the transaction sector by Wallis and North, but this does not seem justifiable conceptually – goods would deteriorate and break down whether or not they are transacted. The servicing sector (as well as personal services) will be counted here as transformation activities.

Another major departure from the Wallis/North procedure will be to include the unemployed in the transaction sector. The Americans neither include or mention unemployment, perhaps because they are so accustomed to it. But we are not accustomed to mass unemployment in New Zealand: it is a quite recent phenomenon, and it would not be proper to ignore a number which has risen from less than 1 per cent of the workforce to as much as 11 per cent in just a 20-year period. All existing models of unemployment – Left, Right and Keynesian – give it what in our context is a transaction-cost interpretation, due to some consequence of specialization and the division of labour. The original rationalization of the Phillips Curve, by Richard Lipsey, had unemployment as a 'structural' phenomenon caused by Keynesian downward wage rigidities impeding the rapid flow of labour between expanding and contracting industries. In monetarist search models, unemployment is voluntary and productive investment in better worker–job matches, and fluctuations in joblessness, arise from misperceptions of prices and wages. In market-power models, unemployment is necessary to discipline the wage claims of employed workers and their unions. In all these explanations, it is specialization and exchange that generates – really, requires – unemployment. There is no unemployment in a single-household economy.

That is, unemployed workers are seen as a reserve of undeployed resources, in essence no different from stocks of refrigerators in the warehouse or canned peas in the pantry: necessary if the continual process of the allocation and reallocation of resources is to proceed without undue fluctuations in prices. Of course, this raises in the New Zealand context the question of why such reserves of labour were not needed before the late 1970s. It is popularly believed (though with little empirical evidence beyond case studies and/or anecdotes about a few infamous government departments, such as the railways, post office and forest service) that there was 'disguised unemployment' in New Zealand during its protected years, in the form of overmanning. In our terms, this means (if it is true) that transformation efficiency was not what it could have been. But from the point of view of transaction costs the old regime appears, at least in this respect, to have been highly efficient, since it was apparently able to do without stocks of unemployed labour. New Zealand was able to escape the Phillips Curve – in modern macroeconomic terms, the 'NAIRU' (non-accelerating inflation rate of unemployment) was about zero.

This conceptual section closes with discussion of three problematic groups: criminals, teachers and soldiers. By definition, criminals are not 'transformers' – that is, they are not producing directly useful goods and services, at least in the eyes of society. Most crime (about two-thirds) is property crime, and so could be assigned to the transaction sector, as one of the byproduct costs of running a system based on formal property rights. But other illegal activities, such as crimes of passion, do not fit neatly into either transaction or transformation categories. We will not resolve this issue here.

Teachers illustrate a number of the conceptual issues raised above. To the extent that they are child-minding while the parents work, they are part of the transaction sector, facilitating the division of labour. To the extent that they are socializing students by teaching them the norms and techniques of participation in economic life, and are contributing to more sophisticated signalling and credentialism exercises justified by costly asymmetric information, they are also performing a transaction-sector activity. But to the extent they are adding to human capital that can be used in transformation activities, they should (along with the producers of physical transformation capital) be classified in the transformation sector. This is quite clear in the case of teaching science and technology, less clear for the teaching of languages. As for social sciences, such as economics, teaching and research in these fields is directed at understanding how (specialized) inputs fit together – surely, a transaction-sector activity. This is not, of course, to say that teaching economics is not *useful* – a point which deserves emphasis. Contributing to a better understanding of how the economic system functions will help towards improving the functioning of the economy, in terms of its ability to deliver goods and services that are directly valued.

Soldiers present an interesting final case. Wallis and North include national defence, which they define as 'the costs of protecting property rights on a larger scale' in the transaction sector, which implies an unusual (for Americans) but probably realistic judgement of the true role of the US military in the world. We will follow this precedent here, though it may be true that neither Australia nor New Zealand's current military resources are capable of protecting their sovereign property rights.

To conclude: the conceptualization of the distinction between transaction and transformation activities is not straightforward and raises many interesting and often quite enjoyable points of definition and delineation. The best we can hope for is to establish a reasonable set of criteria which can be applied in a consistent fashion to the actual data, to which we turn now.

Measurement

If transaction activities are exchanged for money, and if such exchanges are picked up in the national accounts, then, in principle, they could be measured from either side of the accounts as the value of outputs or the value of inputs. In practice, this is possible for coordination activities sold on the market, such as accounting services, but not directly for coordination services buried inside firms and other organizations, such as management supervision and clerical work.

Despite this, Wallis and North do work with an output measure, estimating the value added by transaction-sector activities. For within-firm transaction activities they take the number of employees – an input measure – assume that transaction workers are paid the same as transformation workers within each industry, and take the resulting estimate of the wage bill as the transaction-activity contribution to GNP (value added) from that industry. This is not entirely satisfactory. Some transaction workers are likely to be paid more (managers) and others less (secretaries) than the average wage; and the wage bill measure excludes the contribution of capital services, which of course are included in the directly-measured value added of dedicated transaction industries.

The approach adopted here is the simpler and more direct one of working with an input measure, the number of members of the labour force involved in each type of activity. This approach can be defended not just for its computational accessibility, but also conceptually: transaction activities are an intermediate input to production, and it is the changes in the organizational technology of the economy as reflected in changes in transaction inputs that we wish to analyse.

Apart from this, our general measurement methodology follows Wallis and North, with the specific departures justified in the previous section. We distinguish where necessary between what people do (occupations) and where they do it (industries), and adopt, with one exception, an 'all or nothing' approach, assigning the complete contents of an industry or occupation cell to either transformation or transaction activities. The unit of measurement is full-time-equivalent employment (FTE), with part-time workers converted using the Statistics New Zealand convention that one part-time worker is equivalent to half a full-time worker.

All industries are transformation industries except the following. Within the private sector we distinguish four categories of dedicated transaction industries, following Wallis and North: 'FIRE' (finance, insurance, real estate), and business services (including legal and accounting services, data processing and guards). From the public sector, national and local government contributions to the transaction sector include the police and general administration functions (for example, not teachers but counting the Department of Education in Wellington). Defence employment is also included.

The Input–Output tables are used to net out of transformation industry output that portion that is used by transaction industries as intermediate input. This is assigned an employment numbers-equivalent on the assumption that the labour/output ratios do not differ between production for transaction input purposes and other production.

Unemployment could be classified as an 'industry' or as an 'occupation' – in any case, unemployment FTEs are assigned to the transaction sector. All managers and clerks (which category includes secretaries) are counted as transaction occupations. As noted above, Wallis and North also include all sales and service workers, while admitting that this is an exaggeration. Here, it will be maintained that servicing work (fixing and maintaining things) is a transformation activity, not in essence different from making things in the first place. It directly adds value (lowers entropy).

As for sales workers, having noted above that they are likely to be involved in both transformation and transaction activities, and because they are quite a large group accounting in 1995 for about 12 per cent of total New Zealand employment FTEs, we depart from the 'all-or-nothing' rule and assign them 50:50 to each sector. The share of sales workers in total employment changed little over the 40-year data period, so errors in our allocation will have the following effects. If in fact more than 50 per cent of sales work is properly attributed to the transaction sector, then we will have underestimated the share of that sector in total employment, and overestimated its growth between 1956 and 1995. If the measurement bias is in the other direction, we will have overestimated the size of the transaction sector and underestimated its growth.The measurement procedure is summarized in Table 14.1.

Table 14.1 Typology of transaction and transformation activities

Occupations	Transaction industries	Transformation input to transaction industries	Other transformation industry output
Transaction occupations (managers, clerks, half sales workers)	x	x	x
All other employed occupations	x	x	
Unemployed	x	x	x

Note: Workers fitting into the cells marked 'x' are assigned to the transaction sector.

Data sources and procedures

For both countries the main source of data is the five-yearly Census of Population, held most recently in 1996. The quality of information deteriorates as we go further back in time, in particular with respect to the extent of disaggregation by occupation, by industry and by part-time/full-time status. The earliest years for which reasonable numbers could be constructed were 1956 in New Zealand and 1961 in Australia. Achieving comparability between the two countries forces us to follow Wallis and North and assign all 'Business Services' activities to the transaction sector, even though these include a few such categories as architectural services and consulting engineers which conceptually belong in the transformation sector. Defence employees are included with public administration workers in the transaction sector.

Constructing consistent time series for numbers in the three transaction or partially transaction occupations (administrative/managerial, clerical, sales) is made difficult by periodic major revisions of the occupational classification systems. These affect, in particular, estimates of the number of managers. In Australia, data since 1986 in the 'administrative, executive and managerial' category include 'farmers and farm managers', who, for comparability with New Zealand and with earlier years, should be counted in the transformation sector, and who are therefore removed from the post-1986 Australian figures. In New Zealand the 1990 Standard Classification of Occupations included (correctly) in the managerial category many managerial and proprietorial workers who under the previous (1968) Classification had been assigned to the activity they supervised (for example restaurant and hotel managers classified as 'service workers'). The sales and clerical occupations also required some scaling and splicing to get time-consistent series.

Part-time and full-time workers are aggregated to 'full-time equivalents' by Statistics New Zealand, using the convention that a part-time job is one half of a full-time. We follow this convention in constructing Australian FTEs, even though (a) it appears to overestimate the average hours worked by part-time employees; and (b) the cutoff points differ in the two countries – part-time is less than 35 hours/week in Australia; less than 30 hours/week in New Zealand. Unemployment numbers are Registered Unemployed in New Zealand and Labour Force Survey data in Australia.

Transaction workers use some transformation sector outputs (for example office supplies) as intermediate inputs. We assign the workers involved in producing these outputs to the transaction sector of the economy, using the same procedure for both countries. From various years' Input–Output tables we compute the value of transformation sector output used as intermediate input per dollar of the transaction sector gross output, and also the gross output per employee for transaction and transformation industries in total (using the employment data constructed as explained above). From these two ratios we can get an average figure for the fraction of a transformation-sector worker needed to supply intermediate input to each transaction sector worker. These fractions or ratios are interpolated and extrapolated to get estimates for each of our census years.

To avoid double-counting, we must subtract from our figures for the numbers in transaction occupations those who are employed in transaction industries (for example, bank managers). Census tables giving occupational numbers broken down by industry groups are used to estimate ratios of managers, clerks and (one-half) sales workers to total employment in the private and public sector transaction industries.

Results

Looking first at Table 14.2, which gives the results for our 'control' economy, Australia, for census years 1961–96, the last row shows the ratio of values in 1996 to 1961. As our point of reference for these numbers, note row 5: total (full-time equivalent) employment in Australia increased by 80 per cent over this 35-year period. We see at once from row 1 that the private-sector transaction industries – finance, insurance, real estate and the various business services – grew by nearly 350 per cent – more than four-fold – from 1961, marking, it seems, an increase in the use

Table 14.2 Transaction and transformation employment in Australia, 1961–96 (full-time equivalent worker, 000s)

Sector	1961	1966	1971	1976	1981	1986	1991	1996
1 Finance & business services	225	281	371	425	520	697	876	1004
2 Public administration & defence	131	162	204	270	289	315	333	346
3 Total transaction industries employment	355	442	575	695	809	1011	1209	1350
4 Total transformation industry employment	3679	4144	4652	4773	5056	5252	5558	5928
5 Total all industries employment	4035	4586	5228	5467	5865	6264	6768	7278
6 Admin, managerial workers	314	321	340	351	387	476	575	593
7 clerical workers	511	665	813	896	956	1048	1139	1170
8 Sales workers	417	484	550	586	637	685	776	876
9 Total managers, clerks, sales workers	1242	1470	1702	1833	1980	2209	2490	2640
10 Unemployment	164	79	93	293	381	598	799	780
11 Transformation input to transaction industries, FTEs	40	50	60	66	76	94	134	147
12 Total transformation industry managers, clerks, sales workers	825	966	1088	1136	1186	1262	1365	1376
13 Total transaction workers	1384	1538	1816	2189	2452	2965	3506	3653
14 Total net transformation workers	2814	3127	3505	3572	3794	3896	4060	4405
15 Ratio of transaction/transformation workers	0.492	0.492	0.518	0.613	0.646	0.761	0.864	0.829
16 Without unemployment, ratio transaction/transformation workers	0.434	0.467	0.492	0.531	0.546	0.608	0.667	0.652

of markets and the exchange of property rights. By 1996 about one worker in seven was employed in the 'market-making' sector.

Public-sector administrative employment grew less than transaction-sector numbers, but still by twice as much as total employment, to reach nearly 5 per cent of total employment in 1996. With the two transaction sectors growing more than the average, the remaining industries – the transformation sector – necessarily shrank in relative terms, but still employed over 80 per cent of the total in 1996 (row 4). Rows 6,7, 8 and 9 show the numbers and the total of the transaction and managerial, clerical and sales workers, all of which grew moderately more than employment in total.

One of the biggest growth industries or occupations is, sadly, unemployment – up by an order of magnitude over its 1966 trough, and nearly six-fold over the recession year 1961. We will see results calculated with and without unemployment included as a transaction activity.

Row 14 nets out of transformation employment first, the workers engaged in supplying inputs to transaction industries (row 11), and, second, the managers, clerks and (one half of) the sales workers employed (row 12) in the transformation sector. It is to be compared with row 13, which gives the total number of transaction workers (that is, all employees of transaction sector industries and all transaction workers in other sectors). The shares of these totals sum to more than 100 per cent of total employment because unemployment is included here in the transaction category.

The 'bottom line' is the ratio of transaction to transformation employees (row 15). It begins in 1961 at 0.49 – that is, about two transformation workers for every transaction worker – and peaks at 0.86 in 1991 and falls back slightly in 1996, representing overall a 69 per cent increase in 35 years. Row 16 shows the same ratio with unemployed not included in the transaction sector. Naturally, this reduces the ratio and its growth. As noted above, I see unemployment – no matter what theory you have to explain it – as a quintessential transaction activity (that is, one that would not exist in the absence of a division of labour), but not everyone agrees.

What does all this mean? What these figures seem to reveal is a fairly smooth but eventually quite substantial structural shift in the Australian economy since 1961. Transaction workers grew by 164 per cent; transformation workers by just 57 per cent. Just how significant these changes are, in terms of what they mean for competitiveness, will be assessed in the next section.

Now turning to Table 14.3 with the numbers for New Zealand, there are similarities and differences with the Australian experience. Note first the

Table 14.3 Transaction and transformation employment in New Zealand, 1961–96 (full-time equivalent workers)

Sector	1956	1961	1966	1971	1976	1982	1986	1991	1996
1 Finance & business services	37941	44701	56708	69486	87357	97766	126325	156110	190948
2 Public administration & defence	31817	84807	38428	46375	59461	75532	75969	81205	75785
3 Total transaction industries employment	69758	79509	95136	115861	146818	173299	202294	237315	266733
4 Total transformation industry employment	745278	814152	925039	988381	1107603	1114231	1186518	1038486	1172333
5 Total all industries employment	815035	893661	1020176	1104243	1254421	1287530	1388813	1275801	1439066
6 Admin, managerial workers	27305	33689	44013	55262	73956	89201	141046	156738	184758
7 Clerical workers	90178	105746	131090	147568	167738	173707	196763	175587	189917
8 Sales workers	97345	105157	110576	114900	125758	142913	136928	142896	167409
9 Total managers, clerks, sales workers	214828	244591	285678	317729	367452	405821	474737	475221	542084
10 Unemployment	6596	6898	9107	16168	26337	60255	109191	163770	152121
11 Transformation input to transaction industries, FTEs	7283	8301	11588	14112	19028	23083	41126	36309	40810
12 Total transformation industry managers, clerks, sales workers	147848	168603	198776	219243	253624	281871	330394	305084	338558
13 Total transaction workers	231485	263311	314607	365384	445806	538508	683006	742479	798223
14 Total net transformation workers	590146	637248	714676	755026	834951	809277	814997	697092	792964
15 Ratio transaction/transformation workers	0.392	0.413	0.440	0.484	0.534	0.665	0.838	1.065	1.007
16 Without unemployment, ratio transaction/ transformation workers	0.381	0.402	0.427	0.463	0.502	0.591	0.704	0.830	0.815

(row 5) figure for total employment growth, which, at 61 per cent, is rather smaller than the equivalent number for Australia which had higher population growth over these years. Thus, in general, we should expect New Zealand growth rates to be below those of Australia. This is true of both public and private-sector transaction industries (rows 1 and 2). Interestingly, by 1996 the share in total employment of these industries is, in total, exactly the same in the two countries, with that of the 'market-making' private sector transaction industries still in New Zealand slightly below that of Australia, though the differences probably are not significant, given possible minor differences in definitions.

Thus, New Zealand's 'more-market' reforms do not in fact seem to have required, relative to Australia, larger numbers of workers eventually (1996) devoted to the specialist market-making and market-using industries, and even the growth over 35 years of this sector, relative to total employment growth, is only a little larger in New Zealand than in Australia. But the bottom line of row 15 shows that the overall transaction/transformation ratio in New Zealand grew more than twice as much as in Australia, beginning below the Australian ratio in 1956, and outstripping it by 1981 to end up at about 1 by 1996.

The differences are accounted for a little by higher unemployment growth in New Zealand (from an even lower base than Australia), but mainly by a remarkable discrepancy in the growth of one important transaction occupation – management. Whereas in Australia the number of administrators and executives grew (Table 14.2, row 6) barely more than employment in total, New Zealand experienced manager-number growth of more than 500 per cent, to arrive in 1996 at the situation of one worker in eight being a manager, compared to one in 12 in Australia. 'More market' has actually meant 'more managers'!

Figures 14.1 and 14.2 show graphically the ratios of rows 15 and 16 of the tables. Each figure plots transaction/transformation worker ratios for both countries, with the first including and the second excluding unemployment from the definition of transaction workers. The pictures shown are qualitatively similar. In Australia, the ratio grows fairly steadily up to 1991, and then falls back somewhat in 1996. New Zealand starts below Australia and stays there for twenty years, up to 1976. Then it bursts away, reaching, at the 1991 peak, a level 28 per cent higher than the Australian ratio, before falling back in 1996 as overall employment grows and unemployment falls.

In summary, our 'control' economy, Australia, devoted an increasing proportion of its resources to the coordination of economic activity over

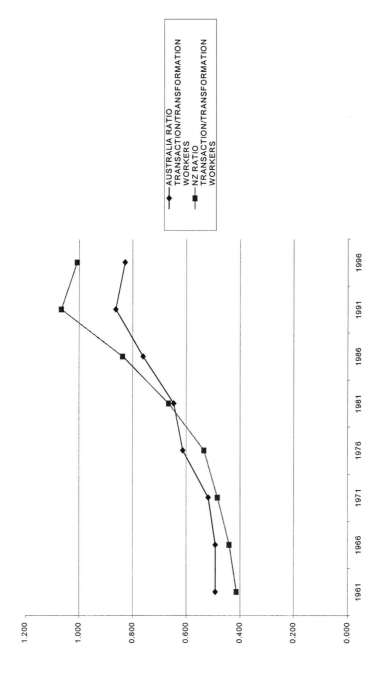

Figure 14.1 Ratio transaction/transformation workers; Australia and New Zealand; 1961–96

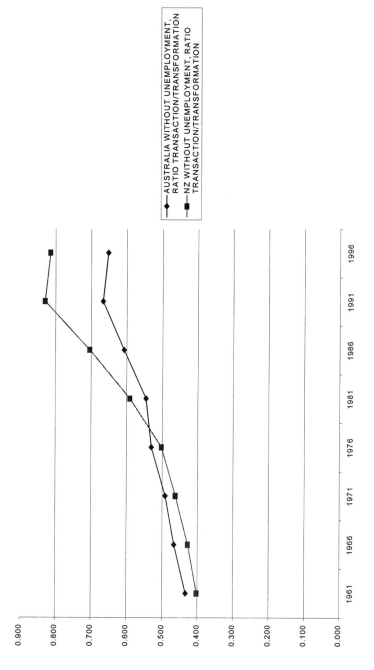

Figure 14.2 Ratio transaction/transformation employment; Australia and New Zealand; 1961–96

the 1961–91 period, with the bulk of this increase (apart from unemployment) coming from growth in the general business-services sector, including finance and insurance. The New Zealand experience with business-services industries growth is actually quite similar to Australia's; the big difference is seen in the occupational category, in particular, with administrative and managerial workers. Whereas the 'old' New Zealand was – in comparison – under-managed, the new New Zealand appears quite strikingly overmanaged compared to Australia.

In both countries the share of transaction workers dropped after 1991, even after netting out decreases in unemployment. This could, of course, mark the start of a new trend, but it may also be a cyclical phenomenon if transaction employees tend to be more 'fixed' than transformation workers. A reasonable inference at this stage might be that both countries have reached a mature stage in their transaction technologies, about three decades after the share of transaction resources in the United States seems to have plateaued (Wallis and North, 1986, p. 121).

Implications

What have we found? We are investigating the importance of transaction technologies in modern and modernizing economies. Taken at their face value, we could conclude from our data (a) that transaction costs are indeed important, accounting in New Zealand by 1996 for fully one-half of the workforce, and (b) that their importance has grown substantially, with the ratio of transaction to transformation workers more than doubling since 1961. Put another way – in, say, 1966, 30 per cent of New Zealand workers were transaction workers; 30 years later, in 1966, 50 per cent were.

To put these figures into perspective, they are quite similar both in scale and rate of change to the proportion of the workforce that is female: 27 per cent in 1966, 45 per cent in 1996. They are larger than another oft-cited indicator of structural change, the decline in the employment share of the manufacturing sector, which fell from 27 per cent in 1966 to just 16 per cent 30 years later. Thus, these transaction-cost numbers are certainly 'big'. But that doesn't in itself mean that they have economic importance, and there is also the question of their statistical reliability. To illustrate the first point, it is probably true that the decline in the proportion of men wearing hats since the 1950s is just as substantial and wide-ranging as any of these numbers, but few would regard this as a figure of any economic significance. I can't yet *prove* that the shift towards transaction employment is important, because no-one has yet 'put the figures to work' – that is, found that they have important linkages with other variables that are generally accepted as being important.

In the introduction, I suggested that the linkage might be with GDP itself; specifically, that the very disappointing GDP growth performance of New Zealand compared, say, to Australia, could be associated with an increase in transaction costs. It is fairly easy to see how this linkage might work, though less obvious how it could have happened.

An additional transaction worker presumably increases the productivity of the remaining transformation workers who actually produce the goods and services that have value, but taking such a worker out of the transformation sector reduces the quantity of inputs available for production. If the reallocation from transformation to transaction activities is excessive, then the net effect of this trade-off could be to reduce total output. But why would this happen? Why would the market allocate too many resources to transaction activities? Well, perhaps the market would not make this mistake, but policy-makers might. There was nothing *laissez-faire* about the New Zealand economic revolution – it was most definitely a top-down, imposed change in regime, and it could have been wrong.

Wrong about what, specifically? Recall that the big difference between Australian and New Zealand experience is not in the growth of the market-making and -using finance and business-services industries, but in the number of managers. This in turn suggests that it may be the 'commercialization' aspect of the New Zealand reforms rather than its liberalization (opening markets) component that is key to the performance differences. Commercialization involves focusing behaviour on achieving specified goals or outcomes, and imposing such behaviour requires monitoring or management. Excessive managerialism could reduce productivity growth by eroding intrinsic work motivation and discouraging cooperation and teamwork. If the commercialization goal is in itself broadly unattractive to the workforce, then imposing it will generate agency problems which will soak up productive resources – the additional monitoring required by principals and the efforts of agents to evade such monitoring. This hypothesis is worthy of further research.

Finally, let us discuss the statistical reliability of the data. There are two issues – the variance or noisiness of the numbers as estimates, and the possibility of systematic bias. The data are all from official statistical agency sources, and so could be taken to be as reliable as any of the official data used by economists, were it not for the problem of definitional changes requiring splicing to get time-consistent series. Changes in industrial classification systems are not problematic at the quite highly aggregated level (1 or 2-digit SIC) used here, but the occupational classification systems are quite tricky, especially in New Zealand where the 1968 New Zealand Standard Classification of Occupations (NZSCO) introduced the odd practice (as noted above) of assigning many specialist managers to the same category (for example 'sales') as the workers they supervise. The 1990 NZSCO reverted to a more sensible and inclusive definition of managers, and we do have a detailed (5-digit) concordance between the two systems to assist in scaling the 1971–86 numbers, but it is a pity to have to do this.

Then there is the issue of the validity of assigning occupations and industries to 'transaction' or 'transformation' activities. It is all very well to invoke the authority of a Nobel Laureate (Douglass North) for this, but one cannot take that line too far, especially given that I choose to go against the Wallis/North procedure in important respects (splitting sales workers between the two activity classes, and putting all 'service' workers into the transformation category), as well as including the unemployed in the analysis. Of course the procedures are crude and must result in errors – the question is whether they are close enough to the target to be useful, and this cannot really be answered without putting the data to work, in a growth model.

What about bias? I expect that there is a conservative bias to the numbers, in that they are likely to underestimate, not overestimate the resources devoted to transaction activities. There are two major sources of transaction work that are here assigned to the transformation sector: farmers and farm managers (about 3 per cent of the workforce in Australia), and all the transaction stuff done by transformation workers – 'paperwork' and dealing with transaction workers. In the other direction, no doubt some of the time of managerial and clerical workers is spent on transformation activities, and there are some industries in the business-services sector which should be classed as transformation: engineering and architectural services and (possibly) some of the insurance industry. It is my expectation that the net effect of these errors is to underestimate the quantity of transaction work.

Notes

1 For an overview and complete listing of the reforms, see Bollard *et al.* (1996).
2 Named for the Finance Minister, and then Prime Minister of the time, (Sir) Robert Muldoon, who intervened directly in the economy with a number of large and distortionary policy initiatives – increased subsidies to farmers; increased pensions; a series of 'Think Big' energy megaprojects. Muldoon called a snap election in 1984 and lost power to the Labour party led by David Lange, and dominated by the reforming Minister of Finance, (Sir) Roger Douglas.

3   Wallis and North include transportation activities in the transformation sector, correctly, in my opinion.

References

Bollard, A., Lattimore, R. and Silverstone, B. (1996) 'Introduction', in B. Silverstone *et al.* (1966) *A Study of Economic Reform: The Case of New Zealand*, Amsterdam: North-Holland.

Dalziel, P. and Lattimore, R. (1996) *The New Zealand Macroeconomy: A Briefing on the Reforms*, Melbourne: Oxford University Press.

Dalziel, P. (1997) 'Evaluating New Zealand's Economic Reforms: A Comment on Evans, Grimes and Wilkinson', paper presented at NZAE meetings, 29–31 August 1997.

Easton, B. (1997) *The Commercialisation of New Zealand*, Auckland: Auckland University Press.

Engelbrecht, H.-J. (1996), 'A Comparison and Critical Assessment of Porat and Rubin's *Informational Economy* and Wallis and North's *Transaction Sector*', paper prepared for the EAEPE Conference, Antwerp, Belgium, 7–9 November 1996.

Fukuyama, F. (1995) *Trust: The Social Virtues and the Creation of Prosperity*, London: Hamish Hamilton.

Hazledine, T. and Murphy, A. (1996) 'Manufacturing Industries', in B. Silverstone *et al.* (1966).

Silverstone, B., Bollard, A. and Lattimore, R. (eds) (1996) *A Study of Economic Reform: The Case of New Zealand*, Amsterdam: North-Holland.

Wallis J.J. and North, D.C. (1986) 'Measuring the Transaction Sector in the American Economy 1870–90', chapter 3 in S.L. Engerman and R.Z. Gallman (eds), *Long-Term Factors in American Economic Growth*, Vol. 51, NBER Studies in Income and Wealth, University of Chicago Press.

Index

Abbreviations used in the index

FDI   foreign direct investment
GATT   General Agreement on Tariffs and Trade
ICT   information and communications technology
LDCs   less developed countries
R&D   research and development